RIVER OF SHADOWS

Muybridge underneath a sequoia near Yosemite Valley, ca. 1872 (photographer unknown).

RIVER OF SHADOWS

Eadweard Muybridge and the
Technological Wild West

REBECCA SOLNIT

VIKING

VIKING
Published by the Penguin Group
Penguin Putnam Inc., 375 Hudson Street, New York, New York 10014, U.S.A.
Penguin Books Ltd, 80 Strand, London WC2R 0RL, England
Penguin Books Australia Ltd, 250 Camberwell Road, Camberwell, Victoria 3124, Australia
Penguin Books Canada Ltd, 10 Alcorn Avenue, Toronto, Ontario, Canada M4V 3B2
Penguin Books India (P) Ltd, 11 Community Centre, Panchsheel Park,
    New Delhi–110 017, India
Penguin Books (N.Z.) Ltd, Cnr Rosedale and Airborne Roads, Albany, Auckland,
    New Zealand
Penguin Books (South Africa) (Pty) Ltd, 24 Sturdee Avenue, Rosebank,
    Johannesburg 2196, South Africa

Penguin Books Ltd, Registered Offices:
Harmondsworth, Middlesex, England

First published in 2003 by Viking Penguin,
a member of Penguin Putnam Inc.

10 9 8 7 6 5 4 3 2 1

Photograph credits appear on page 297.

LIBRARY OF CONGRESS CATALOGING IN PUBLICATION DATA
Solnit, Rebecca.
River of shadows : Eadweard Muybridge and the technological wild west / Rebecca Solnit.
    p. cm.
Includes bibliographical references and index.
ISBN 0-670-03176-3
1. Muybridge, Eadweard, 1830–1904.   2. Cinematographers—United States—Biography.
3. Photographers—United States—Biography.   4. Chronophotography—History.   I. Title.
TR849.M87 S55 2003
778.5'3'092—dc21   2002066384

This book is printed on acid-free paper. ∞

Printed in the United States of America
Set in Guardi with Gill Sans
Designed by Carla Bolte

CONTENTS

RIVER OF SHADOWS

THE ANNIHILATION OF
TIME AND SPACE

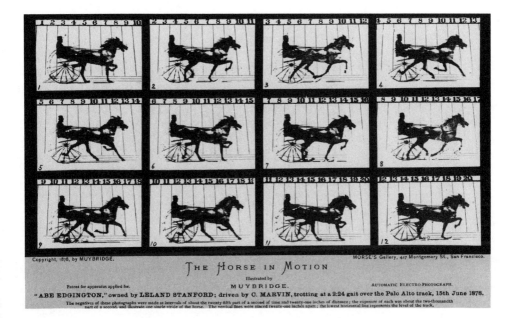

THE HORSE IN MOTION

Illustrated by

MUYBRIDGE.

MORSE'S Gallery, 417 Montgomery St., San Francisco.

Patent for apparatus applied for.

AUTOMATIC ELECTRO-PHOTOGRAPH.

"ABE EDGINGTON," owned by LELAND STANFORD; driven by C. MARVIN, trotting at a 2:24 gait over the Palo Alto track, 15th June 1878.

The negatives of these photographs were made at intervals of about the twenty-fifth part of a second of time and twenty-one inches of distance ; the exposure of each was about the two-thousandth part of a second, and illustrate one single stride of the horse. The vertical lines were placed twenty-one inches apart ; the lowest horizontal line represents the level of the track.

n the spring of 1872 a man photographed a horse. The resulting photograph does not survive, but from this first encounter of a camera-bearing man with a fast-moving horse sprang a series of increasingly successful experiments that produced thousands of extant images. The photographs are well known, but they are most significant as the bridge to a new art that would transform the world. By the end of the 1870s, these experiments had led to the photographer's invention of the essentials of motion-picture technology. He had captured aspects of motion whose speed had made them as invisible as the moons of Jupiter before the telescope, and he had found a way to set them back in motion. It was as though he had grasped time itself, made it stand still, and then made it run again, over and over. Time was at his command as it had never been at anyone's before. A new world had opened up for science, for art, for entertainment, for consciousness, and an old world had retreated farther.

The man was Edward James Muybridge of San Francisco, already renowned for his photographs of the West. In the eight years of his motion-study experiments in California, he also became a father, a murderer, and a widower, invented a clock, patented two photographic innovations, achieved international renown as an artist and a scientist, and completed four other major photographic projects. These other projects are also about time: about the seasonal and geological time of landscape, about the difference between the time that the camera sees and the eye sees, about a war between two societies with radically different beliefs about time and space, about the passage of a midsummer day's sunlight across a city in turmoil. The experience of time was itself changing dramatically during Muybridge's seventy-four years, hardly ever more

dramatically than in the 1870s. In that decade the newly invented telephone and phonograph were added to photography, telegraphy, and the
railroad as instruments for "annihilating time and space." The big corporations were spreading their grasp across wider spaces and into more subtle
interstices of everyday life. The Indian wars were reaching their climax and
their turning point. The modern world, the world we live in, began then,
and Muybridge helped launch it.

Muybridge produced more successful high-speed photographs than
anyone had before. His 1878 camera shutters were a triumph of engineering that made reliable exposures of a fraction of a second for the first time,
a speed at which extremely rapid motion could be captured in focus rather
than recorded as blurs. The photographs were also a triumph of chemistry,
which made the film "fast" enough to record so brief an instant. They froze
motion so that the legs of a trotting or galloping horse, then a leaping man,
and eventually the movements of lions, doves, dancing women, water
spilling, artists drawing, could be depicted as a sequence of still images. At
the same time, Muybridge improved upon the zootrope, a small device invented in 1834 that makes a series of spinning images seen through a slot
appear to be a single image in motion. His zoopraxiscope, as he called it,
projected versions of his motion studies on a screen: moving pictures, pictures of motion. It was the first time photographs had dissected and reanimated actual motion, and it was the foundation of cinema, which emerged
tentatively in 1889, in full force in France and the United States by 1895.
Motion pictures proper were invented by others, but no matter which way
the medium's genealogy is traced, it comes straight back to Muybridge.
And motion pictures changed the relationship to time farther; they made it
possible to step in the same river twice, to see not just images but events
that had happened in other times and other places, almost to stop living
where you were and start living in other places or other times. Movies became a huge industry, became how people envisioned themselves and the
world, defined what they desired and what was desirable. The Russian film
director Andrei Tarkovsky thought that time itself, "time lost or spent or
not yet had," was what people desired and fed upon in the films that became a collective dreamworld inhabited by multitudes. It all began with
photographs of a horse in California.

Occident, the horse that Muybridge photographed in 1872, was one of
the fastest trotting horses in the country. At that time trotting races were a

national passion, and the great trotters were more celebrated than horses that ran their races. Occident belonged to Leland Stanford, who had brought speed to the country in a far more dramatic way, as one of the four masterminds of the transcontinental railroad completed three years earlier. Once, the North American continent had taken months to cross, and the passage was arduous and perilous. In the decade before the railroad the time had been whittled down to six or seven grueling weeks, barring accidents. With the completion of the railroad those three thousand miles of desert, mountain, prairie, and forest could be comfortably crossed in under a week. No space so vast had ever been shrunk so dramatically. The transcontinental railroad changed the scale of the earth itself, diminishing the time it took to circumnavigate the globe. Walt Whitman hailed it as the long-dreamed-of "Passage to India."

The railroad had utterly transformed its builders too, into multimillionaires, buyers of estates, commissioners of paintings and photographs, corrupters of politicians, controllers of much of California, managers of one of the most powerful monopolies this country has ever seen. Stanford was the president of their company, the Central Pacific Railroad, and its most visible figure. Governor, senator, thief on a grand scale, he also became a philanthropist on a grand scale with the establishment of Stanford University on the grounds of his vast country estate forty miles south of San Francisco, the site where Muybridge perfected his motion-study technology in the late 1870s. His sponsorship of Muybridge was his first venture into scientific research for its own sake. Stanford University carried and carries on this venture with a hybrid of commercial and pure research that continues to change the world. Like other immensely powerful men, Stanford affected the world indirectly. In person he seems to have been ponderous and a little dull, a respectable effect he may have cultivated, but his impact was, to use a term of the time, electrifying. Spatial changes on a continental scale, technological innovations, influences on national policy and the national economy, the thousands of men who worked for him, the vast edifices and institutions that arose under his direction, and the countless lives he affected are his real expression. His support and encouragement of Muybridge is not the least of these impersonal effects.

In the spring of 1872, a man photographed a horse. Stanford commissioned the photographs in the hope

11 12 13 14

that they would solve a debate about whether a trotting horse ever has all four feet off the ground at a time. Muybridge's first photographs gave an affirmative answer to that minor scientific question, but by later in the decade he realized that the project had broader possibilities and got Stanford to underwrite his development of them. He told an associate he was going to "revolutionize photography" with the technique he developed, and he did. The story of what Muybridge accomplished with Stanford's support is a peculiarly California story. Much has been written about the artistic and literary modernism that was born in Paris, but only high culture was born there, though that high culture was a response to the pervasive alienations and liberations brought by industrialization. Another part of the modern world came from California, and this part was and is an amalgamation of technology, entertainment, and what gets called lifestyle that became part of everyday life for more and more people around the world and a form of industrialization itself. Perhaps because California has no past—no past, at least, that it is willing to remember—it has always been peculiarly adept at trailblazing the future. We live in the future launched there.

If one wanted to find an absolute beginning point, a creation story, for California's two greatest transformations of the world, these experiments with horse and camera would be it. Out of these first lost snapshots eventually came a world-changing industry, and out of the many places where movies are made, one particular place: Hollywood. The man who owned the horse and sponsored the project believed in the union of science and business and founded the university that much later generated another industry identified, like Hollywood, by its central place: Silicon Valley. Hollywood and Silicon Valley became, long after these men died, the two industries California is most identified with, the two that changed the world. They changed it, are changing it, from a world of places and materials to a world of representations and information, a world of vastly greater reach and less solid grounding. Muybridge's life before those eight years of the California motion studies was a preparation for that phenomenal productivity; his life afterward only polished, promoted, and enlarged upon what he had accomplished in those years. This book is about those years that followed upon that encounter between photographer and racehorse and about that man who seems in retrospect like a bullet shot through a book. His trajectory ripped through all the central stories of his time—the relationship to the natural world and the industrialization of the human world, the Indian wars, the new technologies and their impact on perception and consciousness. He is the man who split the second, as dramatic and far-reaching an action as the splitting of the atom.

Muybridge was forty-two when he began the motion studies, and he had been traveling toward this achievement down a circuitous path. He had been born Edward James Muggeridge on a street in Kingston-upon-Thames paralleling the banks of the Thames, not far upriver from London, on April 9, 1830. An ancient market town, Kingston had a millennium earlier been the place where seven Saxon kings of England were crowned. The lump of sandstone said to be their coronation stone was, with great ceremony, rescued from its long role as a mounting block and raised on a pedestal in the center of town in 1850. On the pedestal below this molar-shaped stone were carved the names of those kings, including two Eadweards. Though Muybridge wouldn't change his first name to Eadweard until his visit to England in 1882, he likely derived it from this monument (he changed his surname twice, to Muygridge in the 1850s and to Muybridge in the 1860s).

His own birthplace and childhood home was a row house only a few dozen feet away from the coronation stone, on the other side of one of the oldest surviving road bridges in Britain, a twelfth-century bridge across a small tributary of the Thames on which locals liked to idle and gossip. At the time, the town's buildings and pace of life seemed hardly changed over centuries: the mayor walked to church amid a procession every Sunday, the market square bustled, a night watchman patrolled the streets, locals got their water from the town pump and their beer from the many public houses. Muybridge's father, John Muggeridge, was a merchant dealing in grain and coal, and the ground floor of the family home had a wide entrance for horses and wagons to come through with their loads. John and Susan Muggeridge and their four sons lived above, in compact rooms whose back windows looked out onto the broad Thames itself, and some of the family business must have been conducted by barge. Like Stanford, Muybridge was born into a quiet commercial family in a provincial town, and like Stanford had he stayed where he was he might have lived and died having made hardly a ripple in history. It

was California that set them free to become more influential than they could have imagined. Or California and the changing world around them, for their fame was achieved by taking hold of those changes and pushing them farther. The year of Muybridge's birth and the years of his childhood saw a set of inventions and discoveries that set the stage for his own.

John Muggeridge died in 1843, and like her mother before her Susan Muggeridge took over her husband's business and seems to have run it successfully, for in 1845 the corn and coal business was listed in her name. Muybridge's grandfather Edward Smith had died when his wife, Susannah Norman Smith, was pregnant with her ninth child. She assumed command of his flourishing barge business and ran it successfully until she passed it on to her older sons, and she presided regally over her large family and larger workforce for decades afterward. When Susannah Smith died at a great age in 1870, she owned more than a dozen houses and considerable other property, though the barge business with its stables of powerful horses seems to have unraveled. Barges had transformed the transport of goods in England before railroads arrived, and the manmade canals built in the late eighteenth and early nineteenth century to accommodate them had transformed the English landscape. Before, most communities had relied largely on local materials for building supplies, provisions, and other materials. Roads were bad and sometimes dangerous, horses were expensive, and each village and town lived in a kind of isolation hard to imagine now. Most people who wanted to get somewhere walked, and many lived and died having never gone farther than a day's walk from home. By the early nineteenth century a carefully coordinated stagecoach system with horses changed every dozen miles or so brought traveling speeds up to ten miles an hour for those who could afford its exorbitant charges, and the coaches seemed reckless and godlike in their swiftness.

Goods moved on barges along canals dug into the landscape, and the barges themselves were a slow-moving business. Muybridge's cousin Maybanke Susannah Anderson recalled that when their grandfather Edward Smith "drove in his gig to London, to buy wheat or coal, he took under the seat of his gig, a carrier pigeon, and in his pocket a quill or two, and when he bought a cargo, he wrote on a small piece of paper the number of barges he needed, put the paper in the quill, tied it under the wing of the pigeon and set it free. Someone watching for the bird's arrival unfastened the quill, took the message to the barges, and they started." Pigeons were the fastest communications technology; horses were the fastest transportation technology; the barges moved at the speed of the river or the pace of the horses that pulled them along the canals. Nature itself was the limit of speed: humans could only harness water, wind, birds, beasts. Born into this almost medievally slow world, the impatient, ambitious, inventive Muybridge would leave it and link himself instead to the fastest and newest technologies of the day. But that world was already being transformed profoundly.

On September 15, 1830, less than six months after Muybridge's birth, the first passenger railroad opened. The celebrated young actress Fanny Kemble had been given a preview of the Manchester and Liverpool Railroad that August. In a letter to a friend she exclaimed, "The engine . . . set off at its utmost speed, thirty-five miles an hour, swifter than a bird flies (for they tried the experiment with a snipe). You cannot conceive what that sensation of cutting the air was; the motion is as smooth as possible too. I could have either read or written; and as it was, I stood up, and with my bonnet off 'drank the air before me.' . . . When I closed my eyes this sensation of flying was quite delightful, and strange beyond description." Thirty-five miles an hour was nearly as fast as the fastest horse, and unlike a gallop, it could be sustained almost indefinitely. It was a dizzying speed. Passengers found the landscape out the train windows was blurred, impossible to contemplate, erased by speeds that would now seem a slow crawl to us. Those who watched the trains approach sometimes thought they were physically getting larger, because the perceptual change in a large object approaching at that speed was an unprecedented phenomenon. Ulysses S. Grant remembered riding on one of the early railroads in Pennsylvania in 1839 with the same amazement that most early travelers recorded: "We traveled at least eighteen miles an hour when at full speed, and made the whole distance averaging as much as twelve miles an hour. This seemed like annihilating space." If distance was measured in time, then the world had suddenly begun to shrink; places connected by railroads were, for all practical purposes, several times closer to each other than they ever had been.

At the railroad's official opening, Kemble returned to ride with her mother, who was "frightened to death" of "a situation which appeared to her to threaten with instant annihilation herself and all her traveling companions." That celebration of a thousand passengers and almost a million onlookers along the route was interrupted by an actual annihilation, the death of the progressive Tory politician William Huskisson. At a stop to take on water for the steam engines, Huskisson got out to stretch and was hit by an oncoming train. It is hard to imagine today the reflexes and responses that made it impossible to step away from a noisy locomotive going perhaps thirty miles an hour, but Huskisson could not. His leg was run over and crushed. Though the duke of Wellington applied a tourniquet to prevent him from bleeding to death on the spot, he died that evening. In Manchester the duke, who had been the hero of the battle of Waterloo and was now the prime minister preventing the democratization of voting, was greeted with angry cries of "Remember Peterloo." The railroad cars had to retreat hastily. It was no coincidence that the first railroad linked two of the Industrial Revolution's primary sites or that the Manchester workers linked the duke and the new technology to the 1819 Peterloo massacre of workers demanding reform. Industrial workers saw the new market economy as bleak and brutal, and they launched a powerful reform movement in the 1830s to gain a voice in it. The agricultural economy was as grim: the Captain Swing riots in the south of England that season of the first passenger railroad's opening protested starvation wages and wrecked reaping machines. An old order had vanished, to be replaced not by a new one but by turbulence and continual change.

Long afterward, Kemble called this railroad "the first mesh of that amazing iron net which now covers the whole surface of England and all the civilized portions of the earth." The Industrial Revolution preceded railroads, but railroads magnified its effects and possibilities unfathomably, and these roaring, puffing machines came to seem that revolution incarnate. Often compared to dragons, they devoured coal and iron in unprecedented quantities, spreading mines and mills wherever they went. In the United States, they ran on wood, and whole forests were fed into their boilers, as though the landscape itself were being devoured by speed. Railroads made possible the consolidation of industries and the industrialization of traditional activities. The fast, cheap transport of goods meant that a town could be given over to shoe-making or beer-making, a whole region to cattle raising or wheatgrowing, and people grew used to depending upon commodities that seemed to come from nowhere. The New England philosopher Ralph Waldo Emerson opined in 1844, "Not only is distance annihilated, but when, as now, the locomotive and the steamboat, like enormous shuttles, shoot every day across the thousand various threads of national descent and employment, and bind them fast in one web, an hourly assimilation goes forward and there is no danger that local peculiarities and hostilities should be preserved." He saw the network of railroads undoing the local character of every place and approved of the erasure. People were being drawn out of their small familiar worlds into one more free, less personal, in which the associations that once attached to each person, place, and object came undone. It was a leap forward of extraordinary liberation and equal alienation.

Grant and Emerson were sounding variations on one of the stock phrases of the day, "the annihilation of time and space," which was applied over and over to railroads and other new technologies. "Annihilating time and space" is what most new technologies aspire to do: technology regards the very terms of our bodily existence as burdensome. Annihilating time and space most directly means accelerating communications and transportation. The domestication of the horse and the invention of the wheel sped up the rate and volume of transit; the invention of writing made it possible for stories to reach farther across time and space than their tellers and stay more stable than memory; and new communications, reproduction, and transportation technologies only continue the process. What distinguishes a technological world is that the terms of nature are obscured; one need not live quite in the present or the local.

Between the time of the Roman Empire and the dawn of the industrial age, wheel-drawn transportation, roads, and ships were improved, but only the printing press made a major alteration in means. Afterward, the devices for such annihilation poured forth faster and faster, as though inventiveness and impatience had sped and multiplied too. Nothing annihilated more dramatically than railroads. As people and goods traveled more frequently and farther, experience was standardized. Distance had always been roughly measurable in time, the stable time of human or equine locomotion, but the railroad transformed those equations, shortening the time and thereby seeming to decrease the distance. The world began to shrink, and local differences to dissipate. People could go much farther because places were not, in terms of time, so far apart, nor was travel so expensive. Distance was relative; a technological infrastructure could shrink it spectacularly. Early in the twentieth century,

Rock Cut Between Promontory and Blue Creek, from the series *The Central Pacific Railroad,* ca. 1869 (one frame of stereo).

when Albert Einstein reached for metaphors to explain his theory of relativity, he repeatedly seized upon the image of a train running across the landscape, a train whose passengers were experiencing time differently than those on the ground.

Railroads transformed the experience of nature, and they transformed the landscape itself. Kemble had been amazed by the cuttings, tunnels and viaducts that leveled the route of the Manchester and Liverpool Railroad, raising the train far above and dropping it below the surface of the earth. "I felt as if no fairy tale was ever half so wonderful as what I saw," she said. Amateur geologists found a rich resource in the railroad cuttings that laid bare Britain's rock and fossils. Geology was the key science of the Victorian era, as physics was of the modern era and perhaps genetics is today, and in that era geology texts sometimes outsold popular novels. One such book was Charles Lyell's *Principles of Geology,* whose first volume was published the year of Muybridge's birth and Kemble's ride. Geologists had begun to debate the age of the earth. Bible scholars asserted that the earth was only about six thousand years old. Its rocks suggested a far greater age to those who studied them, but they did not agree among themselves how old. Catastrophists argued for a comparatively young earth in which forces far more violent than those presently at work had wrenched and welded its topography, and some still claimed Noah's flood had placed aquatic fossils in the heights. The uniformitarians believed that earthquakes, volcanoes, erosion, and other forces still at work must have gradually shaped the earth, and it must be far more ancient than had ever been imagined. Lyell had gone to Sicily to study Mount Etna and concluded that its massive cone was the result of aeons of small eruptions, and that cone sat atop relatively young rocks. His uniformitarian *Principles* portrayed an earth whose age was in the millions of years.

The railroad shrank space through the speed of its motion. Geology expanded time through the slowness of its processes and the profundity of its changes. When they subcribed to the old biblical scale of time, human beings seem to have marched as confidently as elephants, sure they were center stage in a drama whose beginning and end were near at hand and whose set changes were slight. In the new industrial and scientific sense of time, they swarmed and darted like insects, quick but uncertain of their place in a cavalcade of unimaginable length. Expelled from the cozy millenia of biblical time, Lyell's wide audience found itself on a vast plateau of millions of years of geological time. As his colleague George Poulette Scrope put it in 1829, "The periods which to our narrow apprehension . . . appear of incalculable duration, are in all probability but trifles in the calendar of Nature. It is Geology that, above all other sciences, makes us acquainted with this important though humiliating fact. . . . The leading idea which is present in all our researches, and which accompanies every fresh observation, the sound to which the student of Nature seems continually echoed from every part of her works, is— Time! Time! Time!" It was geology, specifically Lyell's

book that he took with him on the *Beagle's* sail around the world from 1831 to 1836, that would lead Charles Darwin to his theory of evolution, and that theory would further transform the place of human beings on the stage of life, more distant from God and closer to the other species. Muybridge, by photographing human beings as "animals in motion" among other animals, took a Darwinian stance.

At the far end of the decade of the railroad's arrival came a third great transformer of time: photography. The Industrial Revolution is most often represented by the bleak textile mills of the British Midlands. But the same steam engines that drove the factories drove the railroads, and though railroads required mines and manufactories, they themselves produced exhilarating effects. Photography is equally a technology of its time, but it generated few such impositions on the landscape or on workers; it was an artisan's technology (though photographic factories came into existence by the late nineteenth century, and every version of the medium has involved toxic chemicals, starting with mercury and cyanide). It did not impose itself on the world but interpreted it, transporting appearance as the railroad transported matter. As a technology, it requires a very different argument about effects and merits than the heavy-duty icons of the Industrial Revolution. For if railroads and photography had one thing in common, it is that they brought the world closer for those who rode or looked. While the dull, repetitive toil of the factories seemed like slavery, these technologies often seemed liberatory.

The brothers Nicéphore and Claude Niepce had begun working on the chemistry of photography in the teens, as had Louis-Jacques-Mandé Daguerre in the 1820s, while the Englishman William Henry Fox Talbot took up the challenge in 1833. Just as the date that counts for the railroad is not that of the invention of the steam engine or the railroad track or the locomotives hauling coal in remote mines, but the date that railroads began to transform public experience, so photography was nothing but a desire, a few premature announcements, and a few faint images before January 7, 1839. That day, Daguerre publicly announced his invention of the photographic method he called daguerreotypy, prompting Talbot to rush to announce his own breakthrough later that January. (In much the same way, the American painter Samuel F. B. Morse and the Englishmen William Fothergill Cooke and Charles Wheatstone invented electric telegraphy at virtually the same time in the early 1840s, and Darwin overcame his long reluctance to announce his conclusions about evolution when Alfred Russel Wallace announced similar conclusions in 1858.)

Photography was in the air. The hope of making images mechanically rather than manually was widespread, and so was the knowledge of the light-sensitive chemicals and the basic principles of the camera obscura, or dark chamber, whose small aperture casts an image of the outside view within its walls. Photography arose out of the desire to fix the two-dimensional image that the camera obscura created from the visible world, to hold onto light and shadow. That desire was compounded of many elements. There was the enormous value placed on realistic images and accurate representations as part of the European embrace of the empirical and the expansion of knowledge and power (a society whose art was abstract or symbolic and whose goal was stasis might never crave this verisimilitude). There was the tendency to replace the activities of the hand by machines, just as the railroad replaced the actions of the traveling foot. And there was the restlessness that characterized modern European and then American society, always willing to overturn what is for what might be, that restlessness of exploration, colonialism, science, and invention, of originality and individualism, the restlessness that regarded the unknown as a challenge rather than a danger, time as something to speed up or speed through. Photography may have been its most paradoxical invention: a technological breakthrough for holding onto the past, a technology always rushing forward, always looking backward.

Photography did not appear all at once as we know it now. Talbot's process, the almost-universal method of photography since the 1850s, produced a negative image and the possibility of printing multiple positives from that negative. But it was Daguerre's process that dominated the first decade of photography. Daguerre had found a way to make direct positive images on polished plates. Each daguerreotype was unique, since there was no negative and no printing, and the images were small and elusive. The mirrored surface that at one angle showed the image at another showed the viewer looking at the image; it seemed phantasmagorical in a way paper prints would not. Compared to painting, early photography was astonishingly fast, but it required exposures from dozens of seconds to several minutes. Morse, who was in

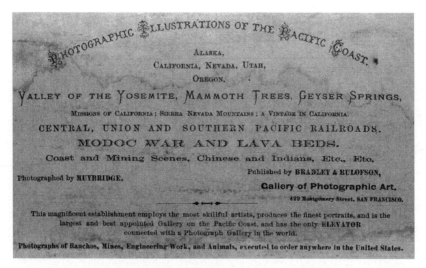

Verso of one of Muybridge's stereo cards, ca. 1873–74.

Paris the spring of Daguerre's announcement, wrote back to New York of the new invention, "Objects moving are not impressed. The Boulevard, so constantly filled with a moving throng of pedestrians and carriages, was perfectly solitary, except for an individual who was having his boots brushed. His feet were compelled, of course, to be stationary for some time, one being on the box of the boot-black and the other on the ground. Consequently his boots and legs were well defined, but he is without body or head, because these were in motion." This man having his shoes polished and the blurry bootblack were the first human beings photographed, and it is eerie to look at them apparently alone, but really surrounded by scores who vanished into speed. Photography was faster than painting, but it could only portray the slow world or the still world. People sat for their portraits with braces to hold their heads steady, and in those old portraits fidgeting children are often a blur. Landscapes were photographed on windless days when the leaves wouldn't move and the water was smooth. The bustling nineteenth century had to come to a halt for the camera, until Muybridge and his motion studies.

Even so, photography was a profound transformation of the world it entered. Before, every face, every place, every event, had been unique, seen only once and then lost forever among the changes of age, light, time. The past existed only in memory and interpretation, and the world beyond one's own experience was mostly stories. The rich could commission paintings, the less rich could buy prints, but a photograph reproduced its subject with an immediacy and accuracy art made by hand lacked, and by the 1850s it offered the possibility of mass reproductions, images for everyone. Every photograph was a moment snatched from the river of time. Every photograph was a piece of evidence from the event itself, a material witness. The youthful face of a beloved could be looked at decades after age or death or separation had removed that face, could be possessed like an object. Daguerreotypes, which were soon sold in elaborately molded cases with cut-velvet linings facing the image that sat within, were alluring objects. Soon countless thousands were lining up to possess images of themselves, their families, their dead children, to own the past. Most daguerreotypes reached out in time to make familiar faces permanent possessions; it was only when the later photographic processes arrived on the scene that photography extended its grasp in space as it had in time. The images piled up, and photography became an industry too. The world was growing larger and more complicated, and photography was both an agent of this enlargement and a device for trying to sort it all out, to own it, to make it manageable. Photography had frozen the river of time, but a torrent of photographs began to pour from the photography studios into homes, pockets, albums, photographs of pyramids, empresses, streets, poets, cathedrals, trees, actors.

Five years after photography, one more technology, telegraphy, arrived to transform time. Telegraph messages traveled almost instantly as electrical impulses over the wires, a technology that telephones and the Internet would only elaborate. "This is indeed the annihilation of space," the *Philadelphia Ledger* exclaimed over the first long-distance telegram in the United States. Many of the early telegraphic lines followed the railroad tracks, and they replaced the railroad as the fastest communications technology. News, words, data, were dematerialized and almost instantaneous wherever the telegraph wires were strung. The distance between places that had once been measured at ten miles an hour or less was wavering, drawing closer, almost dissolving. Karl Marx took up that catchphrase of the day when he wrote, "Capital must on the one side strive to tear down every spatial barrier to intercourse, i.e., to exchange, and conquer the whole earth for its market. It strives on the

18 19 20.

other hand to annihilate this space with time, i.e., to reduce to a minimum the time spent in motion from one place to another." In other words, the more capitalism shrinks space and speeds up time, the more it can profit. In Marx's view, capitalism itself was the engine of the annihilation of time and space, the locomotive its tangible form, and time and space were being annihilated to increase profits. This led to the formation of ever-vaster fortunes and the first modern corporations, even the stock markets whose first major stocks were railroad shares. Capitalism, stocks, corporations, transformed the labor of workers and the materials of the world into that abstraction profit. Labor and materials were themselves abstracted as the one went into the factory to become a series of simple repetitive gestures rather than an authorship of objects, and the objects themselves came to be bought and used by people more and more remote from the process of their making. But these changes also transformed the way everyone touched by the technologies perceived time and space. To use railroad terms, the engine of this cultural and perceptual change was economic.

Before the new technologies and ideas, time was a river in which human beings were immersed, moving steadily on the current, never faster than the speeds of nature—of currents, of wind, of muscles. Trains liberated them from the flow of the river, or isolated them from it. Photography appears on this scene as though someone had found a way to freeze the water of passing time; appearances that were once as fluid as water running through one's fingers became solid objects. Through the nineteenth century, as Darwin worked out his theories about literal evolution, it is as though consciousness evolved from something utterly immersed in this river to something that clambered onto land. There the atmosphere was thinner, the view was farther, and no current forced these mutating Victorians to move at a set pace—but no water bore them up and carried them along either. And there was no going back. The art of the hand had been replaced by the machinery of the camera; the travel of the foot, human or equine, had been replaced by the pistons of the locomotive; bodies themselves were becoming insulated from nature by machinery and manufactured goods; and memory had been augmented and partly replaced by photography, that freezing eye whose gaze soon reached the corners of the world. Appearances were permanent, information was instantaneous, travel exceeded the fastest speed of bird, beast, and man. It was no longer a natural world in the sense it always had been, and human beings were no longer contained within nature.

Time itself had been of a different texture, a different pace, in the world Muybridge was born into. It had not yet become a scarce commodity to be measured out in ever smaller increments as clocks acquired second hands, as watches became more affordable mass-market commodities, as exacting schedules began to intrude into more and more activities. Only prayer had been precisely scheduled in the old society, and church bells had been the primary source of time measurement. In the preindustrial world, most work was agricultural, and the time of the year mattered more, the time of day less. Work was done according to task and available light, and tasks varied from season to season. People worked for themselves or worked with masters who were, for better or worse, more than employers. The new age, with its factories and mobilities, its industrial scale, was to be impersonal as nothing had been before. Tightly enforced schedules came in with the factories whose owners sought to calibrate human labor to machine labor, the machine labor that was speeding up the production of goods, thereby speeding up the raking in of profits, the consumption of raw materials, and on and on—a runaway train of consumption driving production driving consumption. It was these factories and railroads that made knowing the exact time important, that launched the modern world of schedules and bustle. Goods increased in abundance as, for example, Manchester mills generated cheap cotton fabric, but time was becoming scarcer—literally so for workers putting in fourteen-hour days at the mills and slaves growing cotton on the other side of the Atlantic, apparently so for those in the rush of the growing cities, the greater variety of experiences, publications, images, the hectic greed of that era.

The railroad, the photograph, the telegraph, were technologies for being elsewhere in time and space, for pushing away the here and now. They made the vast expanses not so vast, the passage of time not quite so unrelenting. They were celebrated for the very real powers and pleasures they supplied, the real isolations and inconveniences they undid. But there were doubts too about what Thomas Carlyle in 1829 called the Mechanical Age, and the literature of the time is full of it. Hans Christian Andersen's 1844 tale "The Nightingale" compared the drab, independent-minded real nightingale with its bejeweled me-

Thomas Day, Importer of Gas Fixtures, French Clocks, Fine Bronzes, etc., San Francisco. A fine example of Muybridge's commercial work.

chanical imitation, which sang the same waltz over and over. The court music master approved of the machine's predictability: "For you must perceive, my chief lord and emperor, that with a real nightingale we can never tell what is going to be sung, but with this bird everything is settled. It can be opened and explained, so that people may understand how the waltzes are formed, and why one note follows upon another." But it is the mechanical nightingale that grinds to a halt and finally fails the dying emperor because there is no one to wind it up. The live nightingale returns to sing the emperor back to life, out of an affection beyond the abilities of a machine. In a similar vein, Nathaniel Hawthorne's grimly comic short story of 1846, "The Celestial Railroad," sent a group of pilgrims by railroad across the landscape of the great spiritual allegory *The Pilgrim's Progress.* The harsh terrain John Bunyan's Pilgrim had trod on foot sped by pleasantly, but the train ended up in hell rather than paradise. The old world, Hawthorne seemed to argue, was arduous, but it knew where it was going, and it went the slow, sure way. Machines made life easier, faster, more predictable, but they led away from an integrity that people missed from the beginning. It is said that on the first day of fighting in Paris's July Revolution of 1830, the clocks in the towers were fired on simultaneously and independently from several points. The destruction of machinery would be a hallmark of resistance to industrial regimentation and industrial time up through the nationwide railroad riots of 1877, which involved Stanford and, less directly, Muybridge.

Each event and thought itself must have been experienced at a radically different pace—what was slow then was slower than we could now tolerate, slower than we could pay attention to; while the speed of our own lives would have gone by them like the blur of speed before Muybridge's images or been as invisible as the passersby in that first photograph of the Parisian boulevard Morse described. Distance had a profundity that cannot be imagined now: a relative who had moved a hundred or a thousand miles away often seemed to have dropped over the horizon, never to be seen again, and travel for its own sake was rare. In some psychological and spiritual way, we became a different species operating at a different pace, as though tortoises became mayflies. We see much they did not, and can never see as they did. In 1860, George Eliot mourned the transformation of time with an aside in a novel: "Ingenious philosophers tell you, perhaps, that the great work of the steam-engine is to create leisure for mankind. Do not believe them; it only creates a vacuum for eager thought to rush in. Even idleness is eager now—eager for amusement, prone to excursion-trains, art-museums, periodical literature, and exciting novels; prone even to scientific theorizing and cursory peeps through microscopes."

Out the train window, the landscape disappeared into a blur; traveling was no longer an encounter, however awkward and dangerous, but a transport. It was as though the world itself was growing less substantial, and though some doubted the value of the change, many celebrated it. The year before Eliot mourned leisure, the essayist and judge Oliver Wendell Holmes exulted over the way photographs of the material world seemed to eclipse their subjects: "Form is henceforth divorced from matter. In fact, matter as a visible object is of no great use any longer, except as the mould on which form is shaped. Give us a few negatives of a thing worth seeing, taken from different points of view, and that is all we want of it. Pull it down or burn it up, if you please. . . .

Matter in large masses must always be fixed and dear; form is cheap and transportable. We have got the fruit of creation now, and need not trouble ourselves with the core." In Holmes's account, this dematerialization was liberatory. "Everything that is solid dissolves into air," said Marx of that uncertain era, and Holmes thought that dissolving into air was wonderful, that his generation would rise up like birds into that thinner medium, with a new freedom to see the whole glorious nineteenth-century world as a bird in flight might see it, as small pictures of things far away.

Photographic reproduction would make the world's images and experiences as available as the Manchester mills made cotton fabric. It's not hard to see ahead from Holmes's vision of the photographic revolution to cable television with its torrents of nature documentaries and news reports, comedies and advertisements, but behind it lay the hunger and ignorance of a world where images and information were scarce. One way to describe this transformation of the world whose great accelerations came in the 1830s, the 1870s, and the age of the computer is as increasing abstraction. Those carried along on technology's currents were less connected to local places, to the earth itself, to the limitations of the body and biology, to the malleability of memory and imagination. They were moving into a world where places were being homogenized, where a network of machines and the corporations behind them were dispelling the independence of wilderness, of remoteness, of local culture, a world that was experienced more and more as information and images. It was as though they sacrificed the near to gain the far.

There was no simple dichotomy, however, between nature's pace and the railroad, between images and the natural realm of the senses. It was not long before railroad lines were being built to take people into the landscape for scenic excursions and cameras were being used to make landscape photographs. It is as though the Victorians were striving to recover the sense of place they had lost when their lives accelerated, when they became disembodied. They craved landscape and nature with an anxious intensity no one has had before or since, though they pursued it in new ways: with microscopes and rock hammers, with guidebooks and cameras, with railroad excursions and collections of specimens. They filled their houses with pictures of places, but even the close-ups were often as not of places far away. The ideal landscape seemed formed of a wholeness that was no longer theirs. They looked for this wholeness as a place, and so mostly do we. These histories suggest nature was equally a kind of time or a pace, the pace of a person walking, of water flowing in a river, of seasons, of time told from the sky rather than electrical signals. Natural meant not where you were but how you moved through it, and a woman drifting across London on foot could attain certain harmonies not available to those speeding across the prairie on the express train. But the Victorian age had launched a juggernaut, and slowing down was the single thing hardest to do.

This is the paradox of Muybridge's work. He was using his state-of-the-art equipment to feed that ravenous appetite for place, for time, for bodies. He had turned his back on the slow world of his grandfather's barges and pigeons to embrace the new railroad and photographic technology, and with electricity and chemistry he made the latter faster than ever before. But his work is largely a collection of striking still images of the settlements and wilderness of the West through the mid-1870s, then an avalanche of images of bodies, the bodies of horses, then men, then women, children, camels, lions, vultures, reenacting their most familiar gestures. His inventive technology was depicting the place and the bodies that seemed ever more alienated by technological change, as though what had been lost as direct experience could be, just as Holmes dreamed, recovered as imagery. The speed of Muybridge's invention allowed real motions to be recovered at their own pace, though watching them meant stepping out of one's own time. If the experience that was vanishing can be summed up as a person standing alone in a landscape, then photography and, subsequently, film would offer images of that experience. The very essence of that solitary experience in the landscape, however, was its immediacy, its situation in a resonant here and now, while representations are always about there and then, a substitute, a reminder. Yet Muybridge spent much of his adulthood in some version of that experience, photographing the landscape for the market.

In the spring of 1872 a man photographed a horse. With the motion studies that resulted it was as though he were returning bodies themselves to those who craved them—not bodies as they might daily be experienced, bodies as sensations of gravity, fatigue, strength, pleasure, but bodies become weightless images, bodies dissected and reconstructed by light and machine and fantasy. The movements of horses dismayed artists and amused members of the public when Muybridge's in-

22 23 24 2[5]

stantaneous photographs revealed them as much more complex and ungainly than the rocking-horse gallopers in paintings. Then he offered his audience of scientists, artists, dignitaries, and connoisseurs the whole world of everyday gesture back. Those gestures—a gymnast turning a somersault in midair, a nude pouring water—were unfamiliar and eerie stopped because they showed what had always been present but never seen. Set into motion, they were uncanny another way when they undid the familiar distinction between representations, which did not move, and life that did. Through the new technologies—the train to the landscape, the camera to the spectacle—the Victorians were trying to find their way back, but where they had lost the old familiar things they recovered exotic new ones. What they had lost was solid; what they gained was made out of air. That exotic new world of images speeding by would become the true home of those who spent their Saturdays watching images beamed across the darkness of the movie theater, then their evenings watching images beamed through the atmosphere and brought home into a box like a camera obscura or a crystal ball, then their waking hours surfing the Internet wired like the old telegraph system. Muybridge was a doorway, a pivot between that old world and ours, and to follow him is to follow the choices that got us here.

THE MAN WITH THE CLOUDY SKIES

Muygridge ▪ *Helios* ▪ *Muybridge*

■ *Overleaf: The Golden Gate from Goat Island,* probably late 1860s (one frame of stereo).

MUYGRIDGE

"My mother's sister had four sons, one of them was an eccentric boy, rather mischievous, always doing or saying something unusual, or inventing a new toy, or a fresh trick," Muybridge's cousin Maybanke Susannah Anderson remembered of him. "When he left school, the Grammar School of the town, he became dissatisfied. There was nothing worth doing in Kingston, sleepy hole. He wanted adventure, the world was wide, and he wanted to see it. The home of his mother, who was a widow, gave him nothing of interest to do, and at last he announced his intention of going away. But where to go? That question, he could not, or would not answer. No persuasion availed. He wanted to see the world, and to make a name for himself and at last he came to say 'Goodbye,' he was going to America. That was all we were told. When he went to say farewell to his grandmother, she with her usual kindliness, put a pile of sovereigns beside him and said, 'You may be glad to have them Ted.' He pushed them back to her, and said, 'No, thank you Grandma, I'm going to make a name for myself. If I fail, you will never hear of me again.'"

Eventually Muybridge made several names for himself, but his early years in the United States are as obscure as those of any young clerk a century and a half ago. There are only hints from the more abundant documents of his later years. Near the end of his life he wrote a letter to a newspaper in the course of which he mentioned that "while living in New Orleans during the middle part of the last Century, my engagements frequently required visits to the levee, where the steamboats from the up-river country discharged their cargoes of cotton and other merchandise." He may already have been working as an agent for the London Printing and Publishing Company, in which case he may have been supervising books being unloaded on the banks of the Mississippi. In an account he wrote in

1898 about observing the motions of birds, the south crops up again: "The attention of the writer was first directed to the soaring of birds during a southern tour of the United States early in the fifties, when he watched a buzzard wheeling around, at various elevations, for the space of an hour, without the slightest apparent effort of motion." Muybridge tries to imply that he was a man of leisure on tour to see the sights, rather than a roving business representative, but he reveals a real refinement in his pleasure in watching a bird for its own sake long before he was to take up studying the motion of animals professionally. Much of the conflict and contradiction in his life was due to the fact that he valued social standing too much, perceptiveness and talent too little, though he himself had the latter gifts to a rare degree.

Many years later the photographer and gallery owner Silas Selleck recalled that he and the young Muybridge became friends in New York City, and the friendship was renewed when Muybridge arrived in San Francisco in the autumn of 1855. By the spring of 1856 Edward Muggeridge of Kingston had become E. J. Muygridge, bookseller, of San Francisco, and so he would remain through the decade. His cousin thought he changed his name because the new version sounded more euphonious than Muggeridge. It may be too that the prosaic name he was born with seemed to hold him back from his ambition, though it would take him another fifteen years to figure out how live up to that ambition (and more than a quarter century to arrive at the final version of his name). He was an athletic young man with hooded eyes set deep under strong brows and a thick crest of fair hair well weighted with pomade, in the only known photograph of him before a bushy beard obscured the lower half of his face. It's a fierce, strong-boned face with a wide mouth, more impressive than attractive, and its forcefulness contradicts the high collar, velvet lapels, and plump bow tie of his outfit. The rough outdoor clothes of later years suited him better, and when in his late forties and fifties he posed nude for his own motion studies he looked more at ease than in any of the other photographs. Private life was never one of Muybridge's talents, and other than his brief marriage he seems to have formed no profound ties after he left home, though he had many professional friendships. Only a few personal letters of his survive, but business correspondence and courtroom documents depict a proud, driven, solitary man. His photographs are the real journal of his later years, documenting the trajectory of his travels and a sensitivity of perception and dedication to craft rarely evident in the written record. He was to become a truly great photographer, for his acute eye, for his technical genius, and for the scope and originality of his projects. That he was eccentric, immodest, and ambitious does nothing to diminish the testament of those photographs from 1867 onward. But those photographs were far ahead, and far ahead of his own sense of his possibilities in the autumn of 1855.

When Muybridge arrived in San Francisco, it was the capital of the gold rush. The whole Southwest from California to New Mexico and southern Colorado had only been seized from Mexico in 1848, enlarging the nation by about a third and giving it the shape it has today, a wide shield sprawling from the Atlantic to the Pacific. The Southwest was still largely unfamiliar territory to Yankees, and it would be explored as much by those heading east from San Francisco as by those venturing west from the other side of the Mississippi. San Francisco was the capital of the unknown lands, lands where the myriad native nations were mostly unconquered or in the early stages of being conquered. The city was months away from the eastern United States, whether you took a ship the nineteen thousand miles around the horn of South America, took the malarial shortcut across Central America's narrow waist, or trudged months across the mountains, desert, and prairie west of the Mississippi, where the last railroad stopped. Eighty-eight days was the world record time by sea between New York and San Francisco in 1854.

Gold had brought all this about, the gold discovered on the American River in 1848 that brought miners from around the world to try their luck. Nothing like it had ever happened before. Earlier gold strikes on government or private land had not provided opportunities to anyone willing to try. Nor had the transportation and communications system necessary to generate a global rush existed earlier. From Chile and France and China, from Vermont and Tennessee, gold seekers swarmed to the foothills of the Sierra to strike it rich, and for decades afterward California's immigrant population was disproportionately young and male. Isolation allowed these immigrants to develop a different society, with different wages, morality, and opportunities, and the place seemed fantastic not just for the possibility of getting rich but for the possibility of becoming something new and for the wonders already there. Discoveries of the motherlode of gold in the foothills of the Sierra Nevada were soon followed by other revelations of the marvels of the new state, with its balmy coast, snowbound mountains, and, it seemed, outsize everything. In 1851 Yosemite Valley was invaded by U.S. troops and volunteers seeking to eradicate the natives hindering economic development of the area, and the narrow valley's thousand-foot waterfalls and half-mile-high cliffs soon became emblems of California, as did the giant sequoia trees stumbled across by one Augustus C. Dowd, the first white man to see them, when he was out hunting meat for a mining camp. Five men spent twenty-two days felling the largest, more than twenty-four feet in diameter, so that its bark could be sent east for exhibition. Victorians often regarded nature as a cathedral, but they weren't averse to enjoying it as a circus. Easterners suspected the reassembled tree was a fraud, but Californians turned the stump into a dance floor. A cotillion of thirty-two danced upon it, accompanied by seventeen musicians.

Gold rush California was born dancing, but it danced on the giant stump of what had come before. Just as forests were converted into speed in the form of wood fed into locomotive boilers, so the foothills of the Sierra Nevada were converted into money, about 750 tons of it by 1857. The native people of the mother lode were hunted mercilessly, the landscape was shoveled into heaps, the rivers were poisoned with mercury and clogged with silt, and the miners killed each other casually. Some men went broke sifting gravel, and others struck veins that made them millionaires. Within a few years of the start of the gold rush, the democracy of the individual working his claim by hand had given way to large-scale operations with machinery, employees, and shareholders. In San Francisco the fortunes were far vaster, for the real money was seldom in mining per se, but in supplying the stampede, speculating in real estate, or trading mining shares. At the mining camps in the Sierra Nevada, men lived in tents and primitive huts, drank bad whiskey, seldom bathed, and left mountains of tin cans behind them. San Francisco was where the miners came to spend their money, and there was plenty to spend it on.

By 1856 the brand-new city had forty bookstores, including Muybridge's, more than a dozen photography studios, and nearly sixty hotels, along with gambling houses, saloons (537 by 1853, in one count), restaurants, theaters, even an opera. It was a more open society than that of the rest of the nation, and one celebrant wrote, "In California, Catholic and Protestant, Jew and Gentile, all seem to have united in the one effort of establishing a civilization on a broad and liberal foundation, the rules of

Railroad House After the Earthquake, 21st Oct. 1868 (one frame of stereo).

which would not restrict in any way the liberties of any." For women San Francisco was a contradictory place: prostitution was a huge and highly visible industry, and though there were celebrated courtesans in elegant boudoirs, far more women and girls were being worked to death in the "cribs" of Chinatown and the sordid Barbary Coast of Pacific Street that crossed upper Montgomery Street. Yet many women achieved an independence in their personal lives and a role in political, economic, and intellectual life they would have found nowhere else.

There had never been anything like it. Seven miles square, San Francisco is the tip of a peninsula jutting north, farther isolated by a high range of hills across the city's southern end. It is halfway to having an island ecology. There were species of plant and butterfly found nowhere else; and though the city eliminated one of those butterfly species in the nineteenth century (and another in the mid-twentieth), it developed its own rare specimens: eccentrics, visionaries, and radicals. The landscape was full of hills that mostly survived and sand dunes that did not. It had a coastline of inlets and coves, including the great natural cove around which a downtown quickly sprang up. There were so many ships' masts in the harbor that observers compared it to a forest. The ships the gold seekers came in were left to rot as even the sailors deserted, though some were dragged ashore to use as storerooms. There was a land rush, and land in the center of the city near the harbor became so valuable that people took to buying water lots—underwater real estate they filled in with the residue from blasting at the rocks, hauling away the sand, and flattening the hilltops that made up the bumpy topography of San Francisco. The coastline was radically altered, and downtown spread onto it.

Montgomery Street was where Muybridge sold books in the 1850s and his galleries sold his photographs from the late 1860s through the 1870s. It had begun as a waterfront street built partly on pilings, but as the water lots filled in, it ended up several blocks inland. There were shacks and tent cities, but the bustling 1850s town of thirty thousand also had solid multistory buildings clustered around Montgomery Street, the city's great social promenade and the thoroughfare between the city's two gracious residential districts of the 1850s: North Beach and South Park (the latter, where Muybridge would later live, was an oval laid out in the English style around a central garden, on what was then the only flat land south of Market Street). The city burned down a few times in its first few years, and the many volunteer fire departments became important social and political clubs that strove to outdo each other with equipment and uniforms and sometimes fought each other over who would put out a fire while the blaze raged. There were literary magazines and myriad newspapers. Maybe remoteness is why San Francisco gloried in its urbanity, in banquets and music, business deals and political organizations. As someone in San Francisco was listening to opera or buying art books, someone in the gold country was being shot with an obsidian arrowhead or hanged with a dirty rope.

Not that San Francisco was short on murders, lynchings, and executions. The most famous was of James King of William, so called to distinguish himself from all the other James Kings in town. A failed banker who began publishing a small newspaper in October 1855, he had taken on the herculean task of exposing corruption in local government. James P. Casey, a rival newspaper publisher who seems to have got himself elected to city government by openly stuffing ballots, took offense when King exposed his past as an inmate of New York's notorious Sing Sing Prison. On May 14, 1856, Casey gunned down King a few blocks from Muybridge's bookstore. A small vigilance committee in 1852 had attempted to reform the corrupt city government, but the 1856 Committee of Vigilance came to have six thousand members and a dangerous taste for power. On May 20, that committee abducted Casey and a man who likely killed in self-defense and hung them out the second-story window of their headquarters, "Fort Gunnybags." That season San Franciscans could go to the Nahl Brothers' "brilliantly illuminated Railroad Saloon" on Montgomery Street to see paintings of the gold rush and eat ice cream and strawberries or watch men be hung and driven out of town by the vigilantes. Muybridge must have been in the thick of it, but all that is known is that on August 13, he advertised that he had for sale a lithograph of James King of William.

It was not the attacks on his present conduct but the revelation of his Sing Sing past that prompted Casey to murder King. The West presented many opportunities to become what is commonly called a self-made man, a man of wealth, but it offered more profoundly an opportunity to make oneself up, as a fiction, a character, a hero, unburdened by the past. "Oh, what was your name in the States?" went one California song. "Was it Thompson, or Johnson, or Bates? Did you murder your wife and fly for your life? Say, what was your name in the States?" In those days, San Francisco was the capital not only of California but of the West, and the West was for Yankees a place without a past, both a gritty terrain of bare earth and long rivers and a fiction of masculinity and possibilities.

The West had been imagined and publicized by Jessie Benton Frémont more than anyone else. Daughter of the great expansionist senator from Missouri, Thomas Hart Benton, she had caused one scandal by cutting off her hair to pass as a boy and another by showing up for a family wedding in a man's military uniform. Realizing that manhood wasn't available to her, she eloped at age seventeen with the adventurer John Charles Frémont of the U.S. Topographical Corps. Thanks to his father-in-law's political influence, he went off and had the trailblazing western adventures she yearned for, and she rewrote his journals into reports whose literary merits captured the national imagination and made him a hero. The pivotal first-person tales of a man encountering the West were ghostwritten by a young bride in the East. Frémont's own creative contribution was naming. He named everything from the Golden Gate to the Humboldt River to the Carson River, lake, and mountain pass, honoring his chief scout, Kit Carson. By the time Muybridge arrived, the Frémonts were hosting a salon in San Francisco and fruitlessly trying to exploit their huge Mariposa Estate near Yosemite, a seventy-square-mile land grant whose gold reserves enriched more conniving men. Nobody in the West, least of all Frémont himself, seemed dismayed by his court-martial for his conduct in the war on Mexico a decade earlier. In 1856 he made an unsuccessful bid for president, and a downtown San Francisco street on what had once been water lots is named after him.

The early-arriving Yankees named the land they stumbled across as though they had become deities or invented the mountains and rivers themselves. In many mythologies people become constellations and mountains, but in the Yankee West the identities of explorers and politicians were not dissolved into the landscape but affirmed there. Josiah D. Whitney, who directed the state's geological survey in the 1860s, managed to get the state's tallest mountain named after him and had the name transferred to the present Mount Whitney when it turned out they had measured the peaks wrong the first time. This well qualified him for the huge lie he later told for Leland Stanford. When the Central Pacific Railroad was being built, the government payment per mile over mountains was triple that for flat land, so Whitney at Stanford's behest officially relocated the foothills of the Sierra Nevada twenty-one miles farther west. Stanford's name was, before long, given to a giant sequoia tree, a mountain peak or two, and a railroad locomotive. Truth and fiction waltzed with each other across the great western spaces, now one leading, now the other. Carson himself had a definitive experience of this western strangeness when he went to rescue a Mrs. White who had been kidnapped by Jicarillo Apaches, only to find that she had already been killed—but there was a book at the campsite, a largely fictitious biography of Carson in which he was, he recalled, "represented as a great hero, slaying Indians by the hundreds." His story got there before him and did better than he did.

Such frontier heroes as Frémont and Carson were adored for their authenticity, for the physical courage and stamina that made their exploration of the West possible, and for their encounters with the grit of real mountains and real prairies. Yet the details of their adventures and their characters were often fabricated. For the inhabitants of the Wild West they founded, there seems to have been no clear border between the world and its highly embroidered representation. Buffalo Bill and Wild Bill Hickok, respectively an army scout-buffalo hunter and a gunman-lawman, had been the subjects of laudatory fictions published in the East, and they collaborated with the mythmaking by lying extensively about their own lives afterward and acting them out as theater. Perhaps they had become true inhabitants of that murky borderland. A historian of western movies recounts, "Emmet Dalton, the last surviving member of the Dalton Gang specializing in great train robberies, actually collaborated on a book in 1937 (subsequently filmed) entitled *When the Daltons Rode*. This book told the story of how Emmett Dalton had died a romantic death at Coffeyville, Kansas, forty-five years previously." The frontier was the home of the tall tale, from Davy Crockett's boasts when Tennessee was the West, to the antic literature of Mark Twain (real name Samuel Clemens) and Bret Harte during their San Francisco days. It was well populated with liars, delusionaries, confidence men, men disguised as women, and women disguised, for different reasons, as men. Throughout the West, lawmen and outlaws and performers regularly seemed to change place: Wild Bill Hickok, Wyatt Earp, Buffalo Bill, and many others would later try on various of these roles, and much of the West engaged in a more moderate version of this shape-shifting.

The West was to them an arena for their self-invention, and truth was whatever the winner said it was. King's exposure of Casey led to murder because no one was supposed to give away the show, and in San Francisco the show was much appreciated. Joshua Norton, an English Jew who came to California via South Africa, initially made a fortune speculating in foodstuffs. In 1853, he tried to corner the rice market at twelve cents a pound, only to be ruined when Peruvian ships sailed in full of rice at three cents a pound. He apparently cracked under the strain of the crisis, then reemerged in 1859 with a proclamation he gave to the *San Francisco Daily Evening Bulletin* to publish, announcing he was emperor of the United States. Later he added "and Protector of Mexico" to his title. For the next twenty-one years he wandered the city, graciously receiving homage, chastising the disrespectful, and taking tribute in the form of free meals, free clothes, and small sums of money given for his irredeemable bonds, printed for free by local shops. His career as emperor was made by the collusion of the citizens of San Francisco and the newspapers that published his edicts, those old San Francisco newspapers that mixed together poetry and scandals and civic matters. In the photograph Muybridge made of Norton sitting on a bicycle in the late 1860s, he is a solid middle-aged man looking down at his handlebars with a frown of concentration, more serious than his gaudy uniform with its tarnished epaulets. There were dozens more San Franciscans with a drowned past and an invented present. Mary Ellen Pleasant had been born a slave in Georgia, reputedly learned voodoo from New Orleans's Marie Laveau herself, became a major figure in the Underground Railroad, sometimes visiting plantations dressed as a young male jockey to scout out slave escape routes. She started over again in San Francisco as an intriguer who by supplying servants and lovers to many of San Francisco's powerful men became a much-feared power herself, but she also brought a successful lawsuit to integrate the streetcar service. It was not a standard conclusion to a female slave's career, and it might not have been possible elsewhere. For those who came from the East, the West was a place without a past, and amnesia felt like freedom.

Photographic negatives in Muybridge's day were made on glass plates, and glass itself was a valuable material. Photographers sometimes scraped the plates clean to start over, and many of the negatives of the Civil War were recycled into greenhouse plates without being scraped, their images of the harvest of death gradually fading away to let more and more light in on the orchids or cucumbers beneath. When Muybridge's dealer of the mid-1870s, William H. Rulofson, died, his negatives—no doubt including his prizewinning images of Muybridge's beautiful wife, Flora—were bought up by Joaquin Miller to make a greenhouse. Miller was the publicity-seeking author who had conquered London as a representative Californian dressed up in a sombrero and spurs and who had titled his memoir about life among the Pit River Indians of northernmost California *Life Amongst the Modocs,* because the neighboring Modocs had more market value. Rulofson's family secret—that he was brother to a notorious murderer (and distinguished linguist)—was discovered when he died; Miller's real name was Cincinnatus Hiner Miller; Flora Muybridge had sometimes been known as Lily Shallcross, and even her married surname was a made-up version of Muggeridge. The men and women of the West scraped clear the glass of their own lives whenever they wanted to make a new image there, and San Francisco was a hothouse made out of these lives, incubating fantasies, erasures, and new beginnings.

What is striking about Muybridge is how cautiously he launched himself the first time. He had changed his surname, but he had neither rushed to the gold fields nor speculated in the many volatile markets of the city. Little came of his ambition to make a name for himself, unless one considers it a literal operation: his several rearrangements of his own name suggest how consciously he was crafting a self, how ardently desiring to be someone. Nowhere in his long life did he express an interest in or an opinion on religion or politics; science and art were instead his anchors, and in his time science and art stood like twin temples, aligned and almost united in the pursuit of truths that then seemed not so far from beauty. Muybridge's bookstore sold illustrated editions of Shakespeare, a new edition of Audubon's *Birds of North America,* Hogarth's prints, books titled *The Vernon Gallery of British Art, National Gallery, France Illustrated, Pictorial World,* and he seems to have had no shortage of customers. It was workers who were scarce, or his salaries or manner that chased them away: during the five years he was a book dealer he took out forty-four ads for, as the first one put it, "a gentleman well qualified to obtain subscribers for a new illustrated standard work. None but a first-rate canvasser need apply. E. J. Muygridge 113 Montgomery Street."

He became a respected minor member of the city community, showed his wares at the annual Mechanics' Institute Fairs, was elected a director of the Mercantile Library in 1859, a place that was part intellectual organization, part social club. That year he advertised wolfhound puppies for sale and money to lend. His respectable friends later testified he was a good businessman. He must have been a bored businessman, for he handed the business over to his younger brother Thomas, a former seaman who arrived at the end of the decade. On May 15 of that year, he took out another ad in the *Daily Evening Bulletin,* announcing, "I have this day sold to my brother, Thomas S. Muygridge, my entire stock of Books, Engravings, etc., and respectfully request a continuance of public patronage in his favor. After my return from the Yosemite I shall, on 5th June, leave for New York, London, Paris, Rome, Berlin, Vienna, etc., and all orders or commissions for the purchase of Works of Literature or Art entrusted to me, will be properly attended to," and then he listed the terms of the commissions. On June 12, he was still advertising for commissions in the *Bulletin.* No one knows if he got to Yosemite Valley that time, but if he did, he would have been among the first tourists there.

One of those for-want-of-a-nail tales could be told of Muybridge's fateful trip east. He seems initially to have planned to go by sea, and had he done so he might have returned before long still a businessman. Instead, he took the Butterfield Overland Mail Company Stage on its route across the southern states. The company had begun carting mail and passengers from St. Louis to San Francisco and back in the autumn of 1857, cutting the time between the Midwest and the Far West to several weeks. On July 2 Muybridge took passage on the stage, and all went well until the oak groves of central Texas nearly three weeks later. As the *Bulletin* reported from a telegraphic dispatch, "The stage left Mountain Station with several passengers. . . . On leaving the stable, the driver cracked his whip and the horses immediately started on a run. When they arrived at the brow of the mountain the brakes were applied, but were found to be useless. In his efforts to stop the horses, the driver drove out of the road, and they came in collision with a tree, literally smashing the coach in pieces, killing one man by the name of Mackey, a drover from Cassville, Mo., who was on his return from California, and injuring every other person on the stage to a greater or lesser extent."

As Muybridge recalled it, "I left California July, 1860, to go overland, and from thence to Europe; I traveled by stage. I had an accident on the way. After taking supper at a house on the road, I left on a stage drawn by six wild mustangs, and recollect nothing more for nine days, when I found myself lying on a bed at Fort Smith, 180 miles from the place. I found a scar on my head. I had a double vision—saw two objects at once; had no sense of smell or taste; also had confused ideas. These acute symptoms continued three months. I was under treatment about a year. When I went to New York, I was treated there. Then I went to London and consulted a physician named Gull. When I came to my senses at Fort Smith I found an acquaintance sitting on my bed, and he told me of an accident which had happened. I brought an action against the company for $10,000 damages, and they compromised by paying me $2,500. My fellow passenger told me that after traveling half an hour the brake got out of order and the mustangs ran away. I tried to get out of the boot of the stage by cutting the canvas with a knife. Here the stage struck a stump and I was thrown out. Two passengers were killed and all injured. I was in perfect health before that."

Arthur Shimamura, a University of California, Berkeley, neurologist who is an expert on orbitofrontal cortex injuries, makes a strong case that Muybridge suffered injury to this portion of the brain in the stagecoach accident. The cranium is for the most part a smooth case for the brain, but the interior eyesockets are sharp and can cut the orbitofrontal cortex in a high-impact collision. Among the common effects of these contusions are emotional outbursts, inappropriate social behavior, risk-taking, obsessive-compulsive behavior, and a loss of inhibition. These tendencies would be evident in later years, according to the testimony of Muybridge's friends and colleagues, who called him impatient, nervous, irritable, untidy, easily excited, wavering, and eccentric. Sometimes those who suffer this injury also become more creative. Muybridge may well have been one of them. All that is certain is that this accident ended his first foray into America, and that the man who came back to San Francisco nearly seven years later was a different man with a different name.

HELIOS

Before the accident Muybridge apparently intended to return to California directly; instead he meandered for years. He returned to England and sought advice from the eminent doctor Sir William Gull. Prescriptions in that era consisted largely of unhelpful medications and pleasant orders of rest, outdoor activity, and seaside air, and Muybridge seems to have been treated with the latter. (There is still little treatment for his kind of brain injury.) It is sometimes said that Gull prescribed outdoor activity and this led Muybridge to landscape photography, but landscape photography was a brand-new, technically demanding pursuit full of bulky equipment and strong chemicals. It had little in common with idyllic strolls. He came back to New York in 1861 to sue the Butterfield Stage Company and later that year wrote an uncle in Australia that he was going to the continent "on business that may detain me some months." These are hardly the acts of an invalid; he seems to have been casting about for a purpose in life, and he may also having been sitting out the United States' Civil War. His inventiveness first surfaced during these missing years, with a mention of a printing device and a proposal for a washing machine. These practical innovations fall far short of his later creative breakthroughs, and the most important thing he seems to have done during the "missing years" is master photography. He was from the start of this second career a good photographer with superb technical skills. There is no evidence of how much he learned in England and whether he was influenced by any of the great photographers at work there in the 1860s, such as Julia Margaret Cameron, Roger Fenton, and Lewis Carroll.

When he resurfaced in San Francisco in 1867, the *-gridge* that sounded grudging had become a *bridge*. He was Muybridge. But he took his photographs under the nom de plume Helios, perhaps to shelter his new creative life from what was expected of the returning merchant. It was as though he had divided himself: Muybridge took care of the business of selling the photographs, but Helios took the pictures. Helios, Greek for the sun, is not a modest appelation, but Muybridge's aspirations were no longer modest. Early on, photography had been called "the pencil of nature" and "sun drawings," with the implication that nature itself was the artist; with his new name, Muybridge was laying claim to being that nature, that sun. Whether or not photography was an art was debated then, and those who took the photographs were often merely anonymous "camera operators," but Muybridge always insisted he was an artist and put his name on his work. He bought a light carriage that served as a portable darkroom and carrier for the bulky equipment of a roaming wet-plate photographer and had "Helios's Flying Studio" painted on the side, the same phrase he put in his new advertisements.

Having spent his youth on the practical pursuits of a middle-aged man, the thirty-six-year-old had now launched on a life of adventure that would have thrilled any boy. He was one of the new breed of landscape photographers, supplying images for a nation whose imagination swelled into those landscapes and their possibilities. American landscape photography begins in earnest in 1867. That year, the Civil War photographer Timothy O'Sullivan went west to work for geologist-surveyor Clarence King's government-sponsored Fortieth Parallel Survey through Nevada, Utah, and Colorado and made the most subtle and incisive of survey photographs. William Henry Jackson, who was soon to become a survey photographer himself, began his photographic career by purchasing a studio in Omaha, Nebraska, that year. A. J. Russell was making his epic photographs of the Union Pacific Railroad, and A. A. Hart was then doing the same for the

Central Pacific Railroad. That pivotal year, Carleton Watkins, who had been at it longest, went to photograph Mount Lassen and Mount Shasta for the California Geological Survey.

Photography in the mid-nineteenth century took many forms. The images that commanded the most respect were those that most resembled paintings and could be exhibited like paintings: the large-format portrait, genre, and landscape photographs. All photographic prints in that era were contact prints—that is, they were made by laying the glass negative directly on the photosensitive paper. Thus the negatives themselves became vast. The most ambitious and technically difficult landscape images were called "mammoth plates": Muybridge himself eventually made mammoth-plate negatives that were twenty by twenty-four inches. But early on there were also lockets, cameos, and even cuff links bearing small photographic portraits; in the 1860s came the enormously popular cartes de visite, portraits about the size of playing cards produced in quantity; through the 1860s and '70s shows of "magic lantern" slides that could be projected onto a wall or screen flourished; and there were stereographic cards.

The stereograph had been popularized at the end of the 1850s, and the majority of the landscapes taken by Muybridge and many of his peers would be in this hyperdimensional medium. They were made to be seen in a viewer that let two photographic views taken simultaneously from slightly disparate positions merge into one three-dimensional image. The effect was less like the depth of field and dimensionality of ordinary binocular human vision than it was like the pop-out valentines and paper theaters popular in the era. The sense of deep space was exaggerated, but the objects seemed to sit on several flat planes within it. Photographers sought views that would emphasize the stereograph's strong points: deeply receding space with solid objects distributed throughout the foreground, middle ground, and background. Stereographic cards fed a passionate desire to see the world represented as compellingly as possible, a desire that would find its greatest satisfaction in movies. Like cinema and magic-lantern shows, stereographic photography was a medium in which the viewer could lose him or herself, a transporting medium that filled the eyes with a vision of someplace else. Stereoscope enthusiast Oliver Wendell Holmes said of the experience, "The shutting out of surrounding objects, and the concentration of the whole attention, which is a consequence of this, produce a dream-like exaltation . . . in which we seem to leave the body behind us and sail away into one strange scene after another, like disembodied spirits."

Photography was an art, a science involving chemistry and optics, and a business. Studio portraiture was the major source of money, since virtually everyone wanted a picture of self and loved ones, and the work was steady and easy to carry out. Most portrait subjects preferred to appear outdoors than in, and a secondary industry supplied, as the Scovill Manufacturing Co. of New York's ads put it, "balustrades of new designs, good Rocks, in three parts; Rustic Fences in the wood" for these portrait studios. Landscape photography was a far trickier prospect than portraiture both because of the technical challenges and because the market was far less certain. It was this latter branch to which Muybridge dedicated himself—people only appear in his work as either small figures in the landscape or representatives of a particular place or occupation. He documented several groups of Native Americans, a few Chinese miners and city dwellers, army troops, and San Francisco crowds but made no known portraits. His photograph of Emperor Norton on a bicycle is as close as he got—literally as close, for though Muybridge photographed individuals a few more times and made hundreds of motion studies of men and women, he never photographed anyone as close-up as portraiture requires, never depicted them as expressive faces rather than representative bodies. It says much about him that he always kept his distance.

The photographers of the West are sometimes praised for their "untutored genius" in landscape composition, but in the nineteenth century images of idealized landscapes proliferated on teacups and plates, printed fabric, advertising cards, wallpaper, cheap prints, even the motifs on stock certificates, as well as in the art books Muybridge once sold. Landscape was inescapable. Before the Civil War, there had been little photography of the West, but afterward the San Francisco galleries and the government photographers in the interior west sent thousands of images cascading east. By November 1866 the prominent San Francisco gallery Lawrence and Houseworth was advertising over a thousand stereoscope views of California—mining scenes, trees, cities, and of course Yosemite. Most of the major landscape photography of that era was commissioned by government surveys, but the Californians did their best work independently. There was a market for and in California, and landscape and cityscape photography flourished in San Francisco as nowhere else. The images were usually called "views," a term that did not distinguish between urban and rural places.

The wet-plate process that reigned supreme through the 1860s and '70s required that the negative be made, exposed, and developed in quick succession, so all the chemistry went wherever the camera did. At one point Watkins traveled through the mountains with 2,000 pounds of equipment, and Muybridge sometimes had as many as four assistants with him, along with a pack train. The first step in making a landscape photograph was pitching the dark-tent, a small tent of red or orange fabric in which photographic materials could be handled without exposing them (though in more accessible locations, a "dark wagon" might perform the same purpose, and such wagons and tents are sometimes visible in the survey photographs of the era). Inside the tent or wagon, the glass plate was made into a negative by pouring collodion, a volatile syrup of gun cotton and ether, over it and deftly tilting it to coat it evenly (a smudged plate or an unevenly applied collodion would result in a streaked or uneven picture). The coated plate was then briefly dipped into a bath of silver nitrate, drained, and placed into a light-excluding holder to be inserted into the camera for exposure. The photograph had to be taken in the few minutes before the emulsion dried; the exposed negative had to be developed on the spot.

The camera itself was little more elaborate than the old camera obscuras: it was a tripod-mounted wooden box on the front of which a lens mounted on a smaller, sliding box focused an image that appeared upside down on the ground-glass back wall. The photographer, draped under a dark cloth, could see and compose the image that appeared on the ground glass, and when he was satisfied, the plate was slipped in and the exposure was made by taking the lens cap off for an interval ranging from a few seconds to several minutes. There were no shutters, no light meters. Intuition and experience, rather than precise measurements, governed the process. Once the chemicals and darkroom were set up, a fast photographer could make a picture in half an hour from plain glass to developed negative. William Henry Jackson once boasted that he could do it in fifteen minutes.

Muybridge may have set out for Yosemite Valley before he left California in 1860; it was from that valley that he launched his artistic career in 1867. On that trip, Muybridge photographed his equipment sitting among the rocks: the dark tent provided only enough room to stand up in while handling equipment, and the bottles of chemicals stood haphazardly on the rocks. He was already superb at his métier: after he sent a batch of his Yosemite photographs to the *Philadelphia Photographer,* the country's main photography journal, they requested negatives, and a print from one of those negatives became their "picture of the month." Muybridge also knew how to promote his work, and he was never backward about doing so.

It has often been said that California is to the United States as the United States is to the world: an empire of infinite possibility and exaggeration; and it was as true then as now. Yosemite was then the definitive emblem of this version of California, and much of the market for images of Yosemite was in the East (Watkins had already won a medal at a Paris exposition for his Yosemite photographs; Muybridge would win one in Vienna in 1873). In their influential guide to housekeeping published in 1869, New Englanders Catherine Beecher and Harriet Beecher Stowe recommended readers display three chromolithographs for the "refinement of thought" they would impart, including Albert Bierstadt's *Sunset in the Yosemite Valley.* In its epic grandeur, Yosemite had become a national landscape, as Niagara Falls had been earlier in the nineteenth century and the Grand Canyon would be in the twentieth. The height of its rock faces and waterfalls, the verdure of its meadows, the girth of the nearby sequoias, suggested the country's own aspirations to greatness. The United States rooted its identity in its landscapes, as though to suggest that its identity was itself natural, in contrast to the much-denounced artificiality of European culture.

Of course, the ability to appreciate landscape was considered evidence of refinement, and Yosemite appealed precisely because its beauties so resembled those of Europe, or at least of the images inspired by European art. With its greenness, its water, its enclosure, its often misty atmosphere, it was for easterners an island of familiar aesthetic appeal in the ocean of strangeness of the arid plains, deserts, and mountains of the West. It also contrasted with the mined lands all around it. The seven-mile-long valley was officially set apart by an act of Congress in 1864, at the height of the Civil War, one of the world's first landscapes to be protected by any government and the first to be set aside by that government. Two hundred and forty tourists came to the valley that year, 360 the next, and 450 in 1867, the year Muybridge went there with his cameras. A great national symbol of nature, Yosemite was known largely through the devices of culture—paintings, books and articles, and photographs.

Muybridge was one of the first few photographers to arrive there. Charles Leander Weed had been brought in in 1859 to make photographs from which the valley's first promoter, James Hutchings, made engravings for his publications. Carleton Watkins took extraordinary mammoth-plate photographs there in 1861 and 1864–65, virtually the first major landscape photographs in the United States and the first of that technically formidable size. The mild-mannered Watkins had set the standards of landscape photography Muybridge would seek to exceed. Born in upstate New York six months before his rival was born in Kingston, Watkins grew up with Collis P. Huntington, who would become one of the "Big Four" magnates of the Central Pacific Railroad. When Watkins came out to California in 1851, Huntington employed him in his Sacramento business delivering mining supplies, and later he would become Huntington's photographer as Muybridge became Stanford's. After Huntington's store, Watkins found employment with a bookseller, then seems to have stumbled into photography under the aegis of Robert Vance, San Francisco's preeminent photographer of the 1850s. By 1857 he was making landscape photographs in the new wet-plate process.

In the 1860s and 1870s, landscape was a western business, but Watkins came first, and he stood alone. Historian Weston J. Naef calls his 1861 photographs "the first body of work to systematically present the landscape as a wilderness before the arrival of man . . . not the first landscape photographs, but they are the first to present nature from a deliberately assumed artistic posture," and so he can be considered the founder of the major photographic tradition of landscape on this continent. Watkins was a visionary, and the landscapes of his vision had neither the strangeness of terra incognita nor the roughness of the Wild West. They are radiant with a mysterious serenity. For his camera, the world stood still, and the resulting pictures looked like the true world everyone sought but no one else could locate among the mining booms, railroad building, land grabs, mobs, and murders. His landscapes were composed in the aesthetic sense of being harmoniously arranged, but they were composed in the psychological sense as well. They are pictures of reflective water, solid rock, air so transparent even the remotest objects are clear. In that absolute clarity the visual suddenly speaks of solidity, of silence, of warmth, things that seldom find their way into a photograph.

Muybridge must have aggravated Watkins by dogging his tracks both as an artist and an explorer, but he was not exactly an imitator. Where Watkins was tranquil, Muybridge was turbulent, and his greatest Yosemite photographs would be precarious, disturbing, unsettled. Where Watkins was content to make hundreds of pictures of lucid beauty from Washington State to the southern deserts, Muybridge would push on—covering even more ground, inventing new techniques, eventually moving out of landscape photography altogether. He began with 100 half-plate (six-inch-by-eight-inch photographs; full plate is usually eight inches by ten inches) and 160 stereoscope images of Yosemite. While Watkins generally photographed in the flat calm light of midday, Muybridge worked when the shadows were dramatic, and all his Yosemite work shows a strange attraction to debris, to piles of rocks, tangles of dead branches, fallen trees, to a foreground of chaos. He was good but not yet great, and it was his innovations that called attention to his work. He photographed new places, used unusual camera angles, and pushed the possibilities of the camera.

He photographed Yosemite Falls from under the falls. In early November, the newspaper of the nearest town, the *Mariposa Gazette,* reported, "A. M. Maybridge of San Francisco is taking photographs of Yo Semite Valley. In his perambulations about the valley, he discovered a crevice, between the Sentinel and Cathedral Rock, one thousand feet deep, and less than a yard wide." His stereophotograph looking straight down into the crevice that bisects the picture is nothing like a conventional landscape composition. The image conveys a sense of vertigo and of almost anatomical form. With boulders wedged deep within it, this is a sensual cleft and a dangerous one. Other images featured waterfalls, rainbows, and cloud formations; many are centered on some form of water. Watkins captured the eternal; Muybridge chased the evanescent. Still water was a much loved subject of landscape photography, and Muybridge had already learned the trick of showing the watery reflection of the landscape rather than the landscape itself. Moving water was something else altogether. Seen up close, rushing streams and waterfalls turned into feathery white spaces on the film, because the exposures were slower than the flow of the water. Sometimes it looked as though the rivers flowed with milk.

The flyer Muybridge issued in February 1868 announced "views of our world-renowned Yo-Semite Valley, photographed last year by 'Helios.' For artistic effect, and careful manipulation, they are pronounced by all the best landscape painters and photographers in the city to be the most exquisite photographic views ever produced on this coast." Some of the newspapers rose almost to the level of these boasts. The *Alta* praised "just such cloud effects as we see in nature or oil-painting but almost never in a photograph: the rocky faces of the rugged precipices are partly obscured by floating clouds, and in one of the views the valley is filled with low-hanging mists. In another a rainbow is photographed on the spray of the Nevada Fall. . . . The effect of falling water, shown in a photograph of the base of the Lower Yosemite Fall, is also very wonderful, and cannot be sufficiently admired." That year twenty of Muybridge's small images were used to illustrate John S. Hittell's guidebook to Yosemite Valley, a prestigious launch to a new career. Later the writer Helen Hunt Jackson would visit his San Francisco gallery and exclaim in a Boston newspaper article, "Mr. Muybridge's pictures have another peculiarity, which of itself would mark them superior to others. The skies are always most exquisitely rendered. His cloud photographs alone fill a volume and many of them remind one vividly of Turner's studies of skies. The contrast between a photographed landscape, with a true sky added, and one with the usual ghastly, lifeless, pallid stippled sky is something which it is impossible to overstate." It's arguable whether Muybridge was better than Watkins, whose smooth skies contributed to the neoclassical calm of his work, but his landscapes with cloudy skies achieved a very different effect.

The chemistry of wet-plate photography perceived yellows as far darker than they are and blues as far lighter. The sky in most nineteenth-century photography is pale and featureless, because to expose for the land was to overexpose for the sky. Photohistorian Peter Palmquist points out that Muybridge "tolerated more darkness in the foreground" than Watkins; his shorter exposures and darker images improved his ability to photograph clouds in the first place. Too, though a blue sky would come across as very pale, a stormy sky could provide exactly the opposite effect. Muybridge pursued cloudiness in two other ways. First, he created an archive of cloud photographs that he then printed over the pale sky. Some of his clouds were unabashed forgeries, just as were his later "moonlight" scenes, in which the sky was merely a diurnal cloud scene printed dark—what filmmakers call "day for night"—and the moon was the sun seen dimly or a

A Study of Clouds (one frame of stereo).

white circle added to the clouds. What truth meant in photography was not yet settled—retouching was almost a universal practice, and some of the most respected photographers made composite images. No one minded clouds that had been added later. Was the white sky that came from technical limitations truer than a sky full of realistic-looking clouds that just happened to be from another time and place? The clouds were, in a way, the lie that tells the truth, the manipulation that made Muybridge's photographs look more convincing and more "artistic," as art was then imagined. The clouds also made his pictures moodier, more romantic.

Some of Muybridge's clouds were additions, and this had been done before, though seldom so well and perhaps never so extensively. Other of

A Study of Clouds (one frame of stereo).

his landscape photographs with clouds were made with his "sky shade," which constituted an improvement on the existing method for photographing clouds in a landscape. In May 1869 he published an account in the *Philadelphia Photographer* of this spring-operated shutter, which allowed extremely brief sky exposures with longer exposures for the landscape below. (A spring-operated shutter system would later be a crucial part of the high-speed motion-studies technology.) He had made a camera that could see at two different speeds: faster for sky and slower for the earth below. Already the manipulation of time and the refinement of camera technology was on his mind. Muybridge had a passion for clouds. He later made a series of fifteen stereograph cloud studies, a series more akin to a scientist's specimen collection or a painter's sketchbook than to the work of his peers in photography. He may have been aware of the English painter John Constable's cloud studies of the 1820s, art critic John Ruskin's copious 1860s writings about clouds in *Modern Painters,* or American painter Jasper Cropsey's 1855 essay "Up Among the Clouds." Having spent so much time as a bookseller with the cloud-adorned engravings in the art books of the time, he may have had ideas drawn from painting and printmaking about what made a landscape beautiful.

He certainly was thinking about landscape and photography in more sophisticated ways than his peers, and the cloud studies cannot have been made for commercial reasons—the audience eagerly snapping up stereographs as souvenirs of their encounters can hardly have known what to make of them. He continued adding clouds to his landscape photographs as long as he worked in the genre. Like his comment about watching the buzzard fly for an hour without flapping its wings, his photographs of clouds were evidence of his pleasure in observing natural phenomena for their own sake. They are evidence of his persistent passion for the mutable, the fleeting, and the unstable. They put the stamp of his disposition and aesthetic on landscapes of every kind and sometimes even cityscapes. And they were a triumph over the limitations of photography in his time.

MUYBRIDGE

Helios took the pictures; Muybridge sold them. Watkins went into business for himself with the Yosemite Gallery on Montgomery Street and was thereafter torn between taking photographs in the field and minding the store until he went bankrupt in 1875 and his underhanded creditor seized all his negatives as part of the property. Muybridge began by operating out of his old friend Silas Selleck's Cosmopolitan Gallery at 415 Montgomery, but moved in quick succession to the optician Ewing's store at 138 Montgomery, then a few doors away to the Nahl brothers' painting and photography studio at 121 Montgomery. By 1870 he was with Thomas Houseworth's big gallery at 12 Montgomery Street, where optical equipment and "philosophical instruments" were also sold. Whether he was moving up the ladder of photographic success or was restless is hard to tell. He burned plenty of bridges in later years.

In February 1868 Muybridge advertised his Yosemite half-plate photographs at twenty dollars for twenty pictures, and in April he advertised that "HELIOS is prepared to photograph private residences, animals, or views in the city or any part of the coast." Muybridge undermined his vast output of good work with his great work. Had he never made his 1872 mammoth-plate Yosemite pictures, his 1878 panorama of San Francisco, and his motion studies, he might be remembered for his less ambitious landscapes and his many other cityscapes. In the late 1860s he documented San Francisco and the Bay Area more profusely than any other photographer, and his pictures show how the place had grown from a camp to a cosmopolitan city. He took many, many pictures of the shores of the San Francisco Bay, often with a lone figure standing in the distance, as evocative as those in the paintings of the German romantic artist Caspar David Friedrich, and he photographed the ruinous Spanish missions of the California coast with the same melancholy. The bay and the missions were documentary subjects, but the pleasures of ruins and solitude were romantic ones.

Muybridge worked as a journalist, photographing the damage of the October 21, 1868, earthquake and had the results on sale within a week. He later photographed local industries ranging from San Quentin prisoners in their striped uniforms making wheels for the travels of others to the extensive series on Buena Vista Winery he called *A Vintage in California*. He photographed downtown buildings, wharves, and San Francisco's pleasure grounds, including the Cliff House out at the city's wild northwest corner and Woodward's Gardens, the amusement park that had opened in 1866. Woodward's Gardens at Fourteenth and Mission Streets was a comic mixture of the marvelous and the shamelessly commercial, not unlike Muybridge's own work at the time, and for a while he maintained an independent sales room there for his photographs. The gardens had an art gallery with landscape paintings and marble sculptures of nude women a little more nubile than was strictly consistent with art's uplifting agenda. It had a small lake with a round boat much loved by children and a saloon better loved by adults. Badly taxidermized animals from polar bears to tigers and more marble sculptures in various states of undress ornamented its lawns like broken toys. Muybridge photographed the Chinese giant "Chang Woo Gow, 8 ft. 3 in.," who exhibited himself at Woodward's Gardens, looking gracious in his embroidered satin robe, far more at ease than the half-nude Hawaiian performers he also photographed there. San Francisco's female population had increased considerably, and many

Chang Woo Gow, the Chinese Giant, 8 ft. 3 in. (one frame of stereo).

women were to be seen strolling or sitting with parasols there. All in all, Muybridge made more than forty stereoscopic pictures of the place, but he was hardly a local photographer.

He had managed to get a commission to go to Alaska with General Henry W. Halleck in late summer of 1868. They sailed up the coast on the steamship *Pacific,* and Muybridge photographed the Canadian ports along the way, then the Indians and "Russo Greek" priests of Sitka, Fort Wrangle, and Fort Tongass. The general officially accepted the photographs in October with the statement, "These views besides being beautiful works of art give a more correct idea of Alaska and its scenery and vegetation than can be obtained from any written description of that country." For much of the rest of his career, Muybridge advertised himself as "official photographer to the U.S. government," and he did receive a few more commissions. Early in 1871, he photographed the lighthouses of the California coast on commission for the Lighthouse Board. His government work seems to have given him entrée to many off-limits military sites of the Bay Area, including Alcatraz, the San Francisco Presidio, and Fort Point, and the Fort Point pictures were ordered destroyed by the War Department. This was his range, from Alaska to Arizona, from pleasure gardens to gun emplacements, from wildernesses to hotels, and from mediocre to brilliant.

Muybridge loved to work in series and sequences, studying natural phenomena and their changes. In the wilderness his photographs focused on ephemeral phenomena—on clouds and water, rainbows and mist. In the Bay Area he documented sequential change. It is easy to see precursors of the motion studies in this early work. In 1868 he photographed three stages of the sun setting over Mount Tamalpais on the north side of the Golden Gate and three stages of a festive crowd swarming onto Market Street for a Fourth of July parade, and in 1870 he documented several stages of the U.S. Mint being built. He was photographing the passage of time at intervals ranging from a few minutes to a few months. He was already preoccupied with how photography could capture time—not a single moment of time already past, as a single photograph does, but the transformations wrought by time's passage. He was trying to change the tense of photography, and the true subject of these serial photographs is change itself.

LESSONS OF THE
GOLDEN SPIKE

An Eclipse of the Sun ▪
The Transubstantiation of the Bison ▪
Unseen Forces ▪ *The Swirl of the Present, 1872*

■ *Overleaf: Snow Sheds at Emigrant Gap, Looking East,* from the series *Central Pacific Railroad,* ca. 1869 (one frame of stereo).

AN ECLIPSE OF THE SUN

The photograph by A. J. Russell of the driving of the Golden Spike at Promontory Point, Utah, on May 10, 1869, has become an icon of American history. The Union Pacific had laid track a thousand miles west from its terminal at Omaha to join at this remote point with the Central Pacific, stretching more than seven hundred miles farther across the emigrant trail through Nevada, across the steep Sierra with tunnels and trestles, then down to Sacramento. In the foreground of Russell's photograph are several clumps of sagebrush. Farther away across the dusty ground the men who built the railroad are lined up, so many of them that only a few edges of the ties of the actual railroad tracks are visible. The east-running Central Pacific locomotive Jupiter and the west-running UP No. 119 are so close that the men who swarm over them can almost reach out to pour each other champagne. In the unforgiving midday light, the men's clothes look creased and rumpled, fitted to the body by long wear. Shadows turn their eyesockets into black caverns. They are the engineers and managers, the Utah Mormons both railroads managed to avoid paying for their contract work, the directors of the railroad, and the workers, the layers of tracks, drivers of spikes, haulers of loads. It was a moment years in the making. The railroad had been built by hard labor—by former Union soldiers and Irish immigrants on the east, by more Irishmen and thousands of Chinese immigrants (nowhere visible in the Golden Spike photographs, though they had graded the site only two hours earlier) on the west, and farther away by the miners and foundries producing enough iron to bind a continent. But it had also been built as an idea and a political and financial possibility by the men who bribed, lobbied, calculated, gambled, and improvised it into being.

Two other photographers, the Salt Lake City studio owner C. R. Savage and the Central Pacific photographer A. A. Hart, were there with their cameras on that day too, taking alternate versions of the same event. Their photographs of the ceremony made the moment permanent. But telegraphy made it ubiquitous. Leland Stanford drove the spike of California gold with a sledgehammer of Nevada silver that had been wired to connect to the telegraph lines that ran east and west along the railroad tracks. The instant Stanford struck the spike, a signal would go out around the nation. It was the first live national media event. The signal set off cannons in San Francisco and New York. In the nation's capital the telegraph signal caused a ball to drop, one of the balls that visibly signaled the exact time in observatories in many places then (of which the ball dropped in New York's Times Square at the stroke of the New Year is a last relic). The joining of the rails would be heard in every city equipped with fire-alarm telegraphs, in Philadelphia, Omaha, Buffalo, Chicago, Sacramento. Celebrations would be held all over the nation. People felt that to know something as it was happening was to participate in it in some obscure way, even though they could neither see nor hear the ruckus in the remote site on the north shore of the Great Salt Lake. It was, as the *San Francisco Bulletin* put it, "a triumph bloodless, deathless, but no less glorious to the Nation and the State: a victory over space, the elements, and the stupendous mountain barriers separating San Francisco from the world." As an event experienced by a whole nation, the joining of the rails was akin to the moon landing a century later, but that landing made the moon accessible to only a few picked astronauts, while the railroad changed the scale of the continent for everyone.

Railroads had been changing time for years before Stanford lifted his silver sledgehammer, and measuring time had long been a crucial concern for travelers. In 1612, when Galileo improved upon that new device the telescope and became the first to see the moons of Jupiter, he realized that their frequent and reliable eclipses could be used to calculate time and thus location far more precisely than ever before. A traveler equipped with tables of the eclipses, a telescope, and an accurate timekeeping device could observe a Jupiterean eclipse and measure how far east or west of the table's times he—or rarely, she—was. This was the first method of calculating longitude, and clocks were crucial to it. Measuring space by time became crucial to exploration; more than two centuries after Galileo watched those remote eclipses, John Charles Frémont was using the same technol-

Lake Flora (Crater of an Extinct Volcano), Mt. Stanford in the Distance, from the series *Central Pacific Railroad*, ca. 1869 (one frame of stereo).

ogy to navigate his way across the western United States and map the regions he crossed. More precise timepieces—the chronometers of the eighteenth century—made it possible to locate one's latitude even at sea, where Jupiter's moons were not so easy to inspect. It was in the course of these navigational developments that Greenwich Observatory became the ground zero of global time, the point from which time would come to be measured first around Britain and eventually around the world. But railroads brought an entirely new concern with time and how to measure it from place to place. Rather than exactly measure locality, railroads demanded locality be ignored.

Before the railroads, each city and region kept its own time by the sun:

noon was when the sun was highest overhead. Every meridian or degree of longitude corresponds to about four minutes of time; 15 degrees of longitude correspond to an hour of time in the 360-degree division of the world. To travel rapidly across the earth was to see one's watch go out of synchronization with the sun and thus with local time. Early on, most rail lines ran on the time of their headquarter city, which meant they were at odds with local time as soon as they had gone any distance east or west, and the differences between each railroad's time and each town's time made schedules intricately unwieldy. By the 1850s, British railroads were all synchronized to what was then called Railroad Time and is now called Greenwich Time. The breadth of Britain encompasses only thirty minutes of time difference, but many were outraged that they were told to keep time that was no longer solar, no longer true to their own locality. It would take a few more decades for the three-thousand-mile breadth, corresponding to nearly four hours of time difference, of the continental United States to be regulated by railroad time.

In 1869 Pittsburgh entrepreneur Samuel Langley began a precise-time-for-pay system, delivering the time signal from the Allegheny Observatory in that city to subscribers across the east. The celestial time of the transit telescope became the business time of the subscribing institutions. He wrote of the intricately intersecting system of railroads avoiding collisions by careful scheduling, "Time exactly obtained and kept is the regulator of this complex system of moving parts, which, in theory at least, should resemble one great piece of clock-work. To make things 'move like clock work' is not merely a figure of speech, then, here, where our lives depend on the accuracy of a conductor's watch." In other words, the railroads comprised a single machine that wrapped the continent in its iron ribbons and wreaths of steam. Regulating that machine to prevent collisions meant regulating the nation with the precision of a single clock. The Saratoga Springs teacher Charles Ferdinand Dowd proposed a way of doing so. It was he who in 1869 thought up and first laid out the uniform standard time system of four time zones, each an hour apart from the next.

When Stanford lifted his sledgehammer, there was no national time standard. Thus his strike was clocked in at 12:45 P.M. local time; at Washington, D.C., at 2:47; Cheyenne, Wyoming, at 1:53; at Virginia City, Nevada, at 12:30; at San Francisco at 11:46 or 11:44, depending on which source one selected. That most of the clocks concurred in making it approximately fifteen minutes before the hour doesn't reflect the wild variety of times: Boston was, for example, eleven minutes and forty-five seconds ahead of New York. Many railroad stations had two clocks, one for local solar time, another for railroad time. Dowd's system—which with minor modifications was adopted by North America's railroads in 1883—meant that all the minute hands used to tell railroad time would be synchronized; only the hour hands would differ. Dowd had expected the nation to retain its two-time system and in 1870 published an elaborate schedule charting the difference between the two at eight thousand railroad stations. But so powerful were the railroads that their time became the universally recognized time of the United States and Canada, and solar time virtually disappeared. The U.S. government officially adopted this scheme in 1918, and only a few cities held out longer for local time, particularly those whose locations made clock time significantly different than sun time.

In the course of the nineteenth century, time ceased to be a phenomenon that linked humans to the cosmos and became one administered by technicians to link industrial activities to each other. It changed the way people imagined their world. After Muybridge emigrated to the United States, his mother, Susannah Smith Muggeridge, moved in with her brother, John, only a few miles from the prime meridian of Greenwich. He collected clocks and was always striving and never succeeding in making the clocks all over the house strike simultaneously. The one in his bedroom was particularly unreliable, and that this bedside clock was nicknamed "Fanny" suggests how personal clocks had become, this one a mistress who ruled even over sleep. John Smith's desire to bring simultaneity to his own home suggests how difficult the task was, and at the time, how desirable. His was part of the anxiety of an age shifting its rhythms from those of the heavens to those of the machine. What factories had done for work time—impose a standardized, inflexible schedule on workers—the railroads did to the world at large. Midway through that century, Henry David Thoreau was living at Walden Pond, outside the community but near the railroad line. Standard time had not yet regulated America, but the railroad already dominated the experience of time. Thoreau commented, "I watch the passage of the morning cars with the same feeling that I do the rising of the sun, which is hardly more regular. Their train of clouds stretching far behind and rising higher and higher, going to heaven while the cars are going to Boston, conceals the sun for a minute and casts my distant field into the shade, a celestial train beside which the petty train of cars which hugs the earth is but the barb of the spear. . . . They go and come with such regularity and precision, that the farmers set their clocks by them, and thus one well-conducted institution regulates a whole country." The railroad had eclipsed the sun.

THE TRANSUBSTANTIATION OF THE BISON

The railroad barged into the Great Plains as the Industrial Revolution incarnate, and the Native Americans there were not pleased to see their wide-open spaces seamed and domesticated. Even as the meeting of the rails was being celebrated, a stray party of soldiers seeking a Paiute raider stumbled upon the scene by accident, stopped to goggle, and then continued their pursuit and killed their quarry. The 1863 treaty with the neighboring Western Shoshone of Nevada stated in its opening clauses, "It being understood that provision has been made by the government of the United States for the construction of a railway from the plains west to the Pacific ocean, it is stipulated by the said bands that the said railway or its branches may be located, constructed, and operated, and without molestation from them, through any portion of country claimed or occupied by them." But the railroad wars were primarily with the Lakota, Cheyenne, and Arapaho of the Great Plains.

The transcontinental was at the time by far the longest railroad line ever built, and unlike all the others, it had preceded and carried development with it, rather than serving existing enterprise and populations. The U.S. Army had to fight a war on behalf of the Union Pacific, the contemporaneous Kansas Pacific, and the later Northern Pacific railroads across the plains, and the Union Pacific's own men were often ex-soldiers who took up rifles as readily as sledgehammers to build the railroad. In 1872 the Bureau of Indian Affairs reported of the Great Plains nations, "Claiming to own most, if not all, of the Territory of Dakota, and portions of the Territories of Montana and Wyoming, as well as the western part of Nebraska, they used every effort to prevent the settlement of the country so claimed, their hostility being especially directed against the Union Pacific Railroad." The railroad wars had come to a climax in 1867 when General William Tecumseh Sherman was sent to clear a belt for the railways. "No interrup-

Shoshone Indians at Corinne [Utah], from the series *Central Pacific Railroad*, ca. 1869 (one frame of stereo).

tion to work on the line of the U.P. will be tolerated," he trumpeted. "Eastern people must not allow their sympathy with the Indians to make them forget what is due to those who are pushing the 'frontier' farther and farther west. These men deserve protection, and they must have it." The Lakota raided the railroad gangs and sabotaged railroad lines so that engines wrecked and the stranded crew could be picked off, but by 1868 many of the Plains tribes had signed treaties.

Those tribes were up against a degree of industrialization and technology that would devastate them. But they were neither strangers nor enemies to European transformation in its earlier stages. Long before Europeans reached the region, aspects of their culture arrived—diseases and guns from the northeast, horses from the southwest. In the seventeenth and eighteenth centuries, guns in the hands of their enemies had driven the Lakota south and west from their original homeland; horses had made that West of open plains and huge buffalo herds alluring; smallpox had opened up more of that space by decimating the more sedentary tribes who had lived along the river valleys. For the Plains tribes the horse was a technology as transformative as the railroad would be for the Yankees of the nineteenth century. In Cheyenne folklore the god Maheo warned them, "If you have horses everything will be changed for you forever. You will have to move around a lot to find pasture for your horses. You will have to give up gardening and live by hunting and gathering, like the Comanches. And you will have to come out of your earth houses and live in tents." The great horse nomads of the plains came into existence in the eighteenth century. Having abandoned the diversity of hunted, gathered, and grown food sources they previously depended upon, they turned to trading with the remaining semisedentary tribes for foodstuffs to vary their diet and with the fur traders for guns, ammunition, pots, iron arrowheads, and other metal tools. They had been, in a remote and romantic way, assimilated into the vast commercial networks of Europe. This trading was the beginning of the end of the vast buffalo herds, for the buffalo hunters in the market economy had incentive to kill more and more as subsistence hunters did not, and guns and horses gave them the means to do it. Their distant relationship with the market seemed to please them, but the arrival of the Industrial Revolution incarnate threatened to annihilate them and their hunting grounds.

It was the railroad and the white hunters who would bring the bison to the brink of extinction. Secretary of the Interior Jacob Cox declared, "The building of the Union Pacific Railroad has driven the buffalo from their former hunting grounds, [so] that it was impracticable for the Indians to rely upon this natural supply of food, clothing, and shelter." The army shrewdly estimated that annihilating the buffalo would sabotage the nomadic hunting way of life of the Plains Indians and make them far easier to coerce onto reservations. Sherman was using the same scorched-earth policy in the West that he had in the South during the Civil War. The great turning point was 1872. The Kansas Pacific Railroad was finished, and its western terminal at Dodge City became a collecting point for buffalo hides (as well as for cattle; the much-romanticized Texas cattle drives were bringing cows to the railroads; the railroads were transporting them to the vast slaughterhouses of Chicago; and Chicago was reducing them to meat for national consumption: cowboys too were part of the far-reaching new economy). On that railroad line, a train once ran for 120 miles through a single herd. Colonel Richard Dodge, after whom the town was named, conservatively estimated the number of hides shipped east on the railroads between 1872 and 1874 to be about one and a third million. The slaughter was profligate. About a million buffalo a year were killed, according to later estimates. Buffalo skeletons piled up into mountains, and these bones were later converted into fertilizer and other industrial products, though most parts of the dead animals were left to rot on the prairie. It was a golden age for scavengers, until some hunters began a sideline in wolfskins. By the 1880s the buffalo whose herds had once spread to the horizon were almost extinct. They had been killed for sport, for food for the railroad builders and other transients, and for hides to ship east. The unromantic destiny of most of those hides was factories. Before rubberized drive belts, the belts that drove the Industrial Revolution's factories were made of leather, and buffalo hide was thick and durable. The roaming bison herds were being transformed into the relentless churning of machines serving the cash economy.

The late eighteenth through the nineteenth centuries were the golden age for landscape representation, for a passion for nature represented as places beautiful to the eyes. This was also the era of rapacious exploitation, though to recite its particulars is to invoke an almost alchemical transformation from wildness to citified commodities. The beaver of the North American West went first, those dammers of rivers turned into felt top hats for city gentlemen. The gold of the California motherlode went afterward, the secret contents of streams and fossil rivers turned into money in the days when money was still a material medium rather than only numbers in an account or guarantees on paper. The whaling industry turned those titans of the seas into lamp oil for parlors and whalebone for corsets and brought them close to extinction, at least until 1870, when Rockefeller founded Standard Oil and began to pump out the black residue of the Jurassic past in unprecedented quantities. The forests of the nation were being pitched into the boilers of locomotives and smelters of ore, were becoming churches and rocking chairs and crates, and the buffalo were becoming factory belts. Organic material is usually harvested so that it

renews itself year after year, but in the nineteenth century the industrialized world began mining this material—passenger pigeons, bison, beaver,
whales, forests—into extinction or near-extinction. What was vanishing as
ecology was reappearing as imagery. Landscape showed up in the stereoscope cards in parlors, in the floral patterns on dresses and saddles and sil-
verware, in the scenery engraved on pocket watches.

UNSEEN FORCES

Those great landscapists Russell, Hart, and Savage photographed the
physical process of the building of the railroads, and when the line was
open, Muybridge and Watkins both made extensive stereoscope series of
the scenery along the route. Most accounts of the building of the railroad
concentrate on just that: the heroic and unprecedented toils of the laborers and engineers that drew a line in wood and iron across the continent.
But less visible webs were being spun. The transcontinental railroad was
far vaster than any of the manufactories of the East. It required unprecedented strata of bureacracy, unprecedented degrees of managerial coordination, and it reached as far into the political and economic systems of the
United States as it did into the landscape. The Central Pacific and the
Union Pacific were the biggest corporations of their time and the first to
have such extensive dealings with the federal, state, and local governments.
The modern corporation's complex synchronizations first appeared there,
and so did the penetration into the world on such a scale. First the railroads, then the networks for distributing energy, food, and basic goods,
drew people further and further into a system; and more and more of them
became employees of such systems. The independence of the frontier and
the subsistence farmer retreated further and further. This was the moment
in which many Americans first began to feel like cogs in the machine.

The postwar era was spectacularly corrupt, and the railroad barons and
their managers were the greatest corrupters, the issuers of bribes, the buyers of senators and congressmen, the controllers of newspapers, the
despotic monopolists controlling the price of many goods and the profit
margin of agriculture in particular. In 1873, when railroad financier Jay
Cooke got up early one day to shut his Philadelphia bank, launching the
depression that dragged into the late 1870s, President Grant was still
asleep in Cooke's mansion. In 1876, when Republican candidate Ruther-

ford B. Hayes found he had been chosen president after a stalemate in the electoral college, he was riding in the Pennsylvania Railroad magnate Tom Scott's private car. The railroad barons amassed vast fortunes by skimming off the money that was supposed to pay for railroad building and builders, and they made staggering sums from operating the resulting lines. In the West, the federal government gave them alternating sections of land alongside the railroad lines as incentives to build. Such land became far more valuable once it was on a railroad line, and so the major western railroads went into the real estate and development business. By the end of this era, the federal government had given the railroads 204,688 square miles of land, a total amount about a third larger than California.

The railroads were acquiring huge tracts of land while they made it possible to ignore the terrain as encounter and experience: they made place into real estate, and their railroads served to bring out immigrants to buy that land and increase their wealth (in October 1869 Mark Hopkins, Stanford, and the Crockers were on the board of the California Immigrant Union, "for the purpose of encouraging immigration"). These railroads generated and controlled manufacture and commerce, and for decades after the hammering home of the last spike, the Central Pacific and its successor, the Southern Pacific, had a monopoly on transportation in California and the interior West. The coordination that let almost a whole nation celebrate the moment of the driving of the Golden Spike was the coordination of systems of technology with political and economic power. Only the unions, the Indians, and a few poets stood up against the railroads and the system they represented. A whole continent, its indigenous nations, its wildlife, its commerce, its settlement patterns, were being altered for profit, and the profit concentrated in the hands of a few.

Those few who organized and chiefly owned the Central Pacific were Leland Stanford, Mark Hopkins, Charles Crocker, and Collis P. Huntington—"the Big Four"—and their corruption was as vast as their profit. One historian concludes, "A detailed study of the finances of the whole Central Pacific network showed that this railroad and its subsidiaries cost $58,000,000 to build, but since $120,000,000 was paid in bonds, stocks, and cash, there was an excess of $62,000,000. Most of this was clear profit, the Commissioners decided, and was paid entirely to Stanford, Huntington, Hopkins and Crocker, voted to themselves by their own votes. . . . When Hopkins died in 1878 he was worth at least $19,000,000, and in

Long Ravine Trestle and Bridge—113 Feet High, 878 Feet Long—Looking East, from the series *Central Pacific Railroad,* ca. 1869 (one frame of stereo).

1889 Crocker's fortune was estimated at over $24,000,000. Stanford's probably amounted to $30,000,000, and Huntington's over $40,000,000." Throughout the construction of the Central Pacific, they managed to hide their accounts from auditors, and when a later investigation got close to the truth, they burned the ledgers. The four men had been storekeepers in Sacramento, and they had all done well selling goods to the miners of the gold rush. Huntington had once briefly cornered the shovel market; eventually, as the mastermind of the Southern Pacific, he would control virtually the entire transportation industry of California and the West.

Like Huntington, Stanford had been raised in modest circumstances in upstate New York. Trained as a lawyer, he had come west in 1852 to join his brothers in selling groceries and mining supplies. His brothers started him out in rough conditions at a remote mining camp and eventually sold their Sacramento store to him and moved on to San Francisco. There he stayed, moderately prosperous until a lucky accident made him rich. The Lincoln mine in Amador County, to which he had extended credit, went bankrupt and he became its main stockholder. Under better management, the mine started to pay and paid enough to let him become one of the original investors in the transcontinental railroad scheme. His career really began in June 1861, when he managed to become both president of the newly formed Central Pacific Railroad and, thanks to his longtime involvement in Republican party politics and his wealth, governor of California. Conveniently, the CP's headquarters was in Sacramento, the state capital. To say that much of what he did would now be considered conflict of interest is an understatement.

Stanford is something of an enigma. As a young man he had the smoldering good looks of a stage villain, but as he became stouter, he came to look like a badly taxidermized badger. Smart enough to become the seventh-richest man in the United States, he was often regarded as slow and doltish by his colleagues. His speeches were lumbering, pious, and conventional. But he did much to establish the Southern Pacific, the corporation that began by taking over a badly managed California railroad line and ended by assimilating the CP and other railroads, building hundreds more miles of line, and running the state like a fiefdom into the twentieth century. He served as the SP's president until Huntington deposed him in 1890, reportedly still resentful over Stanford's sudden and successful bid for the U.S. Senate in 1885 after the railroad had already picked another candidate. Stanford inspired intense loyalty and intense hatred. He was devoted to his wife, Jane, and eventually gave her so many jewels she was said to have more than any royal family in Europe except those of Russia and Britain (at one point, he annoyed his railroad codirectors by buying her a hundred-thousand-dollar diamond necklace just as the corporation was pleading poverty to Congress).

That devotion would extend to his only child, Leland Jr., born in 1868, after eighteen years of marriage, as the railroad was nearing completion. His son's birth delayed his trip to Salt Lake City to negotiate the final stages of the building of the Central Pacific. Instead, he threw a banquet for his Sacramento friends at which Jane Stanford was surprised by the arrival of a huge silver platter she had not ordered: when its lid was lifted, the Stanford heir was lying there on a bed of blossoms, waiting to be displayed to the guests, like a trophy, a cannibalistic treat, or just another hallmark of the excess of the age. The younger Stanford was raised to be a steward of the vast wealth, and by puberty he was a connoisseur of the arts and collector of ancient artifacts.

While his partners retained their New England storekeepers' thrift, Stanford went in for ostentation, and even his hobbies turned into enormously expensive undertakings. He recalled that he "became interested in thoroughbred horses . . . through ill health. My doctor had ordered a vacation for me and had told me that I must go away on a tour. I could not leave at that time. . . . I bought a little horse that turned out to be remarkably fast, and it was in the using of it that I became interested in the study of the horse and its actions." It was Occident he bought in 1870 for a recreation that eventually became a consuming pursuit. Eventually, he would own nearly eight hundred racehorses at his 8,000-acre Palo Alto estate, where just the carrot crop to feed the colts covered sixty acres. His horses set nineteen world records, mostly in trotting, and it seems as though the obsession with speed and technological innovation that drove the building of the transcontinental railroad carried over into his prime pastime. He was a good judge of horses and as tender of their wellbeing as he was ruthless in his business practices. Fond of technology and ingenuity, he would transform the way trotting horses were trained and claim to be pursuing a higher goal, of breeding improved strains for the public at large. Social Darwinism was a great justification for the rapacious conduct of the great capitalists, and it manifested itself in other forms as well, such as Stanford's interest in scientific breeding (and the Darwinian rhetoric of his university in its early years). Stanford became a scientific horseman, and he studied equestrian gaits. Out of this obscure interest came Muybridge's greatest work.

THE SWIRL OF THE PRESENT, 1872

In the spring of 1872, Stanford commissioned Muybridge to photograph Occident in motion. Everything seemed to be in motion in that year. In May 1872 Dowd had brought to the Western Railroad Association meeting in St. Louis (whose members included the UP and CP) his proposal to create standardized time zones. In June, a hundred thousand New York City workers who had successfully struck for an eight-hour workday celebrated with a victory parade. In July, Greenwich Time became standard for all British post offices. That year, the corrupt Ulysses S. Grant successfully ran for re-election against a trio of easy opponents: the ailing newspaperman Horace Greeley (still remembered for his "Go west, young man"), the renegade feminist and spiritualist Victoria Woodhull, the nation's first female presidential candidate, and the eccentric George Frederick Train. Greeley called Train "an ass, a lunatic, a charlatan and a mountebank." Train had traveled around the world, made several fortunes, and spoken in Kansas for women's suffrage (while wearing lavender kid gloves, reporters noted; being a populist and a reformer never interfered with his being a dandy).

In 1863 Train had been the keynote speaker when ground for the UP was first broken in Omaha, and in 1864 he came up with the scheme for the Credit Mobilier of America, the paper corporation to which the UP directors awarded lucrative contracts whose profits they pocketed. In September 1872 the Credit Mobilier scandal of stolen profits and bribed congressmen broke, and all through the rest of that year and the next railroad investigations filled the newspapers. That was the year the tide turned for the railroads. When the Golden Spike was hammered home, they were still seen as carrying out the will of the nation for the good of the nation. Three years later they were widely regarded as a threat to democracy and as enemies of the people. In 1872 the CP was trying to get the government to give it Goat Island, the small land mass halfway between San Francisco and Oakland, as its western terminus, and the land grab aroused the wrath of many Californians. Even Stanford was on the defensive. The restless Train, however, had long ago moved on from arranging the UP's business schemes. "I have lived fast," he wrote afterward, "I have ever been an advocate of speed. I was born in a slow world, and I wished to oil the wheels and gears so that the machine would spin faster and, withal, to better purposes."

In 1872 Jules Verne published his enormously popular *Around the World in Eighty Days,* drawn in part from Train's circumnavigation of the globe in approximately that time two years earlier. It was the transcontinental railroad that had made such a venture possible, though the Suez Canal, which opened at the same time, helped. Train had sped across the continent, stopped in San Francisco long enough to infuriate a crowd at Maguire's Opera House with a speech on "the Chinese question," and hopped a boat across the Pacific. Verne's character had nothing in common with Train but his travel plans and his belief in the machine age, or perhaps Train represented the mania of the age, Verne's fictional Phileas Fogg its belief in its rationality. Fogg was a devotee of regularity and punctuality, "as exactly regulated as a Leroy chronometer." Verne wrote of Fogg's absolute indifference to scenery and civilizations: "Phileas Fogg, who was not traveling, but only describing a circumference, did not bother to inquire into these subjects; he was a solid body, traversing an orbit around the terrestrial globe according to the laws of rational mechanics. He was at this moment calculating in his mind the number of hours spent since his departure." Train and Verne proclaimed that the once all but infinite earth had shrunk into something that could be encompassed not just by an explorer, but by any passenger with adequate funds. The world could be traversed with indifference, without even looking out the window. The annihilation of time and space had made a great leap forward.

In 1872 the whole world seemed to be in motion, but one moment of stillness punctuated the year. That August, on the Yellowstone River, the Hunkpapa Lakota leader Sitting Bull and his tribesmen were fighting the soldiers protecting the Northern Pacific Railroad builders. A railroad line was being laid through what had been the last remote region, the last place in which the Plains nomads could live as they had lived. Earlier that summer Sitting Bull, whose very name described a buffalo, had declared at a peace conference, "I want those roads stopped just where they are, or turned in some other direction. We will then live peacefully together. If you stop your roads, we can get our game." General Sherman replied, "You cannot stop the locomotive any more than you can stop the sun or the moon, and you must submit." Sitting Bull was not ready to submit.

In the middle of the fight on the Yellowstone River, he laid down his gun and his quiver, walked toward the white soldiers, sat down on the grass, and lit his pipe. Two Oglalas and two Cheyennes came and sat down with him, and he passed them the pipe as the bullets whizzed overhead. Reckless bravery was required for that act, which harks back to the intertribal battles where counting coup and winning honor for bravery were goals as potent as killing the enemy. But it suggests an even more powerful yearning for a reprieve from history and its hectic pace in the 1870s. It was as though through courage and will the five men stepped off the runaway train of history or even stopped it. Perhaps in that interval they had time to see the grass clearly, to look at the sky, to think about where they stood, in the landscape as well as in history, to remember their lifetimes of roaming across such grasslands, fording rivers, following buffalo, of living in what then seemed to be the cyclical time of the seasons before the linear time of history caught them up. It was late to be fighting railroads. In 1872 the Oglala Lakota leader Red Cloud and his followers, who had fought the UP so valiantly, had already taken the train to Washington to pursue their rights by other means. They ended up in the gold speculator Jim Fisk's box at New York's Metropolitan Opera.

In March 1872 the Yellowstone region near the battle had been declared a national park. Its thousands of square miles had been set aside to protect its geysers, geological curiosities, and splendid scenery from exploitation as the railroads made it accessible to tourists. Five years later, the Nez Percé fleeing the U.S. government east would traverse the park, but they, like the Oglala and Hunkpapa Lakota, would end up dead or on reservations. Some of the last remnants of the once great herds of buffalo survived in Yellowstone, but the place was not for Indians and subsistence, but for tourists seeking food for the soul in the spectacle of wildlife and wild scenery. In 1872 William F. Cody, who had been a pony express rider and an army scout and who got his nickname Buffalo Bill for his work supplying bison meat for the Kansas Pacific Railroad builders, went onstage for the first time. He was more or less playing himself in a piece titled *The Scouts of the Plains*. It was the beginning of a career change for him, from working in the West to mythologizing it for the rest of the world. Most easterners loved buffalo and Indians, or at least loved what they represented in the romantic art and literature, even as their government's policies were annihilating them. Even in 1866, when the Union Pacific reached the hundredth meridian amid real battles with Indians, its directors brought out all the politicians and dignitaries that could be cajoled into venturing into Nebraska and treated them to banquets, speeches, fireworks—and a simulated attack on the camp by Pawnee warriors. Indians, buffalo, and open space stood for a freedom and wildness incompatible with the pervasive systems that railroads, factories, cities, and commercial agriculture represented. It was as though they were being kicked out of the real world but invited into art and entertainment, into dime novels, Wild West circuses, paintings, and photographs.

The same fluidity of western culture had made possible Muybridge's many name changes, Emperor Norton's peculiar career, the hundred novels about adventures Buffalo Bill never really had. Nothing was too real to become a fiction, and the rough authenticity that could be dangerous and uncomfortable as actual encounter was wonderful entertainment. In 1883, the year time was standardized across the United States, Sitting Bull gave a public address at the commemoration of the completion of the Northern Pacific Railroad. Abandoning his text, he stood up and told the white audience that he hated all white people, that they were thieves and liars. His army interpreter decided not to depart from the script and translated Sitting Bull's speech as a flowery welcome full of faux Indian clichés. The audience applauded enthusiastically. In 1884 Sitting Bull and his entourage exhibited themselves in a wax museum in New York. In 1885 they joined Buffalo Bill's Wild West circus for a season's tour. Sitting Bull didn't participate in the circus's restaging of the Battle of Little Big Horn, but while he was on display he sold signed photographs of himself on the side. The man who had found a moment of peace amid a bitter war had found a place outside time again, but only as art, as the image frozen forever in a photograph, as the actor forever repeating himself as theater.

Many of the first movies would be about this West, the West dreamt of and imagined all the way into Russia and Italy, Brooklyn and Dublin. The movies would create a community, a profession, and a medium in which the fact and fiction that had blurred in the old West would find its true home: the new West of Hollywood, of art and entertainment. The first movie screening, by the Lumière brothers in France, featured workers leaving a factory and a train rushing at the audience so convincingly they flinched. The first feature movie with a real narrative was *The Great Train Robbery*. Featuring a telegraph operator, a train, and a group of desperadoes who made their escape on horseback, *The Great Train Robbery* was a huge success in its day. Edwin S. Porter, who made it in 1903, had been an assistant to Thomas Edison, and Edison's 1888 meeting with Muybridge had launched his workshop's research into motion-picture technology. Porter's film fictionalized Butch Cassidy and the Hole in the Wall Gang's robbery of a Union Pacific train in Wyoming, though it was shot in New Jersey. The movie industry was not to go west until the end of the first decade of the twentieth century. In 1872 Muybridge was west of the Plains Indian wars, west of the shrinking bison herds, summoned by Stanford to take his first step toward synthesizing the technologies that would make motion pictures possible.

STANDING ON THE BRINK

A Space of Time So Small ▪ *Mountains and Rivers Without End* ▪ *At Midpoint*

A SPACE OF TIME SO SMALL

The builder of the transcontinental railroad that shrank the continent became the owner of one of the fastest horses in the country, and to see it in motion he needed a fast photographer. Muybridge was recommended, and their long collaboration began in the spring of 1872. Muybridge had launched a very different project that year, a return to Yosemite to make what is perhaps the single greatest series of landscape photographs of its era. That year, probably that season, Muybridge also photographed the Stanfords' darkly ornate Sacramento house and their carriages and carriage horses. Some of the latter were photographed at the Agricultural Park racetrack, which Stanford had that February paid to fill, grade and improve into an excellent track.

On May 2, the news was that "Stanford's Charley—reported to have been lately named Occident" was training at the Agricultural Park. Occident was the first racehorse Stanford bought. Born in Sacramento in 1863 to a small bay mare covered with the brands of southern California breeders and descended on his father's side from the well-known pacer St. Clair, Charley/Occident started out as a cart horse. A German grocer rescued him from that fate, fed him well, and found out his capacity for speed. In 1870, early in Occident's racing career, Stanford bought him for four thousand dollars in gold, renamed him, and proceeded to make good on his investment with training and research. In October 1872 the chestnut gelding lost a race to Goldsmith Maid, the champion trotter of her time, but the following year Occident matched her top speed of a mile in two minutes, sixteen and three-quarters seconds. In earlier times racers, human and equine, only competed against each other, but by the late nineteenth century they matched their bodies to ideas and records: they raced the clock.

Clearly Stanford enjoyed the role of a scientific connoisseur of horse-

flesh and the unambiguous fame owning fast horses brought him. He entered into the arcane debates of racing and read up on equine motion. A
friend recollected afterward, "It was a hobby with him to explain the phenomena of motion. He always said that nobody understood anything
about it, and that he was determined to unravel the mystery of motion. He
could not explain it himself, but he was satisfied that all explanations were
unsound." It seems to have been the argument over "unsupported transit"
that prompted his photographic commission. Some of the East Coast's
prominent horsemen claimed that a trotting horse always had at least one
foot touching the ground; Stanford and his West Coast friends claimed
that at some point in their stride, trotters had all four feet off the ground.
Long afterward, a legend arose that Stanford had bet $25,000 on the mat-
ter and hired Muybridge to prove his point, but the railroad baron had his
sanctimonious side, and betting was not a pastime in which he was ever
observed. Besides, he saw himself as a man of science, not a sporting man.
Men prided themselves on their knowledge of horses, and it was useful
knowledge. Racehorses then, like racecars now, were a superlative but not
an irrelevant version of everyday transportation. Stanford understood well
the practical applications of photography and had worked with the railroad
photographer A. A. Hart to document the building of the railroad and
would commission photographers to document other projects, including
the building of his houses and his university. He had been enthralled by
the engineering involved in bringing the railroad, via trestles, grades, and
tunnels, over the Sierra Nevada and pushed for use of the newest technologies. This engagement with applied science carried over to his equine
adventures. Later, it would influence the mission of Stanford University.

The racetrack was ready, the horse was there, and Muybridge was in
Sacramento in late April, but Stanford was so busy it's hard to imagine he
had time for a new project. The former governor was still active in party politics, and on April 25 the Republican State Convention assembled in Sacramento. On April 30 the *Sacramento Reporter* published a long letter from
Stanford justifying the Central Pacific's latest land grabs, a day after the
Sacramento Bee had reported that the Stanfords were heading for the scene of
those land grabs, San Francisco. Muybridge later recorded that he made an
initial attempt that failed and a second attempt that succeeded, though
whether the gap between the two attempts was days or months is unclear.
His statements are contradictory, and so the beginning of the motion stud-

ies cannot be pinned down. Muybridge always asserted that he launched the motion studies in the spring of 1872, often naming the month of May, and Stanford more or less endorsed this. It may be that he carried out the project in Stanford's absence, though the millionaire was an avid witness to many of Muybridge's later experiments with photographing motion.

What is certain is that by April 7, 1873, Muybridge had accomplished what Stanford asked him to do: obtain so clear a photograph of Occident trotting at full speed that the exact positions of the horse's legs and feet were visible. He attempted and failed to assemble a sequence, writing, "Each of the photographs made at this time illustrated a more or less different phase of the trotting action. Selecting a number of these, the author endeavored to arrange the consecutive phases of a complete stride; this, however, in consequence of the irregularity of their intervals, he was unable to satisfactorily accomplish." This may be hindsight. At the time, all Stanford wanted and Muybridge sought was a single image of Occident trotting at the moment all four feet were off the ground. They were not inquiring into the nature of the trot or of locomotion, only seeking to ascertain one small aspect of it at one moment of its cycle.

Afterward, Stanford tried to strip Muybridge of credit for the motion

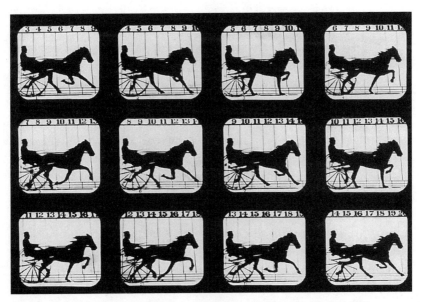

Occident Trotting, plate 35 from *The Attitudes of Animals in Motion,* 1881.

studies. The fragmentary record of the early years of the project suggests that neither of them instigated it. Fred MacCrellish, the owner and publisher of the San Francisco pioneer newspaper the *Alta California,* did, or at least recommended Muybridge as the photographer to carry out the experiment. Five years later, when Muybridge's results had become truly revolutionary, he wrote to the *Alta,* "Editors *Alta*: When you did me the honor of asserting to Gov. Stanford your confidence in my ability to make a photograph of 'Occident' while he was trotting at full speed—providing I could be induced to devote my attention to the subject—I will candidly admit that I was perfectly amazed." In another of Muybridge's many versions of the start of the motion studies, he wrote, "Having devoted much attention in California to experiments in instantaneous photography, I, in 1872, at the suggestion of the editor of a San Francisco newspaper, obtained a few photographic impressions of a horse during a fast trot. At this time much controversy prevailed among experienced horsemen as to whether all the feet of a horse while trotting were entirely clear of the ground at the same instant of time. A few experiments made in that year proved a fact which should have been self-evident."

Why was Muybridge selected? Since the beginning of his photographic career, he had advertised that "HELIOS is prepared to photograph private residences, animals, or views in the city or any part of the coast." Nothing suggests anyone had taken him up on the animals part of this proposition before, but his appetite for diverse projects as well as his unsurpassed technical expertise made him the obvious candidate to try. More than most photographers, he addressed the technical means of the medium, manipulating it with sky shades and darkroom tricks, and perhaps Stanford recognized this. It was, as Muybridge said, "a bold experiment," bringing together two subjects of great curiosity at the time: animal locomotion and instantaneous photography. Up to that point, there had been two limitations on the speed of photography. One was that no quick, reliable shutter was currently manufactured, and photographers had to rig their own devices to make exposures faster than those carried out the old way, by removing the lens cap by hand and replacing it after a suitable interval. The other was that the wet-plate process almost universally used was, in the language of photography, not very sensitive. It required a long exposure in strong light to make a good image. Muybridge had to address both of these limitations to carry out Stanford's request.

Muybridge's achievement is often written about as though it happened in a vacuum, but his photographic peers had long been frustratedly preoccupied with photographic speed and capturing motion. As far back as 1851, photography's coinventor William Henry Fox Talbot had experimented with instantaneous photography, and the word *instantaneous* recurs constantly in the literature of photography, though what it means varies— most often it seems to mean exposures of about one second. In 1859 Oliver Wendell Holmes anticipated flash photography when he declared, "The time is perhaps at hand when a flash of light, as sudden and brief as that of the lightning which shows a whirling wheel standing stock still, shall preserve the very instant of the shock of contact of the mighty armies that are even now gathering." In 1869, the astronomer and photographer Sir John Herschel wrote of his dream "of securing a picture in a tenth of a second of time," by which "scenes of action . . . a battle, a debate, a public solemnity, a pugilistic conflict, a harvest home, a launch," could be depicted. Since the 1860s, there had been "instantaneous" stereophotographs of city streets that, because the figures were distant and the negative was small, allowed walkers to be captured in motion, but this led to no larger possibilities. By the 1870s, the anxiety to achieve instantaneous photography was intense. In January 1872 the *Philadelphia Photographer* had published an article on a quick drop-shutter for "instantaneous effects . . . quick enough to enable me to catch the figure of an animal in rather rapid motion." This was a haphazard device that produced no notable breakthrough, and the situation remained as the *British Photographic News* described it that month: "There is no photographer living, who thinks, that does not sigh continually for the power in his hands to accelerate the exposure in the camera. Especially is this so with the out-door worker, who has for many years been trying every possible way to secure the coveted means. Working in such a short time has become a mania."

By the summer of 1877, when Muybridge announced his second triumph in fast photography, the "mania" was so strong that the *Photographic News* was running an article in every issue on instantaneous photography, and the image that Holmes had used caught on as the term for instantaneous photography. It was to be violent, abrupt, glorious, like lightning, a sudden shock showing a transformed world. The *Philadelphia Photographer* was full of articles about proponents of a "lightning process" that was a hoax or a failure. But even in 1878, an article in that journal condemning the lightning process concluded that "exposures of from two to three seconds to thirty will cover the general working time of a majority of the really good photographers, and the subjects who cannot be kept tolerably quiet for that length of time are few and far between, and it doesn't pay to fuss with them." That year the *Photographic Times* remarked, "for ordinary landscape photography . . . an exposure of from five to ten minutes is quite certain in action and less troublesome in its manipulation." Muybridge was in another galaxy altogether. In order to photograph Occident moving at a speed he estimated as thirty-eight feet a second, he needed exposures measurable in hundredths of a second. If the exposure was too slow, the image would blur. If it was too fast, the film would be underexposed. He settled for underexposure.

In his account, "All the sheets in the neighborhood of the stable" were laid on the ground and behind it to create as bright a background as possible, and Occident was trained to trot over this blinding terrain. Still, the first day, there were no results on the film. On the second day, "with increased velocity in opening and closing" the improvised shutter, "a shadow was caught. On the third day, the artist having studied the matter thoroughly, contrived to have two boards slip past each other by touching a spring, and in so doing to leave an eighth of an inch opening for the five-hundredth of a second, as the horse passed by." This "secured a negative that shows Occident in full motion. . . . The space of time was so small that the spokes of the wheels of the sulky were caught as if they were not in motion." This freezing of motion we take for granted was miraculous then; nobody had undone the blur of speed at close range before. Muybridge's picture was likely only an underexposed silhouette taken in an interval somewhat longer than a five-hundredth of a second, but it showed what was necessary: Occident with all four feet off the ground. Muybridge goes on—in what is clearly one of the many newspaper articles over the years that served him as press releases—to say, "This is probably the most wonderful success in photographing yet achieved, and the artist is as proud of his discovery as the Governor is of the picture taken." Stanford and others marveled at this photograph that Muybridge himself another time called "shadowy and indistinct." Others denounced it as a fraud and an imposture. Since then it has vanished without a trace.

For Stanford, the project was always about the motion of horses. For Muybridge, it was also about the motion of shutters and the speed of film.

He had begun transforming photography into a scientific instrument revealing the secret world of motion. The medium had started out far slower than the human eye, as those famously empty boulevards of the earliest images proved. It was now going to cross a great divide, to bring into visibility, as the telescope and microscope had before it, a world hidden to the eye. Those other worlds had been hidden by scale and space, but this world had been hidden by time. It was the world of everyday things whose motion had always been mysterious. With the railroad, human beings had begun to move faster than nature. With the telegraph, they communicated faster. With photography, they would come to see faster, to see what had been hidden in time, and then to reconstruct those moments in time. It was as though a veil had always surrounded the most basic acts, and Muybridge's photography was on the verge of tearing that veil away forever. Many others succeeded in making instantaneous photographs, but their adventures were like his in 1872–73: anomalous events leading to no profound new knowledge of the world or photographic technique. Only at the far end of the decade would he consolidate his breakthrough into a solid achievement with colossal repercussions.

MOUNTAINS AND RIVERS WITHOUT END

The man who had almost been destroyed by speed when the runaway mustangs smashed the stagecoach in Texas would be reborn by speed, would through his speed become a great progenitor, the Abraham of a whole class of machines and representations, of a brave new world of images rather than things. But that was five years away, and in 1872 he was still working in the slow time of landscape photography. He would spend much of that year in the Yosemite region, making a series of landscape photographs that stand apart from everything he and his peers had accomplished, and perhaps the damage to his brain had something to do with it. Muybridge is an enigma throughout his career, but the character of that enigma comes through in the Yosemite photographs. No one knows how many photographs he made with his new mammoth-plate camera that produced twenty-by-twenty-four-inch negatives, but he published fifty-one of them, along with hundreds of stereoscope images. They are his first moment of artistic greatness.

Time meant something else altogether in the Yosemite pictures than in the motion studies. Though landscape's obvious subject is space, its deepest theme is time. For city dwellers and indoor workers, landscape speaks of leisure, of slowing down, of stepping out of the pace and place of production (though for those who live directly off the land the message may be very different). Images of lush landscape speak of the organic and cyclical time of plant life and the daily cycle of light and darkness. Photographs speak as well of the moment of vision the photographer made permanent, of the split second to minutes the aperture of the camera was open and light poured upon the film. Behind each image is the longer journey of a photographer in search of a subject and possessed of a technology of capturing light. Some of the stereo photographs describe that journey: there are several series of images documenting the route up a steep trail or the circumambulation of a rock formation.

In Yosemite, water and rock became Muybridge's principal subjects. The water spoke of change, of the passing moment, and the rock of what endures, of geological aeons. A river is continually present, but the water in it is forever traveling, forever changed, forever renewed, a permanent instability that is often a metaphor for time. In the images of the Merced's water sometimes stilled to a reflecting pool, sometimes rippled, sometimes a white rush, the river is specifically a measure of duration, of the amount of time passing within the photograph. The still water reflects like a dark mirror, but the rapids and waterfalls are once again white blurs, like cotton, like clouds, like blank places on the map, like forgetting. In the photograph *Helmet Dome and Little Yosemite Fall* the fall is a white rush through a landscape of solid stone into a pool where it becomes dark and tranquil water again. A man, small in that immensity, sits beside the rushing water, his legs and body bent as if to echo its shape, and another man wanders in the distance, so small he's easy to miss. The filmmaker Hollis Frampton, in the best essay ever written on Muybridge, wrote of his "long exposures which produce images of a strange, ghostly substance that is in fact the tesseract of water: what is to be seen is not water itself, but the virtual volume it occupies during the whole time-interval of the exposure."

The river had been photographed before, and the waterfalls were favorite subjects for all the photographers homing in on the valley (nine were at work there in 1872). By that time, many felt that the place was verging on a cliché, both in the celebration of stock spectacles and the use of

Pi-Wi-Ack, Valley of the Yosemite, 21" × 17", 1872.

stock terms of rapture. Muybridge made many departures from what had been done before, went to locations that had never been photographed, and ended with a wholly new version of the place, and he seems to have been reacting against the clichés as well as responding to what else was there (among the novel locations were the top of Yosemite Falls, the back-country up Little Yosemite Canyon, and most of the images from the rim of the rock walls around Yosemite Valley and in the Sierra Nevada far above the valley). He spent months in the region, for the valley pictures were generally taken in the summer, while the pictures in the high country appear to have been taken in the fall.

Yosemite Valley was famous for its landmarks—rock formations, peaks, and waterfalls. Though the titles of most of Muybridge's fifty-one mammoth-plate photographs suggest he has dutifully documented these celebrated landmarks, they are often only a minor element in the background of a study of water or experiment in composition. The Merced River is beautiful, but hardly unusual, yet as the subject of twelve mammoth plates it captured most of his attention in the valley. In *Tutokanula (the Great Chief), "el Capitan" reflected in the Merced,* the colossal wall of rock is visible only as a shimmering, insubstantial reflection in the river. The top of the picture is a solid band of dark trees that doesn't hint at what looms above them. Not only is the granite behemoth upside down, but it exists only as a reflection without a source. The fluctuant, illusory nature of the river has triumphed over the solidity of rock.

The purpose of landmarks is to orient, but Muybridge's emphasis on innovative composition over familiar subjects often has disorienting effects, particularly in the heights. Stability in a landscape image often comes from the more or less horizontal line of the horizon or the inhabitable level space of the foreground. The word *horizontal* even derives from *horizon,* as though one could count on the horizon to be a level line dividing above and below, sky and earth, as though the earth was supposed to be flat. Watkins's characteristic Yosemite pictures have a meadow in their foreground, and no matter how jagged and steep the surrounding rocks, this foreground provides safe ground for the imagination. Even in the heights he generally found a level foreground, a granite lip, and his pictures were largely straightforward—of the landmarks and the landscape seen directly and clearly (though he too was fond of reflected landmarks). Even in his pictures of the Merced, Muybridge brings the river all the way up to the bottom of the picture as though he had been standing in or walking on water, as though there were no place to stand. He chases vertigo and disorientation with the same dedication that Watkins brought to pursuing calmness and stability. In the high country above Yosemite Valley, Muybridge divided his pictures with dramatic diagonal and vertical lines, making them unsettled and unsettling, wild even in their sense of gravity and composition, as well as in the steep and remote places they represent. In

Yosemite Creek, Summit of Falls at Low Water, 17" × 21", 1872.

these eight or so vertigo-inducing mammoth-plate photographs, it is as though the horizon has tipped and everything is in danger of falling.

This dangerousness might have been part of the process of making the pictures, and it was certainly part of the effect intended. "The artist," Muybridge seems to have ghostwritten in a newspaper account of the project, "sparing no pains to get views from points calculated to get the best pictures . . . has had himself lowered by ropes down precipices . . . has gone to points where his packers refused to follow him, and has carried his apparatus himself rather than forgo the picture on which he had set his mind." Retracing the sites of his photographs has proven that some of his vantage points were indeed perilous, amid roaring currents, on the brink of precipices, down steep slopes, far from the trails that had been carved. He gave a sense of what his working conditions were like when he spoke of startling "an eagle from a peak of the Sierra Nevada mountains; the bird gave two or three flaps of its wings, and without any further visible exertion, soared across the Yosemite Valley, and landed on another peak of the range, not less than three miles distant. The time was early in the morning, when there was not enough wind to extinguish a match struck in the open air." Stillness, vastness, and the void were there before him.

Nothing in landscape photography had come remotely close to Muybridge's vision in the high-country mammoth plates, and not much made since has. What they most resemble in elements if not in mood is Chinese landscape paintings, though the two are not historically connected. There is the same enthusiasm for the steep, the vertical, the remote, for intricate detail, for wafting mists and veils. Many of the pictures contain dark slopes in which every rock facet, every pine bough, is exquisitely delineated in low contrast. Like Chinese landscape paintings, these take as their subjects water, rock, pines, and the void. In lusher landscape images, nature is most present as botany, as the annually renewing cycle of growth. In the high-country pictures there are pines, but they are often dead, shattered, bare, skeletal, wind-sculpted, stunted by the scant soil of the crevices to which they cling. Even in the river pictures, dead trees, fallen branches, the debris washed up by the river, dominates the foreground, and in the high-country pictures, nature as the inorganic forces of geology, meterology, and hydrology overwhelms the fragile and isolated signs of life.

One more aspect brings Chinese landscape to mind. In at least a quarter of the fifty-one mammoth plates, one or more small figures are visible. Some are so tiny they vanish in reproduction and are hard to spot even in the full-size originals. These men—for they are always men and were probably Muybridge's assistants and packers—wander on foot, they stand unassertively, they sit. Most of the figures in U.S. Geological Survey photographs are men with clear objectives. Not so with Muybridge's wanderers, and he is far too deliberate an artist for these figures to be accidents again and again. They are not standing in the foreground as if discovering the view, nor are they dynamically engaged in making civilization or domesticating wilderness. The inexorable march of progress in the wilderness didn't seem to engage Muybridge. His figures are not new to the landscape, not conquering it, not standing in for the public, for America, for the rational mind. They are obscure, not connected to each other, not connected to any practical purpose. And in this obscurity lies the great rift between Muybridge, the emigrant who was never naturalized, and his American peers.

In 1872, several of the prodigies who would determine how the western American landscape would be imagined crossed paths in Yosemite. At the summer solstice, as Muybridge was entering the valley on the Mariposa Trail too steep and narrow for wheeled vehicles, another party pulled aside to let him and his heavily laden mule train pass. One member of the waiting party, Helen Hunt Jackson, who had written so enthusiastically about his earlier Yosemite pictures, was pleased to recognize Muybridge. Later she would write *A Century of Dishonor,* an eloquent assault on U.S. Indian policy, and then, disappointed by the ineffectuality of a grim book, write a lushly romantic novel, *Ramona,* about the same subject that became a huge best-seller. Roaming around between valley and mountain peaks that summer was John Muir, whose life, like Muybridge's, had changed course after a terrible accident. Son of a ferociously devout Wisconsin farmer, Muir had studied the natural sciences in his intermittent college career but allowed his genius for invention and mechanics to carry him along into a career as a machinist. In 1867, while he was tightening a belt in an Indianapolis factory, his awl slipped and gouged one of his eyes. His other eye went blind in a sympathetic reaction, and when his vision returned, Muir abandoned his mechanical career and all the values it implied.

He walked out the front door in Indianapolis and didn't stop walking until Florida. Afterward, he shipped for California and found his home, his joy, and his purpose in ranging around Yosemite and the Sierra Nevada. In the mountains he achieved redemption from his father's cruel Christianity and from the grinding productivity of the farm and the factory. His version of nature was a negative image of those things: nature meant solitude, pleasure, freedom, purity, a world outside production and consumption, a world whose variety of physical forms all sang of the spirit. By 1872, he knew the Sierra Nevada region better than any other white man, and he was beginning to acquire a reputation and friendships among scientists and artists. That year he was working as a guide for tourists, including the distinguished Harvard botanist Asa Gray, the photographer J. J. Reilly, and the painter William Keith. He took Keith's autumn party far into the high country and left them behind to ascent Mount Ritter. On that highest peak of the central Sierra Muir trapped himself on a ledge and "became nerve-shaken for the first time since setting foot on the mountains, and my mind seemed to fill with a stifling smoke. But this terrible eclipse lasted only a moment, when life blazed forth again with preternatural clearness. I seemed suddenly to become possessed of a new sense." Something similar to this anxiety and exaltation seems to be present in Muybridge's most precipitous pictures.

In Yosemite Valley itself that summer of 1872 was one of the country's most celebrated landscape painters, Albert Bierstadt, already a friend of Muybridge's. It was Bierstadt who asked him to photograph the Indians in the valley, and he obliged with seventeen stereo images, including two of Bierstadt with his sketchbook among the Indians and their cedar-bark huts. They are among the earliest of the scarce photographs of these people who have maintained a presence in the valley into the twenty-first

A Summer Day's Sport, from the series *The Indians of California*, 1872 (one frame of stereo).

century, though mainstream histories have repeatedly declared them extinct or written them out of the valley's history altogether. Artists, painterly, photographic, and literary, almost always ignored them because they were not the feather-crowned, horse-mounted noble savages of the romantic imagination, and because Yosemite was being imagined as a primordial paradise, not someone else's homeland. The role of these Miwok-Paiute people in the park was a slow-burning controversy over the decades. Simply making their daily lives visible suggested a less romantic, or at least a less American, version of what the valley meant. Muybridge photographed them utterly at home and apparently at ease with the meeting of two cultures: boys swimming, women in cloth dresses grinding acorns, a council meeting, and other evidence of a quiet continuity amid the disruptions of conquest and reinterpretation of their home.

Watkins's Yosemite Valley photographs had been praised because, "In none of these pictures do we see the least signs of man; not a log hut nor an ax-felled tree to indicate his presence: all seems wild, primitive nature, which gives the great charm of these excellent photographs." Muybridge's 1872 photographs would occasionally feature people, log huts, picket fences—and, in *Valley of the Yosemite, from Mosquito Camp,* an ax leaning against a tree in the foreground. A more direct polemic is present in his insistence on using the Miwok place names and their translations in his titles. Thus Bridalveil Falls is, in his version, *Pohono (Spirit of the Wind)* and the triple peaks of the Three Brothers are instead *The Pompons (Jumping Frogs).* This allowed him to call the mountain he photographed reflected in Mirror Lake *Mount Waiya, Pine Mountain,* though it was officially named Mount Watkins by the California Geological Survey in the 1860s.

For instantaneous photography, time meant the control of small increments of the present; for the railroad network and the time system, time meant a standardization of experience across vast spaces. There were other kinds of time at stake in the West of the 1870s. The westerners were weaving stories around themselves to generate a drama in which they played a heroic role. They embraced the idea that the West was ancient in natural time—in geological and biological terms, the terms Yosemite's granite walls and sequioas displayed so well. But they wanted it to be utterly new in human history, and thus they tended to ignore or disparage the history of those who had come before them, the native people and the Spanish settlers. This newness was a vivid part of American identity, the newness of a people who saw themselves just starting out in a landscape of Edenic freshness and infinite resources, infinite possibility. Nineteenth-century Americans liked to contrast this freshness with what they portrayed as the decayed or decadent age of Europe so that lacking a history became a sign of moral virtue rather than cultural poverty. This encouraged the many kinds of erasure of California and western history: the erasure of the Indians, of the personal past, the destruction of resources, species, records. To come west was more often than not to abandon the past.

Muybridge's sins stand out in full sunlight, his virtues hover in the shadows, and his representation of Native Americans arises from those murky virtues. European Americans wanted to see their continent as an unfallen Eden. The explorers wanted to be Adam standing on the brink of an undiscovered continent, Adam naming the animals—or rivers, mountains, and landmarks—before Eve. This is more or less how the surveys operated. They came, they saw, they measured, sampled, and named, and the lone figure in the survey photographs was this kind of pragmatic Adam. In the first stage of this fantasy of newness, the Indians were an inescapable fact, usually represented as brutes to be driven out of Eden, though it was the natives who wished the land to remain as it was, the ax-swinging Adams who were evicting them as impediments to development. In the second phase, Indians were simply erased: both John Muir and Carleton Watkins generally represented Yosemite as an untouched wilderness, a place apart from history and humanity, and it is this transcendentally uninhabited landscape that became the touchstone of the American imagination of nature, of the environmental movement, of later photographers such as Ansel Adams. In the third phase, Indians were romanticized as the original inhabitants of that unfallen Eden, and part of that romanticism involved the voluptuous melancholy of mourning their disappearance (though few tribes ever disappeared from anything but homeland and public view). Bierstadt did paint two small pieces directly from Muybridge photographs, but he ignored Yosemite's native population in the grandiose canvases he was known for. Like most of his peers, Bierstadt wanted Yosemite to be a place whose divine revelation was that a pristine continent awaited the American Adams with their inspired missions, and he specialized in paintings as bombastic as opera, as pious as hymns, full of light like colored syrup.

Muybridge had repeatedly reinvented himself, but his mammoth plates were not part of this fever of nationalistic self-invention. In Muybridge's Yosemite, it is the Indians who are in the foreground and purposeful, the whites who wander small in the distance. The place was in fact well on its way to being the West's major natural tourist attraction, but his small figures are not frolicking tourists either. In this, as well as in their embrace of instability, they are estranged from the photography of their time. Likewise, his almost fifty stereoscope studies of the Merced River come out of affection for a very ordinary kind of beauty at the time when the United States's most celebrated landscape painters made huge brilliantly colored landscapes full of History, Drama, Virginity, Revelation. And in Yosemite Valley itself he didn't edit out the development going on. Like his Bay Area landscapes, his Merced River landscapes sometimes have an unheroic mildness that seems very European: footpaths, picket fences, idling figures are all shown amid the trees and water. Other times they rage with a chaos of downed trees, gnarled trunks, shattered debris, and sharp rocks, the last perhaps shaken loose by the huge earthquake that March. Such debris fills the foreground of many of the pictures. It looks like the wreckage from events of tremendous violence, and though the images are as dramatic as the work of his peers, they bear no traces of their beneficent deity. One stereoscope card from that season is titled *A General Break Down*.

Victorians liked grandeur, and in Yosemite they could look at the half-mile height of Yosemite Falls or the mighty girth of the sequoia trees. But they also derived a more conceptual thrill from the sometimes visible traces of a grandeur of time, of the ancientness of the sequoias (of which, it was popular to say, many were tall trees before Christ was born), of the far more ancient history written in the rocks. The debate was over what story about time the rocks would tell, whether it was a continuous narrative or a series of episodes separated by disasters that erased life and started over again, and how long it took. Since Lyell's 1830s *Principles of Geology,* the study of rocks had been a field commanding great public attention and generating phenomenal new discoveries and ideas. It was in rocks that the history of the earth was inscribed, its age, its species and their evolutions and extinctions, its catastrophes, erosions, and formations.

In 1840 the Swiss geologist Louis Agassiz had proposed the existence of an ice age and connected its effects to the contemporary glaciers of the Alps, still moving, still scouring rock and depositing great boulders far from their place of formation, an aspect of geology Lyell had utterly missed. Glaciers and glacier traces were among the most dramatic episodes of geological history, and they became the center of lively debates and discoveries in the mid-nineteenth century. Ideas about the ice ages became entangled with ideas about evolution and the existence of God. Finding new glaciers and new traces of glaciers became a favorite pursuit among geologists, and in 1870 news arrived of glaciers on Mount Hood and Mount Rainier in the Pacific Northwest. That year, the geologist and government surveyor Clarence King led an expedition that culminated in finding a glacier on Mount Shasta in northernmost California. They promptly named it the Whitney Glacier, after King's old boss, the director of the California Geological Survey. Watkins photographed that glacier for King, who hastened to publish information about it.

Glaciers in the Sierra Nevada were another story. Muir spent 1871–72 in a state of glacier intoxication, conveying in dozens of letters to his friends, family, and colleagues his enthusiasm, his investigations, and his theories about these ice rivers, their traces and impacts. He had been the first to document a living glacier there. In fact, it was news of glaciers that prompted his first small article in December 1872 in what was to become a prolific and influential writing career. Muir argued that Yosemite Valley had been carved out by glaciers, and though he exaggerated their role, he was essentially right. Whitney stubbornly adhered to his assertion that Yosemite's vertical-walled valley had been created by a sudden subsidence, or drop, in the surface of the earth. He even denied that glaciers had ever been present there or that there were still glaciers in the Sierra. He called Muir "a mere sheepherder, an ignoramus" for his glacial theory, though even King agreed more with Muir than Whitney.

In September 1872 King went to the high country southeast of Yosemite Valley with Bierstadt, in search of further evidence of "the eroding power, thickness, and comparative force of the ancient glaciers." While Bierstadt sketched, King and his surveyors measured glacial traces. Muybridge had met with Bierstadt in the valley; he apparently encountered him again in the heights, for the painter requested that Muybridge photograph Temple Peak (now called Echo Peak). He did, and at King's urging, he made three mammoth-plate and several stereoscopic photographs of high-country glacial traces. King had hoped first to hire Watkins and then Timothy O'Sullivan to photograph in the Sierra Nevada that season, and

Glacier Channels, Valley of the Yosemite, 17" x 21", 1872.

perhaps it was because these plans were defeated that he took an interest in Muybridge's high-country work. They most likely met when King was in the high country with Bierstadt—and Muybridge may have met King in San Francisco the previous year, around the time when members of the California Geological Survey visited him and reported that his work "invites comparison with Watkins (or anybody else) in all respects excepting size of picture." It was a year of glacial fever. And it was a time in which artists and scientists saw themselves as alike in their mission of understanding nature, which was why Muir could treat geology and literature as one project, could share a conversation with both Emerson and Agassiz, why Bierstadt and King were exploring together, why King employed great photographers to work with him, why Muybridge never had to distinguish between creative and documentary photography.

In the catalog of Muybridge's work published the following year, the caption preceding the listings of Sierra Nevada stereoscope cards declares for the glaciers in bold terms: "At no very remote period a vast area of these mountains was covered with glaciers on the grandest scale, and in numerous canyons the surface of the rock along the beds of the rivers, and for many hundred feet above, is worn into deep grooves and polished as a mirror by the immense body of ice as it slowly forced its way into the valleys below." In later years, he described the pictures as "illustrating the geology of the Sierras." The turbulence Muybridge had sought visually was also present historically, so he celebrated its traces.

AT MIDPOINT

In 1872 Muybridge photographed a horse and a landscape. Thus described, it's easy to imagine the pictures were about a pure and permanent notion of nature, but both subjects were defined by the controversies of their time. Just as he took on photographic and locomotive debates in the motion studies, so he took on the major controversies of Yosemite when he photographed its resident Indians and evidence of its glaciers. In another way, the projects were radically different from each other. In Yosemite Muybridge photographed place and, like most photographers of the era, largely suppressed the motion that represents time, except for the unavoidable blur of rushing water. In the motion studies, place was literally whited out, with sheets laid over and behind the racetrack, and motion alone was the subject. Too, the Yosemite pictures were about natural beauty of an established kind, however turbulent and uneasy Muybridge's version of that beauty. The documents of motion were not made for that kind of pleasure, though a century later innumerable artists would pay homage to the harsh, unsentimental beauty they found in the gridded sequences. Landscape then and now is often desired and depicted as an escape from politics and society, but those forces were present in many ways in Yosemite: as the characters Muybridge met up with, the controversies he entered into, the definition of nature he achieved when he decided to represent an inhabited Yosemite rather than a virginal one, a turbulent rather than a serene one.

They are not the pictures one might expect from a newlywed at the top of his field. Muybridge had married Flora Stone, a beautiful woman half his age, on May 20, 1871. Of obscure background, she seems to have been obliged to live by her wits, and she mostly chose men to protect her, though she didn't always choose well. She had been divorced the previous December from Lucius Stone, a saddlemaker in the city, on grounds of cruelty. Muybridge had met her at Nahl's Gallery, where she worked as a retoucher. He himself had been changing galleries fast. In the five years of his career, he had gone from Silas Selleck's Cosmopolitan Gallery to Ewing's to Nahl's Gallery, and it was from the last that his prospectus for the Yosemite project was issued. Unlike most photographers then, he was never a gallery employee, only an associate, and when he went to Yosemite, two further galleries, Thomas Houseworth's and Bradley and Rulofson, were apparently vying to publish the results. There's a photograph of Muybridge on that expedition that one of his assistants must have taken. It shows the photographer at the base of a sequoia in a rough suit and thick boots, his beard still brown and not so overgrown as in later years, sitting on a crate labeled "Houseworth" and glowering. The photohistorian Peter Palmquist surmises it may have been taken by Charles Leander Weed, who had been the first person to photograph Yosemite and who could have aided Muybridge with both navigation and mammoth-plate methodology. Another candidate would be the William Towne who appears in a Yosemite hotel register with Muybridge on July 20: they signed in together as "photographic artists," and Towne was likely traveling as an assistant to Muybridge.

Afterward Muybridge moved to Bradley and Rulofson's, the city's largest and most prestigious photography gallery, where Flora sometimes worked as a retoucher. Located upstairs from the Golden City Billiard Saloon at 429 Montgomery, the eleven-thousand-square-foot gallery employed portraitists, darkroom technicians, retouchers, "thirty-four hands all told," including "six Chinese" who were "faithful, industrious, and expert," and boasted of "the only elevator connected to photography in the world." Houseworth retaliated against Muybridge by displaying a badly printed mammoth plate of Yosemite and taking out an ad disparaging the photographs. It became a newspaper squabble. Muybridge's new gallery asserted in the *Alta*, "Messrs. Bradley and Rulofson are much obliged to Mr. Houseworth for giving their names a place in his window; but attaching them to an old, soiled print from a condemned negative of Muybridge's . . . shows to what a wretched strait the poor gentleman is driven in a fruitless effort to compete in business." Houseworth replied in the same newspaper, "The Yosemite View exhibited by us in our window is one of a set of forty furnished to a subscriber by Bradley and Rulofson for the sum of $100." To which Muybridge, straining for a disdainful tone, concluded contradictorily with a fragment of a fable by Aesop about a lion scorning an ass, "Silence and contempt, says Aesop, are the best acknowledgements for the insults of those whom we despise."

Muybridge spent the winter of 1872–73 printing the mammoth-plate photographs or overseeing their printing. It's important to remember that he was a man who spent time not only on precipices and mountain trails but in the darkrooms of San Francisco, and he was a virtuoso at the technical as well as the aesthetic requirements of his medium. In many cases he added clouds to his images, and he must have had an archive of mammoth-plate cloud negatives to draw from. Some of the images exist in two versions, with and without clouds. The results were lavishly praised. Exhibited at the 1873 Vienna Exposition, they—along with Watkins's mammoth plates of Yosemite—were awarded the Medal of Progress. "Landscapes of this size are the exception here, and the thought that Muybridge, with his mammoth camera for plates of twenty-two inches, climbed mountains, fills many a one with admiration and respect," commented the photography critic Dr. Vogel. "Muybridge, above all others, is distinguished by superb cloud effects."

The man who made those photographs had enormous confidence in his own ability to produce for the market. The expense involved in putting together that long mule train hauling his equipment and hiring four assistants would have been considerable. He sold dozens of subscriptions to the series before it had been made, and among his initial subscribers were the Union Pacific Railroad, the Central Pacific Railroad, the Pacific Mail Steamship Company, Bierstadt, most of the principal photography galleries, and some of the leading citizens of San Francisco. However pure his photographs, they were for sale, and for sale to the major players in the molding of the West. "If these pictures are judiciously distributed," commented the *Alta* of April 7, 1873, after much praise, "they will have a great effect in attracting tourists to this State, and we believe it is the intention of the railroad companies to have some of them put into the hotels of the principal cities of the United States and in Europe." If he really sold 170 sets of 40 prints, or 6,800 prints, at $100 a set, it was a spectacular commercial success for a photographer then (though the small quantities of surviving prints suggest the edition was far smaller than the boasts of advance sales). He was a man with

The Artist's Studio, from the series *The Indians of California,* 1872 (one frame of stereo). The artist is Bierstadt.

one eye on the market and his reputation, and afterward he promoted the work with as much florid praise as ever. Around this time, he stopped producing his photographs under the pseudonym Helios and henceforth most often went by the single word *Muybridge.*

Ambition got Muybridge farther into the mountains than almost any previous photographer, but ambition alone cannot account for the originality and the disturbing beauty of the results. The mammoth plates are his most consciously artistic photographs, and because of this they are the most revealing of the man who made them. An utterly original genius is at work in the composition and interpretation, and his Yosemite is distinct enough from the versions photographed by others to reveal his temperament and taste. He liked complex surfaces. He liked water, rock, and the emptiness of huge spaces. He was resisting the obvious commercial subjects when he chose the landscape effects over the famous landmarks, and he was resisting that common Victorian urge to locate a benign God in nature when he emphasized the region's danger and debris. He ignored the lush meadows and was clearly bored by the giant sequoias that presented neither the opportunities for spatial drama nor the dramatic contrast of light and dark he enjoyed in his views. The last photograph in the series, depicting the William H. Seward tree with a small cabin abutting one side of its colossal trunk, is an obligatory nod to the official Yosemite. The man who made those fifty-one photographs was informed about the debates of his time, from glaciers to Indians to aesthetics. But he stood apart from the mainstream ideology of Americans in the West, seeing the place as something more ambiguous than they did, ravishing but not redemptive. Indeed, throughout the photographs, an aloofness comes through, in the sense of space, the detached figures, the taste for the barren over the lush, the turbulent over the calm. Muybridge's Yosemite is lonely, uneasy, and a little tormented.

That a man could make landscape photographs that good and never do so again says more about Muybridge. Seldom has anyone with so much talent valued it so little. In 1873 he planned to work in the mammoth-plate format on the Columbia River and the transcontinental railroad line, but he never took on another landscape project of such ambition or applied such passionate originality to the subject again. Only his 1878 panorama of San Francisco is comparable in its scale, its originality, and its technical genius within an existing genre. For in 1872, just as he was achieving his greatest work as a landscape photographer, Muybridge began the project that would take him away from landscape altogether. At the time, the motion studies he made for Stanford seemed like a minor detour. Five years would pass before he would find the technical means to achieve more and the desire to make photographing bodies in motion his life's work. In those five years, he accomplished much as a photographer, destroyed much as a man.

LOST RIVER

The End of Time ■ *Ghosts and Machines* ■
The Price of Defeat

■ *Overleaf: Toby (the Squaw Who Warned General Canby of His Impending Fate), and Four Old Modoc Squaws*, from the series *The Modoc War,* 1873 (one frame of stereo).

THE END OF TIME

In the Modoc version, the world was once nothing but water, until the creator, Kamookumpts, reached down to the bottom of Tule Lake for a handful of mud. He sculpted the mud into the world around the lake and around himself. "He had shaped and decorated the world as a woman shapes and decorates a basket," said Evangeline Schonchin, the daughter of a Modoc rebel. At the center of the world he sculpted was his seat, the peninsular bluff on the southeast shore of Tule Lake. Around its base are more than five thousand petroglyphs of human and animal figures, of celestial bodies, circles, lines, and zigzags incised in the pale stone, an alphabet of images hard to read now. This wall of markings went straight into the water when the petroglyphs were carved, and the carvers must have approached by canoe. Perhaps they used the same kind of reed canoes as the Modocs did when they fled from Lost River at the north end of Tule Lake to the Lava Beds across the water, at the beginning of the Modoc War, the war that took the Modocs from the center of the world. It was California's most spectacular Indian war, and Muybridge was its official photographer.

There are things that are hard to photograph: guerrilla warfare, the end of an era, the meaning of a place. And there are things it is nearly impossible to photograph: the subtle workings of the human heart, the wandering paths desire and fury take, the bonds of love and blood that tie people together, the decisions that tear them apart, the way that the most unprepossessing landscape can become home and thus speak of stories, traditions, gods that strangers cannot decipher from the rocks and streams. The Modoc War posed a simpler problem, though the meaning of the terrain was part of it. From the first battle in the Lava Beds until nearly the end of the conflict, the U.S. Army fought an enemy so well hidden in the folds and crevices of the landscape that the Modocs might as well have been invisible. Like Civil War photographers, Muybridge depicted no battles, no dramas unfolding, only soldiers in camp, civilians, battlefields, and backdrops, valuable information enough. He showed not a war unfolding but a war's raw ingredients: participants and locations. He appears to have been the first photographer the U.S. Army hired directly to document a war, and he produced its principal images, more than fifty stereoscopic images that were turned into *Harper's Weekly* magazine engravings, sold by Bradley and Rulofson, and later illustrated virtually every book on the subject.

It was his first major project since the Yosemite photographs. The news of his Yosemite and first motion-study pictures was announced in early April 1873; by the end of that month he had left San Francisco for the battlefields by train and then by horse in company with Captain Lydecker of the topographical engineers and Jefferson C. Davis, the commanding general of the *Columbia*. He photographed from, so far as the newspapers tell, May 2 to May 14 (and seems to have been in Sacramento beforehand, perhaps to wind up the first round of motion studies). The war was international news. Because of it, Joaquin Miller's *Life Amongst the Modocs* became a best-seller in England, and even the New York papers eagerly covered the story. "The wide spread and accurate knowledge" of the Modoc war's terrain and participants, Muybridge declared in one of his periodic fits of immodesty, "is due chiefly to the innumerable and valuable photographs" he had taken. Another photographer from the nearby town of Yreka, Louis Heller, got there before him and stuck around to make the photographs Muybridge missed, of the Modoc captives after the war was over.

Though the Lava Beds lacked Yosemite's vertical splendors, Muybridge seems to have found the landscape there to his taste. Muybridge was always a lover of tangles, thickets, and rubble-heaps, of complexity and texture. He photographed three versions of Schonchin Rock, a dark, dramatic outcropping, and made a five-stereoscope-card panorama of the Tule Lake shoreline with the army's tents like little white cones in the distance. He made another panorama of the Lava Beds themselves, twelve images that may constitute one of the most ambitious panoramas in stereo. In the fifty-six-page catalog of his work Bradley and Rulofson produced that year, the war is described not as a history but as a landscape: "The extraordinary system of natural fortifications known as the Lava Beds, are situated in the northern part of the state, on the borders of Oregon. A few miles to the south of Tule Lake are several extinct volcanoes, and from these the lava

Captain Jack's Cave in the Lava Beds, from the series *The Modoc War*, 1873 (one frame of stereo).

probably flowed, which, in cooling, formed upon its surface numerous fissures, caves and rugged valleys and channels, surrounded by natural walls. There are many channels connecting the rivers and lakes of the surrounding country." It was a landscape war. That is, it was a war over land, and it was a war in which the Modocs' profound knowledge of the lay of the land gave them one great advantage. They spent most of the war within sight of Petroglyph Point, in the labyrinthine Lava Beds on the south shore of Tule Lake, a shallow reed-fringed body of water beloved of waterfowl.

During the war, much of this band of ancient petroglyphs was probably underwater, but the bank swallows who live higher up this west-facing cliff must have carried on as though nothing had changed. Even now they fly in and out of their nests, swooping and climbing through the clear air of this arid place as their shadows slide smoothly up and down the rough wall. The flight of the swallows and the steady sound of the wind make it possible to believe that nothing more than this ever happened in this region now known principally for the hundreds of bald eagles that winter in it. But the sound of artillery shells must have echoed from the cliff in 1873, and history didn't start then. Before the whites came, the Modocs warred with their neighbors, and they were fierce fighters. Like the Plains Indians, they were impacted by the guns and horses of white culture before whites were a significant presence in the area, and some sources say that in the quest to find something to trade for horses they began to capture neighboring tribespeople to sell into slavery. But in the Tule Lake region they had bounty enough to stay home for. The area is rich in fish, in game, particularly waterfowl, and in the camas bulbs, water-lily seeds, and other plants that furnished the staples of their diet. From almost anywhere in their pine-studded uplands and sagebrush valleys the snow-covered volcanic cone of Mount Shasta is visible, a fourteen-thousand-foot-high landmark that makes it hard to get lost here (the Lost River is thus named because the river itself disappears and reappears on its route from Clear Lake to Tule Lake). With their guns and horses, the Modoc had already

Panorama of Lava Beds from Signal Station at Tule Lake, Camp South, from the series *The Modoc War*, 1873 (one frame each of five stereos).

embraced the accelerations brought from Europe; what they were not ready for was the concomitant detachment from ritual time and intimate space that came as part of the package. The part they accepted made it easier for them to resist the rest—that is, they could fight with the guns and horses.

The Modoc War had an end on June 1, 1873, but its beginning is hard to trace. Was it inevitable from when the first fur trappers came through the area in the 1820s, or only after the gold rush, when whites began to settle the area in earnest? Massacres, revenges, white encroachments, Modoc resistance, mutual fears, and suspicions piled up like the bones beneath the hawk nests at Petroglyph Point. Something immensely valuable was at stake, but those defending it were not innocents, nor were the lines clearly drawn. The whites were intruders, but some became friends and allies of the Modocs and stayed that way even in the thick of the war. There were atrocities on both sides, and some on each side seemed to believe that harm done by any member of that race could be avenged on virtually any other member of that race. There were also marriages, acculturations, friendships; and many of the Modoc men and some of the women were given nicknames by their white neighbors. The government's translators during the Modoc War and trial were Toby Riddle and her white husband

Frank Riddle. More than thirty of Muybridge's fifty or so pictures of the Modoc war were of the landscape, but he photographed the strong-minded Toby Riddle twice, once with her bushy-bearded husband, once with, according to the caption, four "Old Modoc Squaws." The caption doesn't mention that Frank Riddle and Indian agent Oliver Applegate stand behind the five women. It's a strangely symmetrical image, the figures fixed and impassive like those on playing cards, a royal flush of Modoc women and two of a kind of frontiersmen. Three of the women are wearing the patterned basket hats of traditional Modoc women, though their dresses are calico, and Toby Riddle's and the fourth woman's neatly parted hair shines as smooth as water.

In 1864 the Modocs had been pushed, without a treaty, onto a reservation north of their homeland. The reservation was on Klamath land, and both Klamaths and Paiutes were settled there with the Modoc. As one Indian agent put it, it was expected that "the efforts of efficient and conscientous instructors will advance them rapidly in the customs, arts, and laws of civilization." But they had been set up to lose. Year after year, late frost killed the crops they were instructed to count on for sustenence; the timber mill that was supposed to provide income and building materials never worked right; the conscientous instructors were often little more than profiteers, and the Klamaths, traditional enemies of the Modocs, harassed the latter as squatters and unwelcome guests. A young Modoc leader named Kientpoos but whom history remembers as Captain Jack led some of the Modocs back to the Lost River. They left for practical purposes—to remain was to be hungry and humiliated. But again and again, through years of negotiations, they repeated that they wanted to live on their own land and no place else. Captain Jack and his people remained in their homeland for three years. At the end of 1869, Indian agent Alfred Meacham came to negotiate their return to the reservation, and the forty-three members of Jack's band reluctantly went back.

The Klamath resumed harassing the Modocs on the reservation, and in April 1870 Jack led 371 Modocs back to their land. About 130 more followed suit with Old Schonchin, another Modoc leader, and the Modocs began to move freely between the reservation and the Tule Lake region. Captain Jack obligingly offered to settle his people on a reservation on their own territory from this period through the climax of the war, but nothing came of it. Late in 1871 an Indian agent reported, "I was met by 'Capt. Jack' and 'Black Jim' with twenty of their young men, nearly every man armed with gun and revolver. I lost no time in opening the council: carefully explaining to 'Capt. Jack,' all your instructions; after I had concluded, I asked him to speak in answer to the several propositions, which he proceeded to do as follows.

"'I want to live in my own country, I will live on the East side of Lost River. People in Yreka tell me this is my country, though you want to talk with the President; I and all my people only want to be let alone. My father died here, I will die here, we do not want to kill whites; Soldiers kill for pay; they are not men with hearts; We do not want to live on any Reservation, we want no lines drawn around we [*sic,* meaning us?]; we do not want to see your diagram, gieing [*sic*] us a small place, that place is covered with cattle—we want our Country from Pit River to Lower Klamath Lake— whitemen may have timber, grass, and cold water, but the Fish, Ducks, Roots, and warm Springs we want, we will keep these. This is my talk, I am a good man, and never tell a lie.'

"He then said, 'I am glad you talk about opening farms in our country. . . .'

"I ask him if his people will all stay upon a Reservation, if established in his country. At this he becomes excited, all his men talk at once; after a little while he answers, that he wants the freedom of all his country;

"'We want to live in this Country, to travel and camp anywhere in it, to live among our white neighbors.' The council lasted about three hours, every proposition was answered throughout with about the same speech:

"'We want to live here in our own country.'"

Two different worldviews were in collision, as well as two sets of practical wants. The religion of most Native American communities was tied to specific places; to lose those places was to lose the connection to that power, that spirit, that religion. Stories were inscribed in the landscape; place had a symbolic meaning; seasonal activities were tied to specific locales. The Modoc world had a center. The Indian agents and soldiers with their diagrams, their boundaries, their time determined by the clock were living in a world of abstractions in which one parcel of land was interchangeable with another and religion was as portable as a Bible. (Administrating the Modoc War was made harder by the fact that the forty-second parallel, which is also the state border, runs through Tule Lake, so that the Lost River is in Oregon but the Lava Beds are in California.) After all, the whites had all given up wherever they called home to come to the terra incognita of northeasternmost California and imposed upon it their agriculture with its foreign plants and animals. In photographing Yosemite, Muybridge had celebrated a landscape that was a superlative image and an ideal from Vienna to San Francisco, but to which almost no one in his society had a real relationship. In this light, Yosemite seems like the pinup a lonely soldier tacks up; it's not a place to which its audience has a deep connection but an ideal of place and nature for those who yearn for them. The Tule Lake region's value to the Modocs lay in entirely different qualities, in its familiarity, in its sustenance, in the accumulation of stories around its sites, in things that didn't show up in photographs.

What Europeans and European Americans had lost gradually as the Industrial Revolution loosened their ties to earthly place and celestial time, Native Americans would lose suddenly, as war took them away from familiar places and ancient practices, forcing them into dependence on the government, the cash economy, and domesticated plants and animals. The Europeans had mostly noticed what they were gaining; the colonized who had less to gain kept their eyes on what was being lost. In his speech, Captain Jack recognized the difference between what the two groups wanted from the landscape and proposed that, like two different species, they could coexist, the whites as ranchers and loggers, the Modocs as wide-ranging hunters and gatherers. He was trying to be reasonable. He tried to be reasonable till the end, and he was a peacemaker by inclination, but reasonableness doesn't do much for a person without rights. All he had left to rely on was his own land laden with stories, with meaning, with nourishment, with knowledge. As the situation between the settlers and the off-reservation Modocs deteriorated, topography was his last advantage.

Even when the U.S. Army rode all night through a freezing rain to arrest him at dawn at his Lost River winter camp on November 29, 1872, Captain Jack was moderate: the Modocs there declined to give up their weapons but didn't fire first. The soldiers did, and killed one man. The Modocs in Jack's camp fired back, killing a soldier and wounding several others before the U.S. Army could scramble out of the encampment of about a dozen huts. Across the river, a group of vigilantes who had ridden into Hooker Jim's camp started firing after a scuffle. They succeeded in killing a babe in arms with a shotgun blast. The members of Jack's camp ran for their canoes and paddled frantically for Tule Lake. The Modocs with Hooker Jim scattered after killing another man, a civilian. Both villages were torched, and an old woman unable to flee burned to death in a blazing hut on that morning of hard rain and bitter cold. A local rancher, Henry Miller, had promised to warn Hooker Jim of any military approaches, but the incompetent military men had failed to warn the settlers in the vicinity that a war might break out. Thinking Miller had betrayed him, Hooker Jim vengefully killed him and eleven other men in the neighborhood but left the women and children alone. Always an advocate of violence, Hooker Jim had closed off any option but continued war. Another off-reservation band of Modocs at Hot Creek a dozen miles or so west of the battle, under the leadership of Shacknasty Jim, went to ask a friendly neighbor, the rancher John Fairchild, for advice. They knew that to join Captain Jack's band in the Lava Beds was, in the words of one historian, "to sign their death warrants." But when they tried to go back to the reservation with the helpful Fairchild, they ran into a lynching party and fled for the Stronghold in the Lava Beds, where Captain Jack's and Hooker Jim's bands had gathered.

The Lava Bed Stronghold is as close as nature ever came to making a full-fledged labyrinth. Even the ground is scattered with gray lava pebbles whose fretwork of curving holes seems to echo on a small scale the lacy intricacy of this harsh terrain. From a distance the terrain all across the Lava Beds looks relatively level, but in the Stronghold as elsewhere, pits, gullies, and the occasional twenty-foot chasm open up in the ground. Some of them are actually shallow caves slanting down at an angle into ground that was once hot volcanic magma, and the Modocs used these as shelters. Afterward, Muybridge made four pictures of Captain Jack's Cave, as it is still called, as a dark eye or mouth opening into the dusty landscape. Others of the caves contained water and ice. Higher than the surrounding landscape, the Stronghold gave the hundred and fifty or so Modocs in it superb views of their homeland, of Shasta's pure peak and of Tule Lake coming right to the northern edge of the Lava Beds. Made up of several rings of lava walls, mostly breast-height or higher with gaps that made excellent gun positions, battlements without a castle, the Stronghold was ideal ground to defend, terrible ground to invade.

The army waited until the bitter-cold dawn of January 17 to stage an attack, six weeks after the Modocs had holed up there. Thick fog was everywhere, and wiser commanders might have waited for clearer weather. Almost 350 regular soldiers and local militiamen plugged away until night, but almost no Modocs were seen at all on that foggy day, even by the men who were wounded by them, and though only fifty-four Modoc men were fighting (with women loading guns and otherwise assisting) the soldiers, terrified by their unseen enemy, imagined that many times more held the miles of front line. Nine white men died, a dozen were wounded, and the Modocs easily persuaded the Klamaths who had been recruited to fight to leave guns and ammunitions behind in the Lava Beds. It was from beginning to end an intimate war, fought at quarters so close the Modocs could shout insults at individual whites and blandishments at the Klamath. Not a single Modoc was injured. Curly Headed Doctor, the Modoc shaman in the Stronghold, claimed credit. He had surrounded the Stronghold with a tule-reed rope painted red and promised that no Modoc within the rope's circle would be wounded or killed. The protective rope itself was apparently borrowed from the Ghost Dance religion the Modocs had taken up from their Paiute neighbors.

Despair and desperation had set in among the Indians of the Far West in those years. The 1870 Ghost Dance came out of that feeling, and it spread across western Nevada, southern Oregon, and northern California. It began at the Walker River Paiute Indian reservation in west-central Nevada (as did another version of the Ghost Dance a generation later, when it spread across much of the interior West). In 1869 or 1870 a Paiute prophet named Wodzibob, nephew of the great native-rights activist Sarah Winnemucca, began to preach that the Native dead were coming back and the whites were going to disappear. To bring these things about, believers were to paint their faces, to dance in a circle singing certain songs all night, usually for five nights, and to bathe after dancing. A similar doctrine was preached by a Wanapum Indian named Smoholla or Shouting Mountain, who came from where the Columbia and Snake rivers meet. The Ghost Dance seems to be about wish fulfillment more than anything else: desperate wishes born out of hideous circumstances, out of a sense that nothing less than the apocalypse was needed.

But when the Modocs and the U.S. Army faced each other across ridges of lava, there were no other simple lines to be drawn than Curly Headed Doctor's rope. The Modocs with their rifles and their insults shouted in English do not represent some notion of native purity. They were in transition from a theocracy of shamans, and in Captain Jack's band there was no stable order, only uneasy shifting between fealty and argumentative majority rule. Even the Ghost Dance had much to do with Christianity's vision of the Last Judgment and the Resurrection. "Sometimes," writes one anthropologist, "the 'Supreme Ruler' was to bring the spirits of the dead back to earth; sometimes dead relatives would be returning from the south; . . . sometimes the dead would return in armies from the rising sun; and sometimes the dead would return from their graves." The Modocs were fighting a defensive battle, but perhaps it lasted so long because they kept hoping that the Ghost Dance would save them. Like Sitting Bull snatching a moment of stillness out of the middle of war, the Ghost Dancers during their many months in the Stronghold seemed to be trying to seize time itself, to make it stand still or turn back.

They had danced the Ghost Dance on the banks of the Lost River before the war began. One participant, the son of the leader Schonchin John, recalled half a century later that the Paiutes came to the Klamath reservation "and said all were to believe that the dead were coming back. Doctor George [a Modoc shaman] brought the word to Tule Lake at the mouth of Lost River where Captain Jack's people were. He came in the winter before the grass began to grow. He said the dead would come from the east when the grass was about eight inches high. The deer and the animals were all coming back, too. George said the white people would die out and only Indians would be on earth. The culture hero [Kamookumpts, he who had made the first land] was to come back with the dead. The whites were to burn up and disappear without even leaving ashes. The rules of the dance Doctor George brought were that you must dance or you would turn to rock. They danced in a circle with a fire in the middle and camps around the outside. They danced all night and in the morning they jumped into the river and swam. Some of the men would come out with ice on their hair it was so cold. Some Indians fell down dead [fainted] and began singing and telling what the coming-back people wanted them to do." Another source quoted Doctor George as adding that the dead "will come back, and people will never die anymore. Those who will come back have died once, but they will never die anymore." A man named Jake from the neighboring Shasta tribe was told that the ghosts summoned by the dance had only one more creek to cross before they reached Tule Lake. Apparently the dead were pictured as crossing the landscape on foot, an army of the past marching to cancel out a terrible future. The Modocs were living at the end of time.

GHOSTS AND MACHINES

The Ghost Dance was a technology. Literally, a technology is a systematic practice or knowledge of an art, and though we almost always apply the term to the scientific and mechanical, there is no reason not to apply it to other human-made techniques for producing desired results. Maybe the best definition would be: A technology is a practice, a technique, or a device for altering the world or the experience of the world. To propose annihilating the inexorable march of history and the irreversibility of death was to propose a technology as ambitious as a moon walk or a gene splice. The Ghost Dance had its parallels in the spiritualist movement that began in the 1840s and reached its heights in the years after the Civil War with millions of believers and practitioners in the United States. Spiritualism likewise sought to cross that great divide, death, and even the white raiment women spiritualists sometimes wore to funerals seemed a defiance of death, like the Ghost Dance shirts of the 1890s. This spiritualism had close ties to the feminist movement of the middle decades of the nineteenth century. Women were the principal mediums in spiritualism, and it was something of a women's religion, an alternative source of power and an alternative kind of spirituality. In calling back the souls of the dead to communicate, these spiritualists seemed to politely doubt that the dead were otherwise occupied with heaven, hell, and the authority of God.

The supernatural is nowadays often seen as opposed to technologies, but the technologies of the era often seemed supernatural themselves. In the well-known words of science-fiction writer Arthur C. Clarke, "Any sufficiently advanced technology is indistinguishable from magic." It is only because nature no longer seems so strong and immutable a force that changes no longer seem uncanny. In the beginning electricity seemed spiritual, a form of the life force: it is electricity that brought Frankenstein's fictional monster to life in the teens of the nineteenth century, and a spiritualist machine of the 1840s that was supposed to generate a soul was electrical. Telegraphy was sometimes thought to magically transmit objects rather than signals, and in 1878 the *San Francisco Chronicle* published a story about a man getting evening calls from the dead on that new electrical invention, the telephone, whose disembodied voices still seemed uncanny. "Spirit photography," or photography of the souls who were supposed to appear at spiritualist seances, was often discussed and denounced over the years in the *Philadelphia Photographer,* and even late in the 1870s the photographer John Thomson was reassuring a theoretical listener, "He may be tempted to inquire, What occult science confers on this mystic apparatus the power of picturing objects placed before it, producing an image so perfect that alike no point of beauty, no spot or blemish, escapes its miscroscopic observation? It is some solace to know that the camera and lens—names by which the apparatus are known—lend themselves to no sort of trickery. There is no medium—spiritual—within or without to link the process to the unseen world and works of darkness." The changes brought about by technology seemed supernatural at first, and photography was associated with death both in the many, many images of the dead made during the early years of the medium and in the way a photograph seemed to cheat death by making at least appearance permanent.

Muybridge, when he was photographing the Modoc War, was on his way to inventing a new kind of photography, a photography that with the aid of high-speed electric shutters would make it possible to recapture what had always been lost in the stream of time, not just an appearance but a gesture, a motion, an act, those immaterial events of which time itself is made. Even Thomas Edison, when he discussed the origins of cinema, invoked the supernatural. He wrote, "In the year 1887 it occurred to me that it was possible to devise an instrument which would do for the eye what the phonograph does for the ear and that, by a combination of the two, all motion and sound could be recorded and reproduced simultaneously. This idea, the germ of which came from a little toy called the zoetrope and the work of Muybridge and Marey and others has now been accomplished. . . . I believe that in coming years by my own work and that of Dickson, Muybridge, Marey and others who will doubtless enter the field, that grand opera can be given at the Metropolitan Opera House at New York . . . with artists and musicians long since dead." In other words, cinema would itself be a kind of Ghost Dance. It was and is a breach in the wall between the past and the present, one that lets the dead return, albeit as images of flickering light rather than phantoms in the dark or armies marching across the land. Anyone who watches old movies watches the dead, and Edison was not yet insulated as we are against what is macabre about this. In the first years of cinema, the Lumière brothers made a short film that showed a few men knocking down a wall and then ran in reverse so that the men walked backward and the wall arose whole from its own rubble. For audiences then, it was deeply disturbing and more than a little magical. They were not yet used to time as a toy in men's hands. The Ghost Dance itself was an effort to make time run backward like a film, so the whites vanished, the game reappeared, even death reversed itself.

But the Ghost Dance, which by all objective accounts failed, would settle for nothing less than the return of the people themselves with their bodies, their love, their souls. The technological solution called forth by photography and later mutated into film, television, video, computer animations, succeeded so profoundly that it has become the medium in which we live, but it is only a medium of flickering light and darkness, a river of shadows. Still, electricity and photography were technologies linked and confused with spirituality, and the 1870 Ghost Dance had an ambiguous link to the transcontinental railroad. One apostle of Wodziwob reported long afterward that the prophet had said, "There are a lot of people telling this news but they aren't telling it right. What I said was that a train was coming from the east. My real dream was about that train, but people make it out different." Another member of Captain Jack's band recalled a half-Modoc man named Night Traveler who told them, "The dead were not coming back. He interpreted the message as meaning the whites were coming from the east. He told all about the whites, their churches and houses; how they were coming, like beavers mowing down the timber, like badgers and moles in turning up the earth for their mining, like grasshoppers in cutting down the grass. He said the whites were all around us and we were a little island of Indians, but the whites would come and we should see the truth of what he said. It was the whites and not the dead who were coming from the east." The railroad was bringing them in ever greater quantities. As for the builders of that railroad, grief could make them too turn to the supernatural. When Leland Stanford Jr. died in Italy at the age of fifteen, his devastated parents strove to make contact with him through spiritualism. Jane Stanford retained a lifelong interest in the supernatural, and her secretary remembered, "She prayed so earnestly for light, which meant to behold Leland, that it was pitiful."

They were all technologies of grief, technologies for building a bridge across the painful divide between the living and the dead, between what had been and what is, for defeating the trauma of time itself. The Modocs' grief was for a whole relationship to the natural world and to a specific place, for their culture and community, while the grief of those who produced and profited from their loss was purely personal. While the Stanfords were hosting a pair of spiritualists in their vast estate at Palo Alto, a wealthy neighbor not far to the south was pursuing her own manic version of spirituality through the material medium of architecture. Sarah Winchester, the widow of the man who manufactured the Winchester repeating rifle—"the gun that won the west" as the superb 1873 edition was called afterward—was an ardent spiritualist who spent the last decades of her life, from 1884 to 1922, building a house to ward off the spirits of the Indians killed by her husband's rifles, the technologically advanced repeating rifles whose sale gave her the funds to pay the craftsmen who worked without cease for nearly four decades. A spiritualist medium had told her she would be safe as long as construction continued, and the house came to seem like the emigrant West itself in its insatiable desire for expansion. Her labyrinthine house is often written about as a prefiguration of Silicon Valley, at whose heart it sits, and if all Silicon Valley's suburban sprawl and corporate campuses can be imagined as a larger labyrinth, then Sarah Winchester and her house were the monster, the minotaur, at its center. The house grew to cover six acres and contain 160 rooms, and it was not built to plan, so that skylights open into floors, windows look into other rooms, stairways lead nowhere. It was a labyrinth designed to baffle the souls whose enemy she was, and at its heart was a blue room in which the solitary Sarah Winchester held her séances (and spied on her servants).

The Modocs were at the center of a lava labyrinth surrounded by a shaman's red rope, and there they stayed from their triumph in the January battle through the peace negotiations that stumbled along into spring. Relations worsened during the truce. The Modocs moved freely in and out of the Stronghold, and in the army camps they heard rumors that led them to distrust the appointed peace commissioners. Both sides squabbled among themselves. Captain Jack was for compromise and peace, and many members of his band, particularly Hooker Jim and Curly Headed Doctor, attacked him bitterly for it. Messengers, mostly Modoc women and white friends of Captain Jack, went back and forth through February and into March. At a meeting in late March, Captain Jack reiterated his demand for a home on the Lost River, and afterward the army camps moved in closer to the Stronghold. Another meeting was held. Meacham reported of Jack, "After sitting in silence for a few moments, he replied, 'I give up my home on Lost River. Give me this lava bed for a home. I can live here; take away your soldiers and we can settle everything. Nobody will ever want these rocks; give me a home here.'"

Meacham replied, "No peace can be made while you stay in the Lava Beds; we can find you another place, and the President will give you each a home."

And Jack declared, "I don't know any other country. God gave me this country; he put my people here first. I was born here,—my father was born here; I want to live here; I do not want to leave the ground where I was born."

The stalemate changed at the meeting on April 11, Good Friday. The Modocs had danced the Ghost Dance all night, and the morning was clear and cold. Toby and Frank Riddle warned the three peace commissioners and General Canby to stay away, but they went to the rendezvous site at the western edge of the Lava Beds at eleven in the morning. There Captain Jack, Hooker Jim, Schonchin John, Ellen's Man, Black Jim, and Shacknasty Jim awaited them at a sagebrush fire, and Bogus Charley and Boston Charley were nearby. As usual, Jack asked for land and the removal of the troops. The talks foundered. As Meacham, one of the three peace commissioners, recalled, Schonchin John, "eyes burning with passion," shouted, "Take away your soldiers and give us Hot Creek, or quit talking. I am tired of talking. I talk no more." At a signal, Jack pulled a pistol out of his clothes and turned General Canby into the only U.S. Army general to die in an Indian war. Boston Charley shot the Reverend Thomas, one of the peace commissioners, who died, and four Modocs went after the fleeing Meacham, who was wounded in several places and partially scalped but survived. The third peace commissioner ran for it and lived, as did the Riddles, who weren't targets.

Jack had been pushed into cooperating by the extremists in his band, and he knew that after the murders at the peace tent, they had no good way out of the Lava Beds. It was springtime, the great sky-darkening flocks of waterfowl were migrating over the Lava Beds and landing in Tule Lake on their way north, and normally the Modocs would have been shooting ducks with their sophisticated arrows faceted to skip like stones over the surface of the water. Easter Sunday, the corpses were sent away and seventy-two Indian scouts from central Oregon arrived to join the several hundred troops. The war resumed on Tuesday. Curly Headed Doctor continued to dance, and the Modocs continued to seem indestructible. Their invulnerability and their widespread—but hardly universal—belief in the Ghost Dance made them unwilling to compromise, though their resources were so finite and the government's so vast. A prisoner of war who was allowed to escape so the soldiers would have the pleasure of finally killing a Modoc instead outran the rain of bullets without injury. Eight Modocs held off a battery all day, and the shelling that continued into the night caused no casualties until the second night, when a mortar shell landed without detonating and a naive Modoc blew himself to pieces by examining it. After that, faith in Curly Headed Doctor's power waned, and the

A Modoc Brave on the Warpath, from the series *The Modoc War*, 1873 (one frame of stereo). This image actually depicts a Warm Springs Scout working for the U.S. Army.

Modocs, who were running low on water, left the Stronghold after five months there.

The army was dumbfounded when they gingerly stormed the site the next morning, April 17, only to find it abandoned. The Modocs seemed to have vanished from inside the siege, though they had only walked south one night through the lava trenches. By this time, there was not much mercy left in the Modoc War. When the Modocs captured a young packer, Hooker Jim flattened his head with a rock. When the army found an old Modoc man left behind in the flight from the Stronghold, they cut off his head and kicked it around like a football. Finally on April 26, sixty-four soldiers who set out to look for the Modocs marched into their hiding place without seeing them and sat down for lunch. The ensuing battle was as close to an even match as the Modocs and the U.S. Army ever got: twenty-four Modocs against nearly seventy, and the result was twenty-four dead and many wounded soldiers, no Modoc casualties, and Scarfaced Charley shouting, "All you fellows that ain't dead had better go home. We don't want to kill you all in one day."

It was his own men who finally did in Captain Jack. Black Jim and Hooker Jim argued with him so bitterly that they could not proceed together, and the renegade Modocs split into two bands. The army found Hooker Jim's band first, the Modoc women negotiated a surrender, and Hooker Jim, who would otherwise have been hung for his Lost River murder rampage, made a pact. In exchange for amnesty, he and three others would deliver Captain Jack. They led the army to his encampment. Jack was furious that the men who had refused to let him negotiate when there was more to gain in April had capitulated at his expense and threatened to shoot them like dogs. But the uncaptured Modocs were exhausted and hungry after weeks on the run. In the end, Captain Jack walked out onto a ledge holding his rifle, and the lieutenant in command of the scouting expedition climbed up to receive it. "Jack's legs gave out," he said and handed over his gun, and that was the end of the war. It was June 1.

THE PRICE OF DEFEAT

Afterward, the photographer Louis Heller took Hooker Jim's picture: it shows a youth with a beaded collar whose face is made up of smoothly curving planes and elegantly delineated lines of eyes, nostrils, mouth, a face more graceful than one expects for violence and treachery, though it is a little masklike. Captain Jack, in Heller's portrait, was a tired man in his prime with the same clearly delineated features, high cheekbones, and thick hair cropped at his ears; wearing blue jeans in another portrait, he looks very modern. At ten-twenty in the morning of October 3, after a farce of a trial, Captain Jack, Schonchin John, and two others were hung at Fort Klamath. Two of the Modoc rebels were pardoned from the scaffold and sent to the grim prison on Alcatraz Island in San Francisco Bay. The executed four were buried there on the reservation they had fled, though some stories suggest their heads were sent east as scientific specimens or that Captain Jack's body was preserved and turned into a sideshow attraction.

For the rest of the Modocs the price was not death or prison, but a long ride far beyond the horizon of their native land, to Indian Territory in what is now Oklahoma. Their belief system included a world with a center and places that were irreplaceable, tied to the sacred time of the beginning of the world and perhaps to its end; their war had been against being assimilated into the industrialized world, against the annihilation of this sense of place, this sense of time. The price of their defeat was a ride on the very emblem of the changed world, the transcontinental railroad, shuttling them beyond everything they had known. For the first riders of the railroad the speed of the trains had seemed to annihilate the landscape, drawing them into a limbo that was something new in the world, a being nowhere; the Modocs were now delivered into this limbo. A contemporary Modoc from that eastern Oklahoma territory, Cheewa James, writes on her Web site, "It is doubtful that any of them had even been on a train before. This, coupled with the fact that no one, prisoner or the general public, was to know the destination of the Modocs, must have been a frightening and depressing experience to the subdued group. The Modocs, taken to Baxter Springs, Kansas, were exhausted when they disembarked on November 16, 1873. Records are clouded as to their exact condition. Accounts state that the Modocs arrived half-starved in boxcars." Wodzibob had stated, "What I said was that a train was coming from the east," and it was going back east too. Instead of the glorious end of the world in a spate of resurrections and erasures, there was the quiet end of a world. Most of the Modocs outlived the end of their world, which they must have found harder to imagine than the dead coming back, and more painful. "The lava beds," wrote the historian Hubert Howe Bancroft not long afterward, "which can never be removed or changed, will ever be inseparably connected in men's minds with Captain Jack and the Modocs in their brave and stubborn fight for their native land and liberty—a war in some respects the most remarkable that ever occurred in the history of aboriginal extermination."

The whites who administered Native American subjugation claimed to be recruiting the Indians to join them in a truer, more coherent world-view—but whether it was about spirituality and the afterlife, the role of women, the nature of glaciers, the age of the world, or the theory of evolution, these white Victorians were in a world topsy-turvy with change, uncertainty, and controversy. Deference was paid to Christianity and honest agricultural toil, but more than a few questioned the former, and most, as the gold rushes, confidence men, and lionized millionaires proved, would gladly escape the latter. So the attempt to make Indians into Christian agriculturalists was akin to those contemporary efforts whereby charities send cast-off clothing to impoverished regions: the Indians were being handed a system that was worn out, and it is no surprise that they had trouble wearing this cultural certainty so full of holes. Though the whites were trying to destroy the Indians, by killing them and their culture and by displacing them from the sites for which their skills and beliefs shaped them, the Indians and the whites were ultimately united as, so to speak, passengers on the railroad heading to an unknown destination, to doubt, to destabilization, to our time.

In Europe this state of affairs is called modernism, the cultural reaction to modernization. "Modernization," writes the visual theorist Jonathan Crary, "is a process by which capitalism uproots and makes mobile that which is grounded, clears away or obliterates that which impedes circulation, and makes exchangeable that which is singular." Out west, the complex responses to industrialization and its transformation of time and space include things never dealt with by the impressionist painters and avant-garde poets usually talked of as modernist, include Indian wars and identity shifts, a landscape being claimed and named, photography as art, and a comic literature. But perhaps they were all, cowboys and Indians and impressionists, on the same train anyway. Muybridge was photographing the journey to modernization, for this is what his series of pictures—of the mysteries of movement, of remote landscape, of an Indian war, of an instant city, of the transcontinental railroad line, and other developments of the West add up to. His Modoc pictures are not great expressive works of art; what is important in them is his act of witness and how it connects this history to the other histories he was tied to: the transformation of a world of presences into a world of images. It's usual to talk about artists standing aside, to talk about them being neutral because they observe rather than act directly on what they see. Muybridge's relationship to the history that came through his camera is more complex. He was working for railroads and armies, for tourists and easterners. But he gave them imagery that called their attention to what was just out of reach: the landscapes they wouldn't explore, the cultures they wouldn't encounter, the lives they wouldn't live, the motions they couldn't see, the questions they couldn't answer. Muybridge wasn't neutral. He was independent. He was complicating the record as he made it, inviting doubt into the house.

What was being lost as the real thing was returning as imagery: thus nature was almost the dominant subject of the nature-conquering nineteenth century, and Indians who were chased out of their homeland were finding a shadow home in art and entertainment. The Modocs survived on their reservation, or enough of them did to convert to the Quakers' pacifist version of Christianity. Early in the twentieth century some came back to the Oregon reservation. Few if any seemed to find a home in the northeasternmost corner of California now called Modoc County. Meacham survived his assassination attempt to write a book about the Modoc War and go on a speaking tour with the Riddles, Shacknasty Jim, Steamboat Frank, and Scarface Charlie. He got them to wear face paint and dress up in more "Indian" clothes than they had worn, and he adorned Toby Riddle with the name "Winema, the Woman Chief." Everything spectacular in the West was always being sent east for exhibition: cowboys, Indians, and herds of buffalo in the traveling circuses, stories of the peculiar society of the mining camps, great loads of gold and silver, furs and hides, photographs of Yosemite Valley, the 1878 motion studies that went straight to France.

In the heyday of the gold rush, the immigrants were busy building California's physical infrastructure: dams, roads, cities, farms. At the same time, a more subtle project of construction was launched, of California as a distinct culture. Immigrants bent the place's meanings to suit their needs and dreams, and when they were done, something entirely new had been invented, something that would change the world, a kind of headstrong, rootless sense of heroic possibilities and glamour still summed up by the word *California*. And much that was ancient had been lost, including the way that Modoc culture was tied, with a thousand threads of food and story and name and knowledge, to the place where the Modocs had been as long as they remembered. There are at most two or three speakers of the Modoc language left in the world, and a language is itself a world, creating distinctions and connections, describing time, kinship, place in a unique way. Does something have to come to an end for something else to be born? Did the Modocs make way not only for settlers and miners, but for a new idea of California? Was there room for both a world with a center and California as the center of technological and cultural innovation, or did the latter require a kind of decenteredness and the annihilation of what had come before? To ask this is to ask if there could have been another history, a parallel universe—but the history we have is the history in which the center was uprooted and the machines evolved.

A DAY IN THE LIFE,
TWO DEATHS,
MORE PHOTOGRAPHS

Family Pictures ▪ *A Hand of Cards* ▪ *The Trial* ▪
Flora's Conclusion ▪ *Laundresses and Ruins*

■ *Overleaf:* Detail from page 93 of the Brandenburg album: *Contemplation Rock, Glacier Point* (one frame of stereo).

FAMILY PICTURES

It was a photograph that marked the point of no return in Muybridge's marriage, or rather, it was the inscription on a photograph. On October 17, 1874, he found a photograph of the child his wife Flora Muybridge had borne seven months before, the boy they had called, in a combination of their two names, Florado. The photograph was at the house of Flora's nurse, Susan Smith, and as she told the tale, "Muybridge came to my house Saturday morning and he looked more terrible than I had ever seen him. He appeared as though he had no sleep the night before. He said: 'Mrs. Smith are you busy? I want to see you.'

"I told him I was not. I asked him in; he picked up a picture on the table and said with a start, 'Who is this?'

"I said: 'It is your baby.'

"He said: 'I have never seen this picture before. Where did you get it, and where was it taken?'

"I said, 'Your wife sent it to me from Oregon. It was taken at Rulofson's.'

"He turned over the picture and started, turning red and pale, and said: 'My God! What is this on the back of this picture in my wife's handwriting—"Little Harry!"' He stamped on the floor and exhibited the wildest excitement. His appearance was that of a madman; he was haggard and pale, his eyes glassy; his lower jaw hung down; showed his teeth; he trembled from head to foot, and gasped for breath. He was terrible to look at.

"He cried out: 'Great God! tell me all!' He came forward with his hand upraised.

"I said: 'I will tell you all.' I thought he was insane, and would kill me or himself if I did not. I then told him all I knew."

Harry was unmistakably Harry Larkyns, the man-about-town Muybridge had warned away from his wife, and the photograph's inscription and the nurse's tale clearly suggested that Larkyns, not Muybridge, was the father of the child.

Most of what is known about Muybridge makes him seem a hollow conduit for his work, with only a few vain remarks to personalize the prodigal accomplishments. But like a lightning flash the murder threw that life into dramatic light and shadow. Each of the steps toward it was built out of the flaws and desires of the three adults involved. Harry Larkyns was a rogue whose tales of his life before San Francisco are heroic beyond the reach of credibility. Tall, handsome, and charismatic, he claimed to be from an English or Scottish family of means. After alienating his family by involving himself with the theater, he claimed, he fought with the Italian nationalist revolutionaries Mazzini and Garibaldi. "The spies of Europe knew him. He became accustomed to being escorted across the frontiers by two policemen," recounted one Bay Area newspaper. "When Larkyns came home, penniless but accomplished from his wanderings, his relatives bought him an army commission. He sailed for India to join his regiment. Arrived there, he soon wearied of the routine, sold out his service and started for Central Asia. There his fortune culminated. He fell into the good graces of a heathen potentate, administered his government for him, and finally freed him from all farther care by making himself Rajah. He succeeded to the palace, the harem and the treasury of the man he had expelled, and led a life of barbaric magnificence. After six years of solitary splendor he wearied of the cares of State. He decamped at night and betook himself and a trunk of diamonds to London." He claimed to have lost his diamond fortune in speculation, to have fought with the French army against the Prussians, and to have been made a major and a chevalier of the French Legion of Honor. California believed him at least to the extent of addressing him as Major Larkyns. One of those characters corrupted by their own charms, he squandered his considerable talents and energy on seductions and impositions. As a pure fiction, he was ready for the West, but his first public role in San Francisco was as a common swindler.

On his way west, in Salt Lake City or before, he had befriended and bilked a gullible young heir named Arthur Neil. Larkyns obtained a total of $3,000 from him with the lie that his funds were shortly to turn up and spent that sum on hotels, carriages, fine wines, and other luxuries. In March 1873 Larkyns was jailed and only obtained his freedom because Neil settled with him (with the promise that a probably nonexistent wealthy female relation of Larkyns would reimburse him). Larkyns went to work at various jobs: as a stevedore on the wharves, a translator, an agent for a circus, a researcher in Hubert Howe Bancroft's almost factorylike offices, grinding out western histories at a prodigal rate. He made many friends and at least one bitter enemy. During a stint as a drama critic, he took in a homeless man with the surname of Coppinger and subcontracted some of his writing to him. Coppinger managed to replace him as drama critic by exposing the ruse, but every time they met on the street afterward, "Larkyns would take him by the nose and lower jaw, and spreading open his mouth with a grip of iron, would spit down Coppinger's throat." He was tried for this but once again acquitted—California juries looked leniently on violent defenses of honor and acts of revenge.

Neither of these incidents barred him from San Francisco society, or at least the society of theatrical and newspaper people, nor did his chronic impecuniousness. Muybridge later recalled of his acquaintance with Larkyns, "In the early part of 1873 he came up into the gallery where I was at work. Mr. Rulofson and Max Burkhardt, who were employed in the gallery, had known him for some time previous to this. He wanted to get some of my views for some purpose he had in view; I do not now remember what. My wife, who sometimes worked in the gallery a little touching up pictures, was present, and she introduced him to me. I had frequently heard her speak of Major Larkyns before, but did not know that she was much acquainted with him. I supposed that she had met him somewhere in our social circle and had heard her friends talk about him, but it seems they were better acquainted then than I supposed they were. She afterward told me she was introduced to him at the house of Mr. Selleck, a produce dealer who resides at South Park, with whom I am acquainted. After his introduction to me he frequently came up to the gallery, and I often gave him points in regard to art matters, which he was then writing about for the *Post*."

Flora Muybridge had been born Flora Downs in Kentucky or Ohio and lost her mother soon afterward. A steamboat captain uncle named Stump brought her west and established her with an aunt in California. Another steamboat captain became the foster father whose surname she took when she was known as Lily Shallcross, but she became Flora Stone soon enough. She married a San Francisco saddlemaker named Lucius Stone before she was seventeen and, on grounds of cruelty, divorced him in December 1870 when she was twenty. They had apparently been separated for the last two years of the marriage, and Flora had worked at various jobs to support herself. She met Muybridge when she worked as a retoucher of photographs at Nahl's Gallery and later, as he mentioned, pursued that profession at Bradley and Rulofson's. He helped her get her divorce and married the twenty-one-year-old in May 1871. He was a year short of twice her age and, as one of his defenders recounted it, "He permitted her to go to the theaters and elsewhere and to enjoy herself in ways which had no attraction for him. He loved her deeply, madly, with all the love of a strong self-constrained man."

"We never had any trouble to speak of," Muybridge said afterward. "We sometimes had little disputes about money matters, but they were not serious. I was always a man of very simple tastes and few wants, and I did not spend much money. What I had left over after paying my little expenses I gave to her, and yet she was always wanting more. I could never see that she bought anything with it to speak of, or imagine what she did with it. We sometimes had little spats about the money but nothing serious— nothing more than married people have every day and forget the next."

In the latter days of the marriage, she spent the money underwriting Larkyns's luxurious habits and even took care of his laundry. For though Muybridge didn't mention it, they had another dispute. One night she came home late, and when he asked where she had been, she said she had been at the theater with Larkyns. San Francisco had many flourishing theaters and a lively nightlife and society. The newness of the city and many of the fortunes in it made for more relaxed divides between Boston propriety and Barbary Coast sinning. Historian Kevin Starr writes of San Francisco, "Because of the limited number of women available for social occasions, it became the custom for married women to accept admirers—that is, to attend parties, balls, and the theater in the company of young bachelors. These relationships were intended as sentimental expedients, but they stood in continual danger of developing into something more important." Larkyns often offered both husband and wife theater passes, though Muybridge accepted only once. But when Muybridge was away, as he so often was, Larkyns took Flora out (and apparently when he was home Larkyns would send her matinee passes that she used as a cover for assignations). After the evening when Flora came home late, Muybridge warned Larkyns to stay away with, in his account, the veiled threat, "You know my right in the premises as a married man. So do I, and I shall defend them. If you

transgress them again after this morning I shall hold you to the consequences, and I suppose you know what that means in California."

After the murder, one of the newspapers reported, "Another lady
friend . . . relates that about a year since Mrs. Muybridge, who was then living at 3 South Park, and the Major, began to go out together frequently
and drew upon themselves remarks from the neighbors. They were constantly together at places of amusement, out riding, etc. . . . Mrs. Muybridge she declares to be a thoughtless, impulsive woman, given to fine
dress and flirting, but never suspected by her friends of serious miscon-
duct. She is not a woman of any particular culture or intelligence, but is
possessed of a fascinating address." Flora would have been one of the vast
majority who have disappeared from history altogether had she not created
a scandal preserved in the newspapers of the region. Almost nothing but
the scandal remains of her. There are a few photographs. Bradley and
Rulofson entered six photographs of her in the *Philadelphia Photographer*'s
nationwide competition for a perfect negative and won, and so her picture
appeared on the cover of that magazine in July 1874. The photograph depicts a plump woman with radiant skin, a porcine nose, and a complacent
expression that might speak of nothing more than holding still for the
camera. Her waist was cinched in and her abundant fair hair piled up; she
was bedecked with earrings, necklace, bracelets, a plumed hat, an artificial
rose at her lace-trimmed bodice. The least noticeable of her many orna-
ments was the ring on the fourth finger of her left hand. But the subject of
the prizewinning photograph was never identified by name there or in the
version the gallery offered for sale in a catalog of celebrities. They offered
fifty pages sorted out into "Railroad Men," "Premieres Danseuses," "Communists," "Dwarfs, Giants, etc.," "Magicians, Phrenologists, Spiritualists,
etc." Flora appeared anonymously in the category "Odds and Ends" as
"Gold Medal Picture." A perfect negative Flora remained, but for a few sen-
tences and a letter of hers that were quoted in the newspaper and the Brandenburg album.

In the 1950s a Mr. Melford F. Brandenburg found a spectacular scrapbook in a Bay Area junk shop. Its 138 pages were filled with photographs
from the 1870s. Virtually all of them seem to have come from Bradley and
Rulofson's gallery, and they are about evenly divided between studio portraits of entertainers and views by Muybridge. Nothing conclusively identi-
fies it as Flora's album, but everything points to her as its creator, including

Portrait of Flora Muybridge by William H. Rulofson, from a series of six prizewinning photographs of her, 6" x 4", page 98 of the Brandenburg album.

the presence of one of Rulofson's portraits of her and a few other images that may represent her less glamorously. Few others would have had access to such copious supplies of photographs to treat so casually, and the emphasis on Muybridge's work is also suggestive. The latest work of his in the album is from September 1873, after the Modoc War but before the birth of Florado. It depicts a steamship that had run aground in the Golden Gate, a suitably emblematic endpoint for her involvement with his art. The photograph album was a new thing then, a way of ordering one's family and world into a visual narrative, a coherent picture that was most often a family story but was sometimes a travel souvenir (several tourists' albums full of Watkins and Muybridge images exist). If the Brandenburg album is Flora's, it is an extraordinary self-portrait. The first pages are of sentimental prints and of portraits of performers. Many of Muybridge's 1872 mammoth-plate photographs of Yosemite are present, but they have been trimmed down to fit the ten-by-thirteen-inch pages. It is something of a shock to see them chopped up, but they may have been damaged or reject prints—further evidence that the album was made by someone from within the gallery, for who else would have had mammoth plates to take scissors to? Muybridge's smaller photographs are often sandwiched together with theater pictures in dizzying arrangements that look like portraits of Flora's topsy-turvy world.

Her husband's pictures, if they depict any human beings at all, show them tiny in the landscape, and these small figures are easily overwhelmed by the dozens of studio portraits of male and female performers, all their idiosyncrasies of facial expression and ornament clearly visible. Muybridge himself must have seemed to Flora, with his age, his absences, his lack of sympathy for her theatrical pursuits, as distant as the figures in his own art. There are also Muybridge photographs of Stanford's teams of horses, of the mining magnate Ralston's house, of the resort town of Calistoga, copy photographs of architectural plans—the whole array of his work. One imagines Flora at home while Muybridge was away on an expedition, pasting his work into her album, proud perhaps of her husband's achievements, but altering and arranging them to fit her own vision of the world, making them scenic background to her urban demimonde. Among all the glamour and all the novelty, there is one sad picture that may be of Flora herself. In the prizewinning portraits she tilts her head at a confident angle and her skin glows, but in this one, she is sad, pinched, and apparently pregnant, in a full skirt that makes her echo the shape of the colossal bough next to her that sags with ripe pears, one of those examples of California's amazing fertility then. The pears look heavy enough to break the bough; Flora, sad and peaked and almost haunted, looks ready to break too.

Flora seems to have been trying to patch together a decent life for herself out of two inadequate men: the unsympathetic and often absent provider Muybridge and the charming rascal Larkyns, and for a year or so it worked. She had had three pregnancies during her marriage to Muybridge, and the first two resulted in stillbirths, said Mrs. Smith, who also described the birth of Florado, the third. At two in the morning of April 16, 1874, someone rang her bell furiously. It was Larkyns, "a tall gentleman with a high white hat, and he said that Mrs. Muybridge wanted me immediately. I said that I would dress as soon as possible and go, but he cried out that she was in the carriage. I said that she must be brought into the house as I knew her condition, but he said no, and half lifted me across the sidewalk. Mrs. Muybridge was lying in the carriage (which had, as I learned afterward, just come from the Cliff House) and suffering in the first stages of labor. We drove rapidly, I half clothed, to her residence, on the corner of Howard and Third. The child, a boy, was born at 4 o'clock on the following afternoon. Mr. Muybridge at the time was out of town. I telegraphed for him and he came home the next day. He stayed for a week or ten days, until all danger was past and then went away again. He went to Belmont on business. The day after he left, Mrs. Muybridge wrote a note and told me to take it to the office of the *Evening Post* and inquire for Major Larkyns. . . . He called frequently, and while I was there I was always sent from the room."

The Cliff House was a popular seaside resort at the wild northwest corner of the city where the waves beat against the rocks, "variously the city's most modish meeting place, a favorite hangout for local political types, and a trysting place for gentlemen and their paramours," says one history; that Flora was there so pregnant says much about her insatiable appetite for nightlife (and that Muybridge was nowhere around says much about his satiable appetite for domesticity). Belmont was the location of the luxurious country estates of San Francisco's wealthiest citizens, some of which Muybridge photographed. Three days after Florado was born, Muybridge's mother, Susannah Smith Muggeridge, died in England, leaving fifty pounds to him and the rest of her estate to his younger brother, Thomas, who was reportedly working as a dentist in Walla Walla, Washington, and seems to have had scant contact with the photographer. (He later emigrated to Australia as Thomas Muridge.) Muybridge was planning another expedition to photograph either the route of the transcontinental railroad or Central America, though he loitered long enough in May to photograph the new University of California in Berkeley, a ferry ride across the Bay from the Muybridges' home near downtown. (They moved around the once-haughty and still genteel neighborhood south of Market Street, apparently living in rooming houses rather than setting up house themselves.)

Larkyns, Smith added, "asked why the old man—meaning Muybridge—did not go away on the railroad as he said he would. 'Then Flo and I could have a good time together.'" When the photographer did depart, "Mrs. Muybridge ordered me to bring the baby in for Mr. Larkyns to see. Mrs. Muybridge said, 'Major, who is the baby like?' He smiled and said, 'You ought to know, Flo.' She laughed and made no answer. . . . A negro

Page 104 of the Brandenburg album, including (from left to right, top to bottom): the University of California, Berkeley, ca. 1874; *Falls of the Yosemite*; *Temple Peaks, Monastery Valley*; *Yosemite Studies*; portrait of a woman; *Unicorn Peak, Monastery Valley*; *Tuolumne Valley*; *Yosemite Studies*; *Mount Dana from Tuolumne Meadows*. Album page 13¼" × 10½". All photographs except the portrait are by Muybridge.

was employed to carry letters from him to her. They wrote to each other two or three times a day. On one of his visits Larkyns was standing at her bedside, and she said: 'Harry we will remember the thirteenth of July; we have something to show for it.'"

Muybridge went away for the summer, no one knows where, but he prudently dispatched Flora and the baby to stay with an aunt in Oregon. They left June 15 on the coastal steamer. A month later she wrote to a San Francisco friend that she had not heard from "Muybridge since I came here. I wrote to M last week—don't think he will answer my letter, I also wrote to Rulofson's for some of my photos."

Larkyns took out advertisements in the newspapers asking her to contact him, for apparently the lovers had had some sort of falling out. It may have been nothing more than that Mrs. Smith was holding their letters, since they used her as a go-between. But Mrs. Smith had her own interests to look out for. Muybridge had given Flora money to pay the nurse's bill, but she had spent the money elsewhere. On October 14 Smith took him to court for the money, a little over a hundred dollars. In order to prove she had never been paid, she showed a letter of Flora's admitting this. The letter also mentioned Larkyns "familiarly." Afterward, Muybridge asked for any letters she had, and she obligingly gave them to his attorney, Mr. Sawyer. "As I closed the door," she testified, "I heard a scream and a fall. That was on Thursday morning, and the next evening Muybridge called at my house and told me that Sawyer had told him that the letters did not show anything more than a harmless flirtation with Larkyns." Saturday morning, Muybridge found the proof, in the form of the inscription on the photograph of the child, that there had been more. From there on things happened fast.

A HAND OF CARDS

The day that began with Muybridge's discovery of the "Little Harry" inscription is the most thoroughly documented day of his life, and though it was hardly a typical one, it does convey much about his milieu. Muybridge apparently left Nurse Smith's house and began to set his affairs in order. At one point he spent some time at the San Francisco Art Association, a three-year-old artists' club where he had shown his work and socialized with Bierstadt and many local artists and which he would later use as his address. At half past two or three o'clock in the afternoon, Rulofson ran into the photographer coming out of his gallery. He was immediately struck, because Muybridge, who had hitherto refused even to ride the elevator upstairs, was riding it down, and his face looked like a death mask. Rulofson got him to come back upstairs into the privacy of the ladies' dressing room adjacent to the portrait studio. "He threw himself on a lounge and wept bitterly, moaning like a man in great distress of mind," the photography dealer told the *Chronicle*. "He finally became sufficiently calm to speak, when he said, 'Mr. Rulofson, you have been a good friend to me. I want you to promise me that in the case of my death you will uphold the good name of my wife, and that you will settle our business affairs with her as you would with me.'" Rulofson promised but asked why such a commitment would be necessary. The story, Muybridge replied, "was too horrible to tell." When the photography dealer tried to prevent him from leaving, the account continues, "Muybridge grabbed him, and with almost superhuman strength threw him across the room and started down the stairs." Rulofson ran after him down the stairs, lured him inside once again, and heard the story. Muybridge proposed to hunt down Larkyns, who was near Calistoga, saying that "one or the other of them must die." Rulofson "talked against time," hoping to delay him, but Muybridge frequently checked his watch. Rulofson's own watch, "set to city time," showed that it was four minutes to four when Muybridge left. It should have, the dealer added, taken him about ten minutes to reach the four o'clock ferry to Vallejo, but Muybridge managed to catch the boat. Though Rulofson never mentioned it, he was carrying a pistol.

From Vallejo in the northeast of the Bay, a train went north to Calistoga, and so Muybridge traversed the seventy-five miles or so from San Francisco to the resort town in four hours. (On horseback it would have taken two days or more, but the Bay Area had been modernized in a hurry.) He went to the stable of a liveryman he knew and persuaded him, though it was a dark night, to rent him a horse and buggy. The man also told him that Larkyns was not, as he thought, at Pine Flat but at William Stuart's Yellow Jacket Mine—the region was undergoing a minor boom of silver and mercury mining, the latter element an essential ingredient for refining gold ore then. The driver, a young man named George Wolfe, recalled that he drove "from Calistoga to the Yellow Jacket Mine to the residence of Mr. Stuart in a vehicle drawn by two horses that night, and arrived there about half past ten o'clock. On the journey I did not notice anything strange in his manner or appearance or conversation. I noticed no excitement or nervousness and his conversation was natural and rational so far as I knew—on our way defendant said to me that he would give me five dollars if I would get to the Yellow Jacket Mine before Mr. Stuart. I told him it was impossible as Mr. Stuart had a half hour the start of us." The suspicious Stuart had apparently left to warn Larkyns, though if he arrived in time, it had no effect. "As we were riding along," the driver continued, Muybridge "asked me if there was any danger of being stopped by robbers. I told him no, I had driven there often and such a thing was not thought of. He asked after the lapse of some little time whether it would scare the horses if he fired his pistol off. I told him no and he discharged his pistol."

Larkyns had begun a new life outside San Francisco, as a correspondent for a minor newspaper, the *Stock Reporter,* and as surveyor for what was planned to be a detailed map of the quicksilver and silver district north of San Francisco. He spent the summer and early fall traveling around the region, visiting the various mines and sending back reports that were more literary than the subject seemed to warrant. That he signed them "Ishmaelite" suggests that his exile from San Francisco was not altogether voluntary, though what bridges he may have burned there remains unknown. He sketched a portrait of the same stagecoach driver, Foss, whose partner rented Muybridge the buggy and who Robert Louis Stevenson would a few years later portray in *The Silverado Squatters,* his book celebrating a honeymoon spent camping on the slopes of Mount St. Helena. Farther along the west slope of that four-thousand-foot-high hummock was the Yellow Jacket Mine, whose scenery Larkyns celebrated for "a view over the whole of Knight's Valley and far beyond; water is abundant, and on one of the creeks is a most picturesque spot, known as Acacia Falls, which has been immortalized by Virgil Williams and other of our artists." Like much of the rest of coastal California, Calistoga was a landscape of grasslands and gentle hills studded with oaks and creeks, but up as high as the Yellow Jacket Mine the terrain is rougher and pines begin to appear among the oaks.

The new moon was setting by the time Muybridge arrived, and no scenery distracted him from his purpose. The driver waited with the horses while he knocked at the door. Another man answered and invited him in, but Muybridge asked for Larkyns, saying, "I will only detain him a moment." Larkyns was with a group of men and women playing cribbage in the parlor. He came to the doorway and asked of the figure obscured by darkness, "Who are you?" The photographer, who must have seen only a silhouette before the light, answered, "My name is Muybridge and I have a message for you from my wife." At the word *wife,* he squeezed the trigger of his revolver. The bullet pierced Larkyns an inch below his left nipple. He clapped his hand to his heart and ran through the house and out the other door, collapsing under a large oak tree. Another man at the scene covered Muybridge with his own gun and disarmed him. Muybridge never tried to resist or flee. He was taken to the parlor, and he apologized to the women there for "the interruption." When he was taken out of the room, Larkyns's body was brought in. Flora's lover was dead.

THE TRIAL

Three of the men at the Yellow Jacket Mine that night took Muybridge to the sheriff in Calistoga, one driving the two-seated wagon, one holding the lantern, and one guarding the murderer. Lynching was talked of, but Muybridge was safely locked up in the Napa Jail. Monday morning the story, with its sensational combination of adultery, murder, and celebrity, was in the headlines of all the region's papers. Larkyns received a showy San Francisco funeral, and as the coffin left the church, "a well-known actress of the California Theater leaned from her seat and, sobbing violently, put a handsome bouquet upon the coffin and, following it to the grave, was the last person to leave the vault." Muybridge read a lot during the months before the trial that began in the town of Napa on February 3 and had his meals sent in from a nearby hotel. His friends visited, and he said in the interview he granted the *Chronicle* near Christmas that he had received a great many sympathetic letters. The reporter declared, "Muybridge is forty [actually nearly forty-five] years of age, but looks at least ten years older than that. His full, unkept beard is deeply tinged with gray, and his hair is white. He has mild blue eyes and a face which a physiognomist would invariably pass by in searching for one likely to do deeds of violence or death. His manner is quiet and reserved, his dress plain to a degree somewhat out of keeping with his profession and standing, and any one unacquainted with him would readily mistake him for a quiet, good-natured old farmer. . . ." Muybridge never seemed to think he had done much of anything wrong or

Page 93 of the Brandenburg album, including (top to bottom): *Contemplation Rock, Glacier Point* (uncut stereo); portrait of an actor (left and right); *Glacier Rock, Yosemite* (uncut stereo). Both top and bottom photographs are by Muybridge; the former may show Muybridge himself in the position of which Rulofson spoke when testifying to his madness.

expressed any real regret, and the fact that he killed Larkyns was never in question. When he went to trial he was represented by three good lawyers, led by William Wirt Pendegast, a former state congressman and florid orator. Because Pendegast was a friend of Stanford's, it is sometimes proposed that the railroad baron aided Muybridge from a safe distance. The trial was a great show, with many reporters, onlookers, and friends present—including Muybridge's friend, the former Yosemite promoter and hotelier James Hutchings, writing for the *Sacramento Daily Union*. At times there was a standing-room-only crowd.

Muybridge was on trial for first-degree murder, for which the punishment was death. The lawyers used an insanity defense, much to the benefit of history. Mounting the defense meant asking several of Muybridge's friends to testify about his character, and the newspaper reports citing them offer a stark portrait. It was in court that Muybridge told the story of his stagecoach accident and head injuries, and the picture his friends and associates painted may represent the consequences. Mrs. Smith, the nurse, who was described as tall and plainly dressed but for a flower-adorned hat, told about an incident the spring before, when Muybridge came back to town, "seemed happy, then turned suddenly and looking at two canaries hanging in the room, said to the nurse, 'Why do you give those birds hempseed when I told you not?' I replied, 'You gave that to your birds last night yourself.' 'Ah, dear me,' said he. 'I feel bad here sometimes,' tapping his forehead." Her daughter, who had worked at the gallery with Muybridge and was one of Flora's best friends, said that as a husband he was "always kind and indulgent" but that he was "very eccentric and peculiar, easily excited and very nervous." Rulofson testified next that Muybridge would make a bargain one day and break or forget it the next and had done so thirty to forty times in the two years they had been working together. It may be that his dealer was trying hard to make a case for insanity, but he seems to have found all unbusinesslike conduct lunatic. He testified that Muybridge spurned money and "would never make a view for money if he did not see beauty in it but would drop his tools and pack up at once." When Crocker, one of the Big Four railroad barons, questioned a bill for $700, Muybridge dropped the matter rather than argue. The photographer "would stay up all night reading—generally some classical work." A final damning sign of madness was Muybridge's posing for a photograph on the brink of one of Yosemite's precipices.

The music dealer M. Gray "saw a marked change in him" when he returned from Europe in 1867: "He was formerly pleasant and agreeable; afterward, irritable, more careless in dress and not so good a businessman. . . . He was untidy and his hair turned gray." Silas Selleck testified that he had known Muybridge since the autumn of 1855, almost twenty years before, and (in the condensed transcription of the newspapers) said, "Before the trip [in 1860] his disposition was good and his manners genial; he was a good businessman, sound and vigorous of health. When he came back . . . he had changed so entirely that when he stood in my store, on his return, I could hardly recognize him—hardly know him. In some respects do not consider him of sound mind; his brain is affected." Like Rulofson, Selleck considered disdain for profit a sign of madness. And, Selleck concluded, often Muybridge would, "lost in vacancy," fail to recognize him. Some of this behavior may be the signs of frontal lobe damage that the neurologist Arthur Shimamura points to; some is a sign of being more an artist than a businessman; some may be merely evidence that his friends were doing their best to exonerate him. Useless for the jury's purposes, the testimony is priceless for history's: it shows a man who was a member of a sophisticated commercial and creative community, a dweller in boardinghouses, an indulgent but hardly understanding husband, a restless traveler in pursuit of pictures who must have owned his pistols for the dangers of his journeys in those days when California had both grizzlies and highwaymen. He was an eccentric but not quite a solitary. The testimony also makes it clear that whatever damage he had suffered, his crime was not an act of impulse but a carefully laid plan adhered to for the several hours from when he retrieved his pistol through his odyssey from gallery to ferry to train to town to buggy to the doorstep of the manager's house of the Yellow Jacket Mine that dark night.

The insanity defense certainly didn't impress the jury, though Pendegast's closing argument on Friday afternoon, February 5, did. "The speech was one of the most eloquent forensic efforts ever heard in the state," the *Chronicle* reported, and at the end the large audience "broke into a storm of applause, notwithstanding the previous caution of Judge Wallace." Muybridge occasionally sobbed in the course of the speech, whose tone was that of Victorian melodrama. Pendegast intoned, "I cannot ask you to send this man forth to family and home—he has none. Across the arch of his fire place where once was written the words Home—Wife—Child—

Ancient Sacrificial Stone, Guatemala, 1875, from the series *Central America Illustrated by Muybridge* (one frame of stereo).

Content and Peace, there now appears as a substitute for all, placed there by the destroyer, the single awful word 'Desolation.' But I do ask you to send him forth free—let him take up the thread of his broken life, and resume that profession upon which his genius has shed so much luster—the profession which is now his only love. Let him go forth into the green fields, by the bright waters, through the beautiful vallies, and up and down the swelling coast, and in the active work of securing shadows of their beauty by the magic of his art, he may gain 'surcease of sorrow' and pass on to his allotted end in comparative peace."

With this, the defense rested. The prosecution pointed out that neither the law nor the Bible condoned killing adulterers and concluded, "The virtue of women rests not on their husband's revolvers, but in their own purity. You have no right to ignore the law, and you must find the prisoner guilty unless you conclude he is insane." The trial ended at half past nine in the evening, and the jury began deliberations at quarter to eleven. They deadlocked in the small hours of the night, five for conviction and seven for acquittal. In the morning they deadlocked again, and then one man changed from conviction to acquittal, and with that the rest followed. In direct violation of the law and the judge's written instructions, they found him not guilty without finding him insane. Afterward it was said that they were all married men, and the jury foreman convinced them that they would have done the same if they found their wives had lovers. It was a little after noon when they delivered the verdict, and all eyes turned to Muybridge, who had spent more than three months in confinement not knowing whether he was to hang or go free.

When his exoneration was delivered, "a convulsive gasp escaped the prisoner's lips, and he sank forward from his chair. The mental and nervous tension that had sustained him for days of uncertain fate was removed in an instant and he became as helpless as a newborn babe. Mr. Pendegast caught him in his arms and thus prevented his falling to the floor, but his body was as limp as a wet cloth. His emotion became convulsive and frightful. His eyes were glassy, his jaws set, and his face livid. The veins of his hands and forehead swelled out like whipcord. He moaned and wept convulsively, but uttered no word of pain or rejoicing." Like Mrs. Smith the morning he discovered the baby photograph's inscription, the reporter found that Muybridge's "face was absolutely horrifying in its contortions as convulsion succeeded convulsion. The judge discharged the jury and hastily left the courtroom, unable to bear the sight, and it became necessary to recall him subsequently to finish the proceedings. The Clerk hid his face in his handkerchief." Nothing records whether Muybridge found his fits deeply embarrassing or whether he was oblivious to their effect. He recovered so well that he managed to walk out of the courtroom to be greeted by a cheering throng. That evening, he reached San Francisco to celebrate his freedom with a dinner attended by many friends.

FLORA'S CONCLUSION

It was as though the gun functioned as a camera. Shooting Harry preserved him forever at the moment when Flora loved him. Had Muybridge done nothing, Larkyns might have abandoned her, or Larkyns and Flora might have run away to Britain as he promised her, to live more or less happily ever after, or let their passion burn out. Flora Muybridge came back to San Francisco with the child in the months after the murder, and on December 14 she filed for divorce. She cited grounds of extreme cruelty, asked for alimony, and asserted that her husband was worth from $5,000 to $10,000 and earned upward of $600 a month, a handsome income in those days. Flora continued asking the courts for a divorce in 1875, but she could never explain the real nature of her husband's cruelty: that he had murdered the man she loved. Divorces were easy to get in San Francisco then, and women often availed themselves of the courts. Out of 600 applications for divorce in 1875, 350 were granted. For many women, California's skewed ratio of men to women was a source of power, and dozens of maverick women made their mark in nineteenth-century San Francisco. Flora never freed herself from convention to become, as they did, a poet, a novelist, an actress, a behind-the-scenes politician, a saloniste, a celebrity. The status of women was itself much contested in the 1870s, part of the uncertainty and conflict of the era.

The women's rights movement was then closely identified with "free love." Though many of the feminists of the day abhorred the free-love ideology, others, such as the spiritualist and suffragist Victoria Woodhull, embraced it. "The doctrine," writes Barbara Goldsmith, "of free love and women's rights had much in common: The concept of equal relations between the sexes was identical and led to the fight for many reforms, including the vote and the liberalization of marriage and divorce laws. But free love was abhorrent to many women as well as men because it openly acknowledged equal female sexuality." The free-love feminists pointed out that the current system linked women's economic well-being to their sexual submission to men, as wives or as prostitutes, and they proposed a more idealistic and freer expression of sexuality for women. There was a Darwinian side to it, a belief that women should be free to choose the best possible fathers for their children. Woodhull's sister Tennessee Claflin declared, "Mothers of humanity, yours is a fearful duty, and one which should in its importance lift you entirely above the modern customs of society, its frivolities, superficialities and deformities, and make you realize that to you is committed the divine work of perfecting humanity." It would be a stretch to say that in choosing the handsome Larkyns, Flora was selflessly improving the species, but she was asserting in her acts an independence whose ideology seems to have escaped her. San Francisco seemed less concerned with the principles than the practice of free love, and a considerable number of women led unconventional lives without persecution, but they were careful to set their own terms.

Had Flora boldly left Muybridge for Larkyns, had she asserted her right to go where her heart led her, the outcome might have been different than that which transpired from the wrenching discoveries she left for Muybridge to make. As their marriage was unraveling, another case of adultery was under far more scrutiny. On January 11, 1875, less than a month before Muybridge's trial for murder, the civil trial of *Tilton v. Beecher* began in Brooklyn. Theodore Tilton, a prominent journalist, sued Henry Ward Beecher, the most popular and powerful clergyman of the day, for having slept with his wife, Elizabeth Tilton. The charismatic Beecher was a sneaky lothario among his congregation's women but confidently denied all charges in the trial, which ran for nearly six months and made the front pages of newspapers across the country. Woodhull, tired of being attacked for her advocacy of free love, had helped to expose Beecher, hoping to force his support but only succeeding in alarming him into a deeper hypocrisy. The parallels between the two trials were often drawn, and that a husband who sued was greeted with less public sympathy than one who shot was duly noted.

Flora sued repeatedly for alimony and divorce, but she could not come up with sufficient grounds for a divorce on grounds of cruelty. With a baby to care for, no source of income, abandoned by husband and bereft of lover, she seems to have become increasingly desperate. That she had come to hate Muybridge is evinced by the more and more bitter testimony she offered. Despite his assertions the previous December that he would never let her want, he was apparently not providing support for her and Florado. It is not known whether they ever met again, but they never met in court. Though his trip to Central America is sometimes depicted as nothing more than an attempt to lie low, he had planned it before the murder, and the timing was only opportune. Flora apparently intended to seize

Muybridge's cameras in order to secure alimony, but he dispatched his crates of equipment to the steamship and had himself rowed away in a small boat that caught up with the steamer as it approached the Golden Gate. The *Chronicle* gloatingly reported how Muybridge had snuck out of town not long after the trial: "While the relentless wife was taking steps to lay an embargo, her estranged husband vanished in the mists hovering over the bar." Finally in May she was granted alimony, but there was no way to collect it, and her time was running out.

Muybridge had been living a largely impersonal life among men, ideas, and outdoor subjects. Flora dragged him into a drama of beds and birth and kisses and lies, and his response to her passions incarcerated him for several months. But it was she, like the adulterous women in the novels of the era, who paid most for her pleasure. *Adam Bede, David Copperfield,* and *Tess of the D'Urbervilles* are only three of the best-known books in which young women who have sex outside marriage pay a huge price of death or permanent exile, the price Woodhull protested and, with ostracism even from her feminist peers and exile to England, paid herself. Flora went into a decline. On July 18 she died in St. Mary's Hospital of, in one account, "a stroke of paralysis," in another, "a complication of spinal complaint and inflammatory rheumatism, which baffled the skill of physicians." The ever-attentive *Chronicle* reported that "the poor woman was out of her mind a great portion of her time and was unconscious at the time of her death. Two sisters, who attended her with the greatest of care and tenderness, also sought to minister to her spiritual welfare, and in her lucid moments she afforded them evidence of the success of their labors in that direction, professing a change of heart and peace with God." A girlhood companion recalled many years later that a friend of her foster father, Captain Shallcross, visited Flora on her deathbed, where her last words were, "I am sorry." The funeral was held in a friend's home on Clementina Street rather than a church, and the body was buried in the Cosmopolitan section of the Odd Fellows Cemetery in western San Francisco. Flora was twenty-four.

LAUNDRESSES AND RUINS

Because they still had not divorced, Muybridge became an unwitting widower several thousand miles away. Florado Muybridge was left in the care of a French family. In September 1876, several months after his return,

Muybridge moved the toddler from a Catholic orphanage to the Protestant Orphan Asylum, a large building that he had photographed earlier. It isn't clear whether Muybridge regarded him as a son. He occasionally visited the child and made no effort to change his name, but did little further for him and did not remember him in his will. If Larkyns was the child's father, he was truly an orphan, and Muybridge made him one. At the age of ten, Florado Muybridge was discharged from the orphanage and sent to a ranch, where he grew up working with horses. No one ever found much good to say about his abilities, but his successive abandonments may have had much to do with this. In a photograph of Florado in late middle age, the craggy bones of his face suggest that Muybridge may have been his father after all, as if he were a slow-developing photograph, a late piece of evidence. He was killed by a car while crossing a Sacramento street in 1944.

Muybridge was gone for most of 1875. The Panama newspaper the *Star* wecomed him on March 16, and he spent two months there before moving on to Guatemala, his principal destination. He had traveled with the Pacific Mail Steamship Company and had an agreement with them: they apparently supplied free transportation and other support, and he was to provide photographs that would further their economic interests. Like his arrangements with the U.S. government, it was an ambiguous agreement in which he retained his artistic autonomy and his negatives. The Pacific Mail Steamship Company had been a powerful entity before the transcontinental railroad took away much of its business, and it sought to revive itself through the new population of passengers and new cargo Muybridge's photographs could encourage. When he arrived, Guatemala was in transition from the three-decades-long reign of President-for-Life Rafael Carrera, who had done much to promulgate a real version of democracy that respected the indigenous majority's land ownership and other rights. Carrera died in 1865, as the country was shifting to a coffee-exporting economy for whose benefit the indigenous population was being reduced to the form of slavery known as *mandamiento,* or forced labor. Historians of Central America still prize Muybridge's documents, perhaps the most extensive early body of photographic imagery of the region.

On October 1, 1875, Muybridge advertised in Guatemala his "vistas fotographicas de este Republica" and signed himself Eduardo Santiago Muybridge. The photographic albums he made afterward include what in a film might be called "establishing shots," pictures of the principal cities, plazas, and administrative buildings from Panama City to the highland villages of Guatemala. Toward the end of his trip, he spent an extended period at Las Nubes, the coffee plantation of the Pacific Steamship's agent in Guatemala, William Nelson. There he photographed the entire process of coffee production, from clearing rain forest through the stages of cultivation and harvest to shipping. The steamship company was interested in the coffee economy, since two-thirds of the crop was exported to the United States. This combination of commercial documentation and self-expression is typical of Muybridge, who photographed Yosemite, the Modoc War, wineries, lighthouses, the transcontinental railroad, in ways that officially served the market but often diverged from its interests and interpretations. The photographs range from coastal scenes and cities to mountain and jungle landscapes, from indigenous laborers to soldiers in formation and aristocrats at leisure. Certain subjects recur with a frequency that seems to suggest Muybridge's own sensibility. He photographed again and again the baroque ruins of churches, landscapes with still and moving water, dense thickets, and jungle foliage, and he photographed the laundresses often to be found at that water or at the fountainlike laundry sites in the city. These indigenous women were often as not bare-breasted, and though a certain anthropological prurience emanates from the photographs, their subjects seem as somber as the ruins. These pictures have been compared to Eugene Atget's uncanny documentation of Paris a few decades later, and they contain a similar tension between subjective response and documentary mission. Many of the landscapes have added clouds that make them moodier.

Ruins had been a stock subject for romantic self-expression for a century, but there was more than crumbling stone in the photographs. Muybridge's image of the church of San Miguel depicts a ruin on a hilltop framed against the sky with spiky plants growing out of one tower and foliage creeping around the whole edifice. On the stone steps below, a nude child whose dark skin almost blends into the lichen-spotted steps stands behind a seated woman dressed in white. Churches crumbled, plants grew luxuriantly, volcanos punctuated the horizon, and only the water was the same floating whiteness it had been so many times in Yosemite, the water and the isolation that had returned to embrace him. Small isolated figures are almost swallowed up in their surroundings, solitaries stand with their backs to the camera, and there is an unusual lack of contact between pho-

Ruins of the Church of San Miguel, Panama, from the album *The Pacific Coast of Central America and Mexico; the Isthmus of Panama; Guatemala; and the Cultivation of Coffee,* 1875.

tographer and subject and between subjects. In one splendid picture, ten Pananamian hunters stand, each with a rifle, apart from each other, ankle deep in large leaves and with a wall trailing dry vines behind them. Some blur, one hams for the camera, but they all look off in different directions, as though each were alone. In another, a rough slab of stone with a hole piercing it stands in a field of dry and crumpled cornstalks, and through the hole can be seen the grim, gleaming face of a native man. Muybridge called it *Ancient Sacrificial Stone, Naranjo, Guatemala,* though it was really an astronomical observation device. The gridded regularity of Central American urbanism lent itself to many pictures emphasizing vanishing-point perspective, including an avenue of mausoleums in Guatemala City and a view down one of the straight streets.

He came back with nearly 200 large and 150 stereo images of Central America, and he assembled several albums of the former, most containing about 140 pictures. One went to the Pacific Steamship owners, one to Mrs. Stanford, one with an inscription of fervent gratitude to the widow of William Pendegast, the lawyer who so effectively defended him and died soon after, one to Johnston, another of the defense lawyers, and one to Frank Shay, which must have been given when Shay was Stanford's secretary from 1879 to 1882. Muybridge offered portfolios of Central America prints for sale and showed them in the usual places over the next few years, and he began to do something new in his career—give magic-lantern shows of the images, transferred to glass slides. The Central America pictures ushered him back into public life, and after the initial blizzard of coverage, no publication during his lifetime seems to have mentioned his marital crisis and murder.

It is impossible to admire Muybridge without reservation. His flaws are many and obvious. He worked for the monopolies and robber barons of the day and genuflected before power—though so did the rest of the western landscape photographers, who had only the colonizing, conquering government as an equally generous patron. He was boastful, though his exaggerations are delicately tinted things in the blazing era of Mark Twain, Buffalo Bill, Calamity Jane, Wyatt Earp, Joaquin Miller, Victoria Woodhull,

Picking Coffee at San Isidro, from the album *The Pacific Coast of Central America and Mexico; the Isthmus of Panama; Guatemala; and the Cultivation of Coffee,* 1875.

George Custer, Gertrude Atherton, and Emperor Norton. He was a murderer. But it is impossible to despise and dismiss him. He was a damaged man, an isolated one, and apparently one who suffered deeply. If he had been pure prodigy we could label him such and file him away in one of history's commodious drawers. If he were nothing but a charlatan or a criminal, the same would be true. That he is all of these things means he is not so easily got rid of.

The contemporary question arises of whether, in estimating artistic merit, an artist's personal life should be weighed along with the work. It is the ethics within the work, rather than the biographical clutter, that counts—though the two are never unconnected. There are always traces of the artist in the art. The alienation that is a hallmark of Muybridge's personal life is evident in his photographs; the independence of vision in the photographs also characterized his maverick life. But the masterful clarity of Muybridge's photography is in stark contrast to the emotionally overwrought man on exhibit in the trial. The "great man" version of history has been much attacked in recent years, but Muybridge is worth examination not because without him there would have been no movies but because with him we can start to understand something about their source. The great gifts might have occurred elsewhere, but the peculiar fingerprints on such gifts would not. Muybridge demands a mixed reaction, and this makes him a perfect parent for the age of image streams in which we live, an age of wonders, banalities, degradations, gorgeous spectacles and evils, irreparable losses and spectacular gains. This parenthood he undertook in earnest in 1877, the year after he consigned Florado to the Protestant Orphan Asylum.

SKINNING THE CITY

Traveling in Pictures ■ *The Great Strike* ■
The View from the Top

■ *Overleaf:* Detail: Plates 7 and 8 from *Panorama of San Francisco,* 1878, looking east down California Street. The central building is Stanford's stable; St. Mary's Church is at far right; Goat Island (now Yerba Buena Island, where the Bay Bridge touches down) is in center right, Oakland hills beyond it.

TRAVELING IN PICTURES

In July 1877 Muybridge's first large panorama of San Francisco was published. Early the following month the *Alta* announced his next breakthrough in instantaneous photography with the headline "'Occident' Photographed at Full Speed." He was moving forward on two fronts as he had in 1873, when he simultaneously released his first photograph of Occident trotting and his Yosemite mammoth-plate masterpieces. These city panoramas are his most complex investigation of the subject of time before the motion studies, in the way the individual images develop a sequence and in the way they depict San Francisco on the verge of an uncivil war. These panoramas were, too, part of his restless experimentation with the technical possibilities of the medium. The seventeen-foot-long 1878 panorama, his farewell to the photography of place, is generally considered to be the greatest achievement of its kind.

It is now hard to recall how ravenous the appetite for spectacle, for image, for information, once was, and how inventive and varied were the means of feeding it before films and television and computer imagery arrived to sate it. From the seventeenth century on a whole panoply of innovations strove to make more compelling, more believable, even more frightening images, to make them move, to make them luminous, to make them fill whole rooms. In the eighteenth century the panorama, one of the most successful of these innovations, arose. *Panorama* is a word coined in the late eighteenth century out of two Greek terms, *pan,* or all, and *horama,* or view. It describes a 360-degree painting of a scene, urban or rural. The panorama paintings were theaters without action into whose elevated center a paying audience entered, and for half a century they were popular enough to generate a steady succession of huge circular views (IMAX movie theaters might be their most direct descendants). One of the curious aspects of the painted panorama is that it cannot be seen all at once; the unity expected from conventional painting is irrelevant. It is a picture to be seen by traveling, whether by rotating in one place or by walking its length.

Another version of the entertainment was created by Louis-Jacques-Mandé Daguerre, who earlier had been a panorama painter and then a celebrated set designer. In 1822, seventeen years before he announced the invention of photography, he set up his Diorama theater in Paris. It featured, rather than the full circle of the panorama, two vast but comparatively flat paintings that were transparent in places and augmented by lights and other special effects that created illusions of changing time and movement. The passage of a whole day was reduced to fifteen minutes, and those who might not care to watch the changing skies loved to see their imitation, just as they flocked to see the Diorama imitating a nearby church they could have visited in actuality for free. This is one of the great enigmas of modern life: why the representation of a thing can fascinate those who would ignore the original. Perhaps it is the skill, the medium, the technique, the promise of resolution, or perhaps it is merely that someone has already decided to pay attention to a subject, and the representation invites you to commune with this attention as well as its subject. And this power of the image that eclipses reality is what links Daguerre's work in theatrical productions with his research into photography.

Since its inception, photography has been discussed largely in relationship to painting, but in many ways it was more closely related to what could be called entertainment, that hybrid and ever-evolving mix of sophisticated technique and populist content. Before and during the early years of photography many "philosophical toys" that played with perception were invented. Some of them contributed to the understanding of the nature of vision, and they along with panoramas, dioramas, projections, and camera obscuras are photography's and cinema's forebears and cousins, but they were also popular entertainments. In Muybridge's time, stereocards meant to be seen through a viewing device and magic-lantern slides were important aspects of photography. Both these media, like panoramas and dioramas, satisfied that yearning for a more overwhelming experience than was supplied by a flat image on a wall, in an album, or in the hand.

Not long after the invention of photography, panoramic photographs had been attempted, but in this medium panorama meant merely a broad view, not a full-circle one. The painted panorama itself had mutated by

Panorama of San Francisco, 1878, plates 1 through 3. Thirteen photographs, 24" × 17' 4" total. Crocker's mansion with spite fence is center right of plate 3, behind Huntington's mansion.

midcentury, at least in America. There the round panoramas had a limited audience, but long ones—thousands of feet long at times— that could be moved past the audience on rollers were enormously successful. Writes a historian of the panorama, "The moving panorama anticipated, in art, the speed of travel which the railroads would soon make a reality. In the American moving panorama, viewers were no longer surrounded by a canvas that only appeared to present an open vista on all sides; rather they saw the vast landcape of their continent unrolling before their eyes, as if they were traveling westward." The moving panorama was a form of travel in which the viewers sat still, distinct from the European panorama that viewers pivoted and strolled to see.

It was images of the West that Americans craved, whatever their own location, and though the great canvas panoramas seemed to represent the Mississippi more than any other subject, photographic panoramas flourished most in San Francisco. As the capital of the gold rush, as for many decades the biggest city west of the Mississippi, as a town that grew like wildfire and burned like it too, San Francisco was of considerable interest throughout the nation, and panoramas were made both for locals craving a record of their own experience and easterners curious about the Wild West. In 1851 no fewer than five daguerreotype panoramas were made from Nob Hill, then known as California Hill, after the street that ran straight west up its steep face (the monicker Nob Hill came after the Central Pacific's Big Four—the Nobs—moved there). The pioneer photographer George Farndon made a seven-part panorama from this slope in

Panorama of San Francisco, 1878, plates 4 through 8, with the Golden Gate, Marin County, and Alcatraz in the background of 4 and 5.

1855, just before Muybridge arrived to begin his career as a bookseller there. Charles Weed made a ten-card stereoscope panorama in 1858 or 1859, and all of Muybridge's panoramas before 1877 are in this format.

At first it seems contrary: the usual photographic panorama is a long ribbon almost like a Chinese scroll that offers a sense of spatial continuity. The stereocard panoramas suggest that the viewer would instead, while keeping the stereoscope clapped to his or her eyes, change the cards in sequence to create what cinematographers call a "pan" of a place, and some stereoviewers were designed to feed a sequence of cards into the viewer. (Another cinematic precursor is a sort of peep show in which a series of stereocards depicting a place or a narrative are mechanically changed as the viewer watches.) Thus, the ribbon panoramas allowed one to travel the panorama as space, the stereocard panoramas to travel it in time. Their makers already understood some of the ways that time and space become one another, how the eye could travel through individual plates joined either in proximity or in sequence. The circular panorama had been a static construction viewers traveled by sight or by foot, while the diorama and moving panorama changed over time, but the essence of each was a picture that could not be seen at once: a four-dimensional image.

Muybridge made a seven-stereocard panorama of San Francisco from Rincon Hill south of Market Street early in his career, probably 1868, when that hill was the center of wealthy society; he made two panoramas in the Lava Beds in 1873; and a five-stereocard panorama of Guatemala in 1875.

Thus in 1877 he was already an old hand at what could be called temporal panorama but relatively new to spatial panorama. Carleton Watkins made one of the first large panoramas of San Francisco from the same slope in 1864 and returned to the subject many times in many places, in large-plate, mammoth-plate, and stereoscope formats. Muybridge may have once again been competing with Watkins when he decided to make a large-format panorama of San Francisco, but he may also have been inspired by the thirty-foot photographic panorama of Sydney, Australia, that was briefly exhibited in San Francisco before its arrival at the 1876 Philadelphia Centennial Exposition (where Watkins and Muybridge both had mammoth-plate photographs of Yosemite on exhibit).

Muybridge went to Nob Hill in the summer of 1877 to make his second full-plate panorama (he also made a seven-image panorama from the windows of the Stanfords' Nob Hill home that year). He was able to go high above the city, up into the turret of Central Pacific Railroad magnate Mark Hopkins's unfinished mansion atop Nob Hill, and from there he made a 360-degree panorama. Such a view had rarely if ever been attempted photographically. It was seldom possible to get high enough in the center of a city to see in all directions at once, and until the 1870s virtually the whole city of San Francisco lay east of that promontory anyway. Too, the usual 180-degree view reconstructed what could be seen in a single glimpse, including the latent areas at the far edges of the field of vision. It made sense to the eye. But Muybridge's Nob Hill panoramas are an impossible sight, a vision of the city in all directions, a transformation of a circular space into a

Panorama of San Francisco, 1878, plates 9 through 13.

linear photograph. As filmmaker Hollis Frampton put it, "He condenses an entire rotation of the seeing eye around the horizon (an action that must take place in time) into a simultaneity that is at once completely plausible and perfectly impossible."

Strange anomalies arise from the structure of the full-circuit panorama. California Street is visible stretching east in plates 1 and 11 and west in 5 and 6. Only careful analysis reveals that the multiple stretches of street heading for different vanishing points are one street. The city has been flattened out like the skin of an animal. A flayed skin can be seen as a single surface as a live animal cannot, but the dimensions of its original form must be reconstructed in the imagination. Muybridge had skinned the city with elegant aggression. Making the full-circle panorama was a spectacular technical feat. Careful calculations divided the horizon into equal segments (though in the 1877 version, the first and last plates overlap considerably), and much skill was employed to pivot the camera correctly. Muybridge must have had a temporary darkroom set up in the Hopkins mansion and assistants to help with preparation and development of the negatives, but the task was nevertheless demanding.

With a modern video or movie camera, the horizon could be scanned in seconds, but Muybridge spent the better part of a day aligning his camera and exposing his wet-plate negatives. It is conceptually dizzying to realize that several hours of the day are on view at once, and that the hours are not necessarily in order. To look at the panorama is to look at time, not a moment of it but several moments separated by long intervals (akin in a way to

Timothy O'Sullivan's contemporaneous photographs from a fixed vantage point of a canyon at different times of day or to Muybridge's sequences of the sun setting or the Mint being built, which is to say, akin to the motion studies he was soon to make). Just as viewers are seeing in several directions at once, so they are looking at several separate moments at once. Like a movie, the 1877 panorama was edited together out of many discontinuous pieces of time into a plausible but fictitious continuity. The shadows between the first and second plates appear to have shifted, judging by the way they don't match up on a building split between the two pictures. Muybridge used a negative from an alternate version of the panorama he made at the same time, in what was called boudoir format, for the third plate of the full-size panorama. And he made two different versions of plate 5, the view east down California Street.

These versions are easy to detect because the clock of St. Mary's Church is clearly visible: in most versions the clock is at quarter to two, but in a few the clock is at nearly five-thirty in the afternoon, the shadows are deeper, and the tide has changed so that the ships in the harbor have shifted and one more has sailed in (that light is still pouring down this eastern slope onto the clock face is one sign that the picture was made near midsummer; there are other, more technical ones). This is one of the great enigmas of the panoramas. There is not a clear-cut reason why one plate was used rather than the other, since neither is seriously flawed. All that is clear is that after Muybridge came down from the Hopkins tower, the experiment continued in the darkroom. But despite its flaws, this first version was recognized as remarkable. On July 13, 1877, the *Daily Evening Bulletin* announced, "PANORAMA OF SAN FRANCISCO.—Mr. Muybridge the well-known photographer, has published a panorama of San Francisco, as seen from California Hill. There appears to be no limit to the triumph of possibilities of photographic art, and certainly Mr. Muybridge has advanced very far on the road to perfection. As a picture of the city this is by far the best we have ever seen."

THE GREAT STRIKE

That week the country exploded, and the next week San Francisco followed suit. Since Jay Cooke had closed his Philadelphia bank in 1873, the country had fallen into a depression, and those whose diminished wages were inadequate to feed and clothe a family and those who had no work suffered, simmered, and occasionally struck. They regarded the big capitalists with bitterness, and none were more visible or more hated than the heads of the largest corporations of the day, the railroads. In July 1877 railroad after railroad cut wages that were already savagely low, and the anger boiled over. The Great Strike broke out spontaneously across the country, in Baltimore, St. Louis, Louisville, Pittsburgh, Scranton, Reading, Cincinnati, Cleveland, Toledo, Buffalo, Albany, Binghamton, Terre Haute, Indianapolis, Kansas City, Chicago, Manhattan, and many smaller towns. It began at the railroad town of Martinsburg, West Virginia, when the militia shot a railroad striker on July 17. In response, workers shut down the train traffic until 600 freight trains were idled there. Women, children, the unemployed, all sorts of citizens, poured into the streets to join the railroad workers in Martinsburg, as in so many other towns.

In places, soldiers were called out against citizens, bringing the country close to a civil war, though this time the divide was not between North and South but between rich and poor. Sometimes the militia and police refused to attack, instead joining in the uproar, giving away goods from the freight cars that had been idled, or skulking away in fear. Sometimes they shot into crowds, and by the end of July the death toll was at least a hundred. Even in towns where there was no strike, citizens gathered in groups on the corners and in front of the newspapers and telegraph offices to talk and listen, and ordinary life came to a halt. The strike was about the pervasive power of the railroads and the pervasive hatred of them, and it was spread by the wire-service news that made it possible to read daily accounts of what was going on across the country and to act in concert with those far away. Half a century earlier such widespread coordination would have been inconceivable. Nothing quite like it had ever happened before in the United States, and nothing quite like it has since. There would be other strikes, but none so spontaneous, so widespread, so shocking to those who for a few weeks no longer ran the country. Half the nation's railroad traffic was shut down, and its citizens were out en masse flexing a power they had seldom felt before. The Civil War represented an America of ideologies and a North-South split; the Indian wars an America of westward incursion; but the Great Strike portrayed it as an industrialized nation whose schism was social.

In Pittsburgh, railroad workers and union men were soon outnumbered by thousands of others, looting freight cars for, according to one list, "corn in sacks, cotton in bales, wool in bags, bread, crackers, fruit, sugar candies and confectioneries, hides, leather, shoes, queen's ware, glass ware, clothing, hay, whisky, alcohol, tobacco, coal, coke, silks, jewelry, even assorted volumes of Chambers' Encyclopedia and a number of Bibles." In that grim industrial city, 104 locomotives and 2,152 railroad cars were destroyed—eleven and a half miles of train in total. Twenty-four people, including four soldiers, died in the turmoil. In Harrisburg the militia gave their guns to the crowd and were sent home; in Reading the railroad tracks and cars and even a bridge were methodically destroyed. In Cincinnati the crowd stopped every railroad in the western portion of the city. In Chicago youths convinced the railroad, factory, and dockyard workers to shut down their workplaces. There the police shot into a crowd of thousands, and eighteen died. Comparisons were made to the French Revolution and to the Paris Commune of 1871, when workers took over the city, and in St. Louis something akin to a Paris Commune arose after the railroads and virtually every other industry were shut down, and workers organized to run the city. But as a historian of that general strike wrote, "The 'communists' of 1877 were interested not in setting up an ideal republic, but in matters far more disturbing to the manufacturers . . . wage rates and hours of labor." Red flags flew on Manhattan's Bowery, and a socialist meeting in Tompkins Square was attended by twenty thousand people.

The headlines in San Francisco's *Alta* on July 22 were:

The Great Strike
It Extends to All the Trunk Lines
Militia Called Out in Three States
A Conflict in the Streets of Baltimore
THE TROOPS STONED AND FIRED ON
They Return the Fire, Killing Eight Persons and Wounding Several

A few columns to the left, the headlines were

THE INDIAN WAR
Regular and Volunteer Cavalry Find Joseph in Ambush
Two Scouts Killed and Two Wounded
RETREAT OF THE PURSUERS
Joseph Recrosses the Clearwater—Howard Preparing to Attack Him

Joseph was Chief Joseph, one of the leaders of the Nez Percé, who were fighting for much the same reason the Modocs had fought: because they had been lied to, because they wanted to stay in their homeland, because they saw no other course of action open to them but starvation and imprisonment on a reservation. The conflict had begun on June 17, and before it was over the Nez Percé—men, women, children, livestock—had fled 1,300 miles from their home in eastern Oregon to the Canadian border of Montana. The war was directed by telegram from San Francisco, where General Irvin McDowell, the commander of the West, was headquartered, and supplementary troops were sent east on the Central Pacific. Much fuss has been made over the idea of the frontier, as though it were a line advancing from east to west, but the West was settled piecemeal, and Indians fled in many directions to escape the tightening noose of the railroad lines and towns.

The headlines about the Nez Percé War marched side by side with those of the Great Strike that summer, and when President Hayes convened his cabinet to discuss the strike, he had also just received news that twenty ranchers had been killed by Lakotas in the Black Hills. Urban workers and Native Americans are separate subjects on bookshelves and in universities, but it seemed that summer as though they were engaged in the same war, a war against the central institutions that were taking away their power, their freedom, even their ability to feed themselves, to survive. It was as though every kind of population were being subjugated to the might of the industrial age, to its control of resources, to the brutality of regimented jobs and locked-down lives that still didn't provide enough to eat, whether it was railroad workers on twelve-hour shifts or Indians forced to till the inferior land of the reservations. Removing the Indians opened up their land as an exploitable resource; keeping the laborers subjugated supplied the already-industrialized zones with the cheap labor that made such heinous profits possible. Five years earlier Sitting Bull had sat down to smoke a pipe in the middle of a battle. In the summer of 1877 hundreds of thousands were doing something similar, and from Buffalo to the wilder parts of Montana they succeeded in shutting down the industrial complex and defying the military.

There was other news in the *Alta* that day, July 22. A smaller headline read

A PANORAMIC CITY AND STATE

and a glowing account of Muybridge's panorama followed. "The photograph of San Francisco," it began, "suggests to us that, among the many wonderful features of our city, the panoramic character of its topography is not the least deserving of attention, though it had generally been overlooked." Among the other features of the city was the anti-Chinese movement, which burst into action that week as San Francisco's warped version of the Great Strike. San Franciso had changed considerably in the years since the joining of the rails. Completion of the railroad threw thousands out of work, and the new link to the East undermined the superb working conditions the region had enjoyed during its decades of isolation. Speculation in railroads, mines, real estate, and the growth of industry made some wealthy, but there were more and more poor too. The city was growing, but it was growing apart. In its golden age, San Francisco had seemed to have few such gaps and to offer that American dream of universal opportunity. In what, in honor of the huge mines in Nevada, was christened California's silver age, many had woken from that dream to the bitterness of institutionalized inequality, declining wages and opportunities, rising land prices and working hours. Many hated the railroad barons, but hatred for the Chinese served to buffer the railroads and their owners from the direct action taken in Pittsburg and Martinsburg—as did the Central Pacific's quick revocation of the wage cut they too had applied in early July.

The Chinese immigrants who made up about 8 percent of California's population had long been excoriated as undercutters of wages and thieves of jobs that rightly belonged to white men. They themselves were exploited both by the railroads and factories that paid them pitiful salaries and by the Six Companies, the Chinese-controlled conglomerates that shipped in and controlled most of the Chinese labor in the state. In another time white laborers might have regarded the improvement of the Chinese condition as key to their own, but in the 1870s they scapegoated these workers known as coolies, Celestials, John, and, after a poem by Bret Harte, "The Heathen Chinee" (Muybridge made a series of photographs in the 1860s with that title). On July 23, 1877, ten days after Muybridge's panorama was first announced, the day after the *Alta* praised it, about eight thousand workers gathered in the "Sandlot," the vacant lot next to the new city hall. Those at the center of the meeting studiously listened to the talk of solidarity with the eastern strikers. Those on the edge set out to attack the Chinese laundries scattered throughout the city, augmented by a band from an anti-coolie club marching by. (That white workingmen were not competing for laundry jobs is one of the small ironies of their racial fury, and they proved the utility of ghettos by cravenly attacking only outlying Chinese buildings and people. Chinatown could and did fight back.) The conflict turned into a pitched battle with the police on Rincon Hill and many arsons in what was to become a season of arson. Several Chinese died in fires and attacks. As one San Franciscan noted, "As among the twenty-seven thousand houses, more than four fifths were wooden, and three hundred Chinese laundries were scattered throughout all the wards, this threat caused much uneasiness. If an anti-Chinese mob should get control for a few hours, the destruction of San Francisco might be the result."

On July 24, businessman William T. Coleman, who had headed the 1856 Committee of Vigilance, revived it with about six thousand status-quo sympathizers armed with the weapons that gave them the nickname the Pickhandle Brigade, and there were confrontations in the streets. Under the following night's full moon, a huge fire sprang up on the wharves and in the warehouses, and thousands who were out on the streets watched. More than a hundred barrels of whale oil caught fire, and the burning oil ran over the docks, torching piles of lumber. A quarter of a million dollars worth of primordial material from ocean and forest went up in flames. The young rowdies who tried to interfere with the firemen were assaulted by the Pickhandle Brigade. Three died in the incident. Within forty-eight hours, the militia had been called out, and three naval gunboats had been ordered to the city's harbor in readiness for a full-fledged civil or class war.

THE VIEW FROM THE TOP

This was the climate in which Muybridge released his first big panorama and planned his last. Panoramas were expressions of civic pride. They were an attempt to define the city, to make of its complexity a single commanding image. And Muybridge's definition, like those of the photographers who ascended Nob Hill before him, was of the city as a collection of buildings and an arena for light. In the turmoil of 1877 this was a polemical or even a wishful position, because a city is also its residents, and in San Francisco the city as citizens was close to annihilating the city as architecture. The photographic city is silent and still, but the actual city had been alerted by the shriek of the powerhouse whistle blowing the riot signal and the swarms of people roaming the streets. Muybridge was literally standing on the territory of the robber barons as he pivoted his camera in Mark Hopkins's tower, and when the fog of their racial fury lifted, the members of the newly formed Workingmen's Party turned to these millionaires.

That first day after the Sandlot riots, the *San Francisco Examiner* declared that the Great Strike was not, "as the hired advocates of Stanford and Co. would have us believe, a contest against Railroads, for no one is so foolish as to depreciate their value; but it is a contest against the audacious usurpations, the monstrous tyranny, the unparalleled robbery, of the Railway Companies. . . . The tyranny with which we are threatened is greater than that which our forefathers rose against and resisted and overcame after a bloody war of seven years. If the people do not unite and overcome it now, in a very short time the masses of Americans will be reduced to the condition practically of serfs." This was an important point: the riots were not against the technology itself, but the social consequences of its implementation for the benefit of a few. The *Examiner* had special vitriol for California's own railroad corporation, "the chief corruptor of public morals in this State," charging it with "a deliberate systematic conspiracy to defeat the known will of the people. These practices threaten all good government and all popular rights."

San Francisco Appraisers Building under construction, southwest corner of Sansome and Jackson, November 11, 1875 (date according to inscription). On more than one occasion, Muybridge documented buildings being erected over extended periods from a single vantage point, and in their depiction of change these serial images prefigure the motion studies.

The owners of that railroad were busily aggrandizing their holdings, not only with political maneuvering but with the building of the Southern Pacific, which would become one of the most powerful corporate monopolies in American history. By 1877 they had built a line to the Arizona border; eventually they would control all the land and some of the sea transportation from the far West, setting prices so that agriculture retained just enough profit to continue being bled. From the 1870s until the twentieth century, the railroads were widely hated as the first giant American corporations, the first to corrupt and control the government. Nine years after the Great Strike, the Southern Pacific would open the way for the rise of the modern corporation with the Supreme Court case of *Santa Clara County v. Southern Pacific Railroad*. In a historic decision, the court awarded Southern Pacific all the rights and privileges of a "natural person," though

San Francisco Appraisers Building under construction, southwest corner of Sansome and Jackson, early 1877 (date according to inscription). From a series of four or more photographs. Note the very large poster that can be seen advertising a theatrical "tour of the world in 80 days."

corporations lacked human vulnerabilities and possessed aggregate powers only governments could match. Given human rights and privileges as well, they became truly fearsome. California historian Kevin Starr remarks of the Southern Pacific at the turn of the century, "The SP offered the most obvious instance of what was grossly wrong with California: a very few of the super-rich virtually owned the state—its land, its economy, its government—and were running it as a private preserve."

None of this was visible in Muybridge's panoramas. In fact, they seem strangely deserted, though the pictures were taken in the best hours of fine summer days. Again it is slowness that has emptied out the city, slowness and scale. A few waiting horses and carts are visible; a few antlike figures can be found in the distance. Photographs didn't stop time as Sitting Bull attempted to: they did not resist history but seized a piece of it and made it permanent and widely available. It could be argued that this too can be radical. In 1877 Muybridge was making Hopkins's commanding and expensive view available to all time and to all comers for eight dollars (for a rolled panorama) or ten dollars (for one accordion-folded and bound like a book). On August 2 of that year, the newspapers announced that the key to the panorama had been published—a reduced version of the original in which more than two hundred notable sites, including the homes and businesses of many leading citizens, were indicated. Clearly the panorama was being marketed as the patrician view of San Francisco. (It also recalls Jeremy Bentham's Panopticon, a late eighteenth-century proposal for a circular prison in which all prisoners could be watched by a central guard: the railroad magnates, and Muybridge as their guest, occupied the place of the guard.)

Charles Crocker's property had been designed to eliminate one sight, that of the house of funeral director Nicholas Yung, who had refused to sell his small portion of the city block to the railroad magnate. Infuriated by this resistance to his will, Crocker built his famous "spite fence," a forty-foot-tall wall surrounding Yung's small house, both as a way of putting Yung out of sight and of shutting out his air and light. Not easily intimidated, Yung mounted an outsize coffin with a skull and crossbones atop his house, facing Crocker's, though he eventually moved without selling the lot; the spite fence outlived both Yung and Crocker, surviving until the 1906 earthquake and fire razed that section of the city. The spite fence made visible the bullying of the railroad barons, just as their houses made visible the incredible profits they had wrung out of the railroad. Hopkins's house was the most elaborate and the tallest, but Stanford's mansion next door, with its marble, its gardens, its mosaics, was more opulent. Only the spires of the Hopkins house are visible in the panoramas, but Crocker's house across California Street and to the west is clearly visible with its spite fence, and portions of Stanford's house are too, as is his three-story stable farther down California Street.

Finally, that strife left the sandlots and the Chinese laundries to march straight up Nob Hill. On October 29, the demagogue who led the Workingmen's Party, Denis Kearney, stood atop Nob Hill and inveighed, "I will give the Central Pacific just three months to discharge their Chinamen, and if that is not done, Stanford and his crowd will have to take the consequences. I will give Crocker until November 29 to take down the fence around Yung's house, and if he doesn't do it, I will lead the workingmen up there and tear it down, and give Crocker the worst beating with the sticks that a man ever got." Kearney was a master of the empty threat, and a few nights later, he declaimed, "But I tell you, and I want Stanford and the press to understand, that if I give an order to hang Crocker, it will be done." It wasn't. One of Stanford's guests tells of visiting his mansion, which cost an estimated $2 million in those days when a railroad man made less than two dollars a day. Stanford led him on a tour of its many luxurious art-works, including paintings, mosaics, and a monumental Sevres vase. Say-ing it had cost $100,000, he urged his visitor to examine the vase more closely, and the appalled guest reports that it was inscribed, "'De Marie Antoinette au dernier Marquis de Villette.' I had no sooner read this in-scription than a great howl went up in the street nearby. To my look of in-quiry, the Governor answered, 'Oh that's nothing unusual. It is Kearney and his crowd. They've adjourned their meeting at the sandlots so as to give the residents of Nob Hill a taste of their peculiar oratory,' and he treated the matter as a joke."

Muybridge had gone back to work for Stanford, apparently because he had new ideas about how to solve the problem of instantaneous photogra-phy. He didn't share the widespread anti-Chinese sentiment—one of the reporters on the murder trial recounts his jailhouse tale of defending a Chinese man who "one of the 'hardened' was abusing. 'Stop that' said Muybridge. 'None of that here. I will not allow it. No man of any country whose misfortunes bring him here shall be abused in my presence,'" and he threatened to stop the harrassment by force if necessary. As a skilled professional, Muybridge would not have seen the Chinese as competitors, and his dealers Bradley and Rulofson—whom he left shortly before the first panorama was published—employed Chinese workers with whom he must have been familiar. Defending the Chinese was as disinterested an act as cultivating the Big Four was strategic.

Not long before he made the first Hopkins panoramas, he made a deluxe album of the Stanfords' Nob Hill home, in which almost every room seems airless, endless, sepulchral, and obsessively ornamented, the Pompeian Salon as dead as its original, the library with its books sealed up but its chandeliers dangling low, the art gallery with its arctic and Sierra landscapes and its figures in marble. The two or three photographs of each room are nothing more than dutiful. The upper hall has frescoes symbolizing all the continents as though the house were the center of the world, and certainly the house had a commanding view. Only the pictures Muybridge took from the windows seem free of the weightiness of wealth, and from one balcony he took a seven-plate panorama of the view south and east. Clearly the view was what made Nob Hill attractive to the railroad magnates, the lofty perch on which they could both see and be seen, and both Hopkins and Crocker had observation towers, while the Stanfords had their panoramic windows.

The *Bulletin* had reported that the men grading the foundation for Stanford's house used explosives, as they would have in building a railroad grade, and the shower of rocks "created some indignation in the neighborhood," since rocks flew through a window in which two children had been playing a few minutes before. While the house was being built, Stanford told a newspaper, "I shall hope to live to sit up yonder balcony and look down upon . . . cars from the city of Mexico and trains laden with the gold and silver bullion and grain that comes from Sonora and Chihuahua and from Washington Territory and Oregon on the north. . . . I shall look out through the Golden Gate and I shall see fleets of ocean steamers bearing the trade of India, the commerce of Asia, the traffic of the islands of the ocean." Stanford's city was a global capital of commerce, not a community. A deluxe leather-bound copy of the 1877 panorama was given to Stanford, and a lavish version of the huge 1878 panorama was inscribed, "Mrs. Leland Stanford with compliments of the Artist." The photographer had embarked upon his life's great work, the motion studies, and only Stanford had the horses, the grounds, the technicians, the interest, and the wealth to support such an ambitious project.

Picture Muybridge atop the unfinished turret with its lacy iron railings, the precarious highest point in the central city; picture him standing there with his addled brain, his furtive heart, his boundless ambition, his tangled beard, his incomparable eye, looking out over his own history and looking into the question of what a panorama could be. There he stood for most of a day, once in the summer of 1877 and again a year later, seeing his city as almost no one but Mark and Mary Hopkins and a few carpenters had seen it before. Or seeing it as no one had, for he would have been standing behind a tripod, stooping under the dark cloth to gaze at the tiny upside-down theater of the camera's back wall. It must be remembered that Muybridge was a man who had grown used to looking at the world upside

down, grown used to looking at a world in color and imagining it in mono-
tones. He could see Goat Island, which the city had fought so bitterly to
keep out of the hands of the Central Pacific; see Mission Bay, where the
Southern Pacific centered its operations; see the house of Coleman, the
leader of the vigilantes in 1856 and 1877; see Montgomery Street, where
most of his professional life had been spent; see the bold letters announcing Ackerman's store, where Flora had worked before they married, and St.
Mary's Hospital, where she died; see off in the southwest the tall Protestant
Orphan Asylum, where Florado languished; see theaters, synagogues, the
Barbary Coast, the Bohemian Club; see directly below him Chinatown,
which was under virtual siege that year; and see the elaborate dome of the
new city hall next to the sandlots where that siege was organized; see the
laundry on the rooftops that day in 1878 that might have been a Monday
washday; see the ships in the bay and the hills beyond. The young Edward
Muygridge who had come to a boomtown at the end of the world to deal in
books had vanished as profoundly as had that frontier town of thirty thousand souls housed in shacks and shanties amid the dunes. This metropolis
of about two hundred thousand people had the largest hotel in the world,
had monuments and spires, and it spread far in all directions from Muybridge's perch.

Muybridge was at the height of his powers. That summer of 1878 he
made his breakthrough with the sequential-motion studies. There is an
oft-repeated tale that an early 1878 fire had burned down his gallery and
destroyed his Central America and panoramic negatives, prompting him to
rephotograph the latter. It would fit neatly into San Francisco's historic up-
heaval if Muybridge's work had been incinerated in the volatile city he was
photographing, but a letter he wrote in 1879 makes it clear he still had the
Central American negatives, and he used the panorama key published in
1877 to accompany some of his 1878 panoramas. Too, he had in 1877 announced a fourteen-panel twenty-foot panorama that almost certainly did
not yet exist; it was more likely a general description of the monumental
panorama he planned than a work that burned without leaving a trace.
The earlier panoramas had likely been studies for this feat, and it was far
more than a replacement for them. And no primary source for the fire has
turned up.

The national turmoil continued into 1878. By February the headlines
were full of new sources of unrest. Popular opinion had turned against the

great landholders who had seized control of much of California and of the hydraulic gold mines, whose discharge was silting up the rivers and flooding the riverside towns and farmland (the successful 1884 lawsuit against the hydraulic mines would be one of the first restraints of industry in the public interest, a landmark in environmental legislation). Nineteen months after the Lakota victory and the extermination of Custer's troops at Little Big Horn, a war was anticipated with the Hunkpapa Lakota led by Sitting Bull. Kearney was still staging oratorical attacks on Stanford and the Chinese. Between the Indian wars, the Klan atrocities in the post-Reconstruction South, and the anti-Chinese violence up and down the Pacific Coast, the United States was as fraught with racial conflict as it was with class war in the explosive year between the two panoramas. With the hungry clamoring outside Nob Hill's mansions, Nez Percé riding across Montana, hydraulic mines washing away the mountains, and barrels of whale oil afire on the docks, it was a garish, gorgeous, violent, unjust time, though only the gorgeousness makes it into the panoramas.

Muybridge was coming more and more into the Stanfords' orbit, and his mammoth-plate 1878 panorama is something of a farewell both to landscape photography and to the city it depicted. There is an old crafts tradition in which a journeyman makes a superlative work to signal the end of his apprenticeship and the beginning of his mastery; this panorama, which signaled the end of Muybridge's work in the field and the real beginning of his work in the studio, may have something of that significance. It was to be an incomparable, an extraordinary, a unique panorama. In a stroke of genius, he ignored the instinct of nearly every panoramic photographer before him. A panorama is nothing if not a colossally horizontal picture, and panoramic photographers assembled their image out of horizontal photographs. But Muybridge turned his mammoth-plate camera—perhaps the same camera with which he had photographed Yosemite six years before—on its side and made vertical pictures. He had done his calculations brilliantly this time, and thirteen of the vertical photographs measuring sixteen inches across (when cropped) perfectly circumambulated the horizon of San Francisco. The vertical format gave the panorama a grandeur, an airiness, that no panorama before had possessed; it made the finished work huge; and it allowed him to show everything from the nearest buildings to the hills far away.

It was twenty-four inches high and seventeen feet, four inches long, far too long to see all at once. Only the wealthy would have had a table or even a room in which it could be laid out flat, and to see it whole would be to lose all detail. Like a book, it could be viewed page by page; like a long Chinese scroll, it could not be seen in all its detail at once. It was on a scale to be traveled through in time, not taken in at a glance, and in this it resembles the small stereo panoramas and prefigures cinema. Probably only the wealthy saw it then, for this panorama was never publicized and marketed as the previous one had been. Of the nine known copies, only one is known to have been sold, and it was sold many years later; five are known to have been given away, one to Mrs. Hopkins (whose husband had died in March 1878), one to Mrs. Stanford. The panorama was made when Muybridge had already largely given up making photographs for the marketplace to devote himself to the motion studies, and he was already leaving San Francisco for a sojourn at the Stanfords' Palo Alto rancho and for the nomadic years that followed.

Another way to look at the panoramas is as a series of pictures akin to the motion studies' multiple images. Each picture is of both a different time and place, and the series of pictures is assembled into a whole that tells a story. In the motion studies, the story is clear: a horse ran, a man jumped. In the panoramas it is implicit: an unseen man followed the light of midsummer around a city over the course of the day. The motion studies were sequences of photographs showing the progression of a gesture or an act across a gridded space (they were taken with multiple cameras so that each image represented a different camera meeting its subject in a different location—though the cameras were often little more than a foot apart), and the panorama strung together thirteen photographs to show the progression of another movement, that of the sun across the city, a fitting motion study for the man who had begun his artistic career under the name Helios.

In the panorama of 1877, Muybridge had used alternate plates of California Street east. In the panorama of 1878, he replaced the view just to the north, plate 7, with a plate made later in the day, creating a clash of shadows in what is otherwise one of the most seamless photographic panoramas of its era. It may be that the first version, the one taken in sequence so that the light and shadows would match up, was damaged or flawed. But the fact that in 1877 he had substituted a plate taken later in the day when it wasn't necessary suggests there may be a more complex, unfathomable story behind the substitution. Perhaps like quilt makers and Navajo weavers who traditionally subvert the flawnessness of their patterning with one reversed or divergent detail, he wanted to take one step back from perfection. No one will ever know. It means that the panorama is not what it appears. To the casual eye, the panorama seems to be what Hollis Frampton described, "an impossible simultaneity." To the careful observer, this great panorama is a discontinuity that appears to be a continuity, many hours of the day masquerading as a single supreme moment, like a film in which segments shot at various times are edited into a believable narrative. The most careful observer of the panorama in modern times, the photographer Mark Klett, who in 1990 made his own panorama of a very different San Francisco from the same location, says, "If he had to remake a photo due to this technical limitation, or even if he had to remake a broken or scratched plate 7, I like the result visually and conceptually. It blows holes in the notion of a seamless and omnipotent view and opens the door on space and time."

STOPPING TIME

Speed ■ *Pleasure and Joy* ■ *Revolutionizing Photography* ■ *Time Does Not Stand Still* ■ *After Stanford*

■ *Overleaf: Photograph F: The Experimental Track at Palo Alto,* from the album *The Attitudes of Animals in Motion,* 1881, showing, on left, the whitewashed wall and, on right, the studio from which Muybridge photographed the equestrian motion studies.

SPEED

Picture a racetrack in 1877 with a racehorse running its oval circuit of brown earth. For the horse the race is from nothing but perhaps a touch of the whip to nothing but the end of the exercise. For the driver, the trainer, the owner, the horse is attempting to minimize the amount of time it takes to travel from one place to another, to defeat the limits that nature places on the movement of bodies, to dissolve the weight of matter and the binding force of gravity, to fly, to become instantaneous, to annihilate time and space. The horse is training. That is, it is alone on the track, racing the clock rather than other horses. Muybridge will seize hold of that running, stop it on film, take it apart and put it back together like a Chinese puzzle. It takes the speed of a technological breakthrough to capture the speed of the horse so that like a machine it can be understood, and this speed is not a change in degree but a change in kind, a speedup that takes humanity across the threshold into a new world of knowledge and representation. Past a certain point everything, anything, disappears into the visible imperceptibility we call a blur, a veil of speed covering up the erotics of motion. Muybridge would bring the blurred back into sharp focus, and it would turn out that stripping speed of its veils had more far-reaching possibilities than anyone had imagined.

Speed is a basic survival skill for both predator and prey. But races have neither predators nor prey, only competitors. The race simulates the conditions of survival and awards those found most fit not with survival itself but with glory and money. In the nineteenth century a confusion of language arose between the activity and the category of the race, for Europeans and European Americans perceived progress as a race that they, the white race, were winning. The fundamental metaphor of this culture is one of travel, movement, progress, exploration, discovery, of going somewhere in search of something new, a metaphor that links Columbus in his boats and Fremont on his trails with the Faradays, the Edisons, the Bells, in their laboratories. Muybridge's restlessness seems partly personal, an unhappiness or dissatisfaction that keeps him from standing still, but partly cultural, a curiosity and ambition that keeps him moving onward, both geographically and technically. For a culture that believed it was exactly where it ought to be and had everything it needed, the race could never be so resonant, and this may have been one of the huge differences between the two sides in the Indian wars.

Speed hovered below the horizon of consciousness and culture as an absolute virtue questioned by only a few poets and theologians. Endurance was admired too, and the 1870s were full of pedestrian races of up to 500 miles, in which for days on end the competitors could not break into a run and could only stop for brief intervals. The point of the races was obscure, for they were not glorious like a horse straining to do his utmost, though there were ladies' races that provided, as contemporary accounts make clear, at least the reporters with voyeuristic pleasures. These races on sawdust tracks were numbingly repetitious, and they must have in some faint way echoed the repetitious labor in the factories where men, women, and children performed ever-more-reductive tasks as servants of the machines, working twelve or more hour days, six days a week, every week of the year, until the body failed as those of the pedestrian racers sometimes did when they literally dropped from the competition.

In the Industrial Revolution speed becomes efficiency: time is money, and the less time used in manufacturing or shipping, the more money amassed—the annihilation of time and space Marx spoke of. The competitors strive to smooth the world for their own advantage and to outrace each other, and the clock is made out of money, the ticking of dollars into the till. The Union Pacific and the Central Pacific raced each other to build the most track across the great American outback because they were paid by the mile. Eventually immobilized by poor health, the lumbering Stanford built his fortune on speed, on the incredible global speedup that the transcontinental railroad provided, even the speed with which it was built, epitomozed by that famous competition in which the CP workers laid ten miles of rail in a day. The race was a metaphor for industrialism too, but nobody said what the goal or the prize was, except riches for the owners. The theory of machinery is that it saves time, but Stanford himself noted of such machinery that "if you could limit man's wants it might be called 'labor saving,' but as there are no limits to his wants, the machinery really increases the power of production." That is, the industrialized world wants more goods, not more time, and so the machinery doesn't increase freedom and leisure, it increases production and consumption.

In the summer of 1876 Stanford had bought the first portion of his Palo Alto estate from George Gordon, the developer of San Francisco's South Park, and in subsequent years he bought more and more surrounding land until he held 8,000 acres of what is now Stanford University. Most millionaires spend their profits on something that disguises, gilds, or contradicts their source: paintings that speak of the leisure, education, and joy so far from the harsh labor that bought them, tranquil estates built on armaments profits. Sometimes anxiety about the source of the fortune is revealed in its expenditure, as with Sarah Winchester's fearful house. But Stanford's most visible expenditure, even beyond his $2 million pile on Nob Hill or his 55,000-acre Vina Ranch in north-central California, was his racing stable, and these horses enacted as pleasure and recreation what the railroad enacted as business: speed. They set nineteen world records and even eventually became profitable. The railroad business was full of bodily destruction—Chinese men killed in dynamiting, railroad workers missing fingers and limbs from operating dangerous machinery, the occasional boiler explosion that killed stokers and engineers, the squatter-farmers shot down in Mussel Slough by agents of the Southern Pacific. The Palo Alto ranch was a peaceable kingdom celebrating the perfectibility of the equestrian body. The estate staff, which eventually numbered a hundred and fifty (one-third Chinese), was forbidden even to speak harshly to the horses, which eventually numbered near eight hundred. A man was fired for striking one. "Few of Stanford's charges knew the meaning of fear," a biographer writes: tenderness in sight, brutality over the horizon, and speed everywhere.

To race the clock is to race time itself in the present and the historical record of the past, to attempt to break the record as though it were a real thing like the ribbon broken at the finish line of a race. It's to race against an idea. To encourage that possibility, the terrain over which the horses run is reduced as far as possible to a smooth, even surface. Just as railroad lines smooth out the landscape to make a straight track—one that neither ascends nor descends too steeply nor turns too sharply—so the racetrack

Horses, Running, Sallie G., plate 43 from *The Attitudes of Animals in Motion,* 1881.

allows the horse optimum conditions, only the horse is going nowhere, going in circles. It is as though the ideas of time and competition become more and more real, the actualities of place and substance less and less so. Muybridge, a man who had spent his life photographing somewhere, whether it was a cliff face or a war zone or a pleasure garden, was going to give the rest of his life over to nowhere, to the neutralized places in which he could match the machine speed of photography to the cadences of bodily movement. Time in his photographs had been expansive too—the time of history, of geology, of a passing day—but he was to shift his focus to events that unfolded in a second or two. To represent movements in real time, machinery had to move faster than the human eye, both in capturing fragments of motion and in reassembling them into a continuity. This is what cinema would be made out of, the speed of the projector matched to the speed of the camera. It took extraordinary speed to reproduce, say, the plume of cigarette smoke slowly uncoiling above a heroine's face, the tail of a hero's coat swinging as he turned around. But it didn't begin as heroines, as fictions, as cinema. It began as photographs of horses in motion.

A horse in 1877 was still state-of-the-art power for war, agriculture, and transportation, a biological technology that had been much improved with careful breeding and such inventions as stirrups, bits, and harness. None yet foresaw that within half a century the horse's practical uses would be largely superseded in the industrialized world. Relying on horses for everyday transportation meant that human beings were still in collaboration with the organic world, a world of unpredictability and mystery. Muybridge and Stanford were approaching the horse in an ambivalent way, seeking to study it to make it more like a machine. A machine must first be imagined and understood before it can be set to work, while nature can be utilized for millennia without giving away its secrets. It was a contrary impulse akin to the one that reveres wilderness while planning to map and develop it. And understanding the gaits of a horse in a mechanical way enhanced the possibility of tinkering with it, through breeding, training, and other forms of management. For Stanford, the experiment would allow him to further shift the essence of the horse from the mysteries of nature to the manageable mechanics of industrialism.

PLEASURE AND JOY

It isn't clear whether this second time around Stanford approached Muybridge or Muybridge approached Stanford, though the latter seems more likely. The photographer had, he said, engaged in some "very rapid work in the southern country" of Central America that made him eager to resume pursuit of what he had attempted with limited success earlier in the decade: images of Occident in motion. Another time he said he had "had occasion to make a series of experiments in photographing scenes offshore from the deck of a rolling vessel. These experiments resulted in the construction of an apparatus and the preparation of chemicals so as to permit the photographing in outline of a rapidly moving body." Thus far, little had changed; he was attempting to take a single image, and his main breakthrough was apparently in the area of chemistry—not in a new chemical formula but a new precision, concentration, or other shift in the existing formulas ("iron was employed in their development," one source reported). This time around, the shutter was triggered when the horse broke a thread across the racetrack. At first, Muybridge apparently worked at the Sacramento Union Racetrack; evidently Stanford had not finished moving his racehorse operation to the ranch he called Palo Alto, Spanish for "tall tree," after some redwoods there. During the interim, Occident may have been housed in the luxurious California Street stable that shows up so prominently in the Nob Hill panoramas. It is known that Stanford liked to drive his own team at top speeds in San Francisco's Golden Gate Park, where he would sometimes race Charles Crocker, and one source suggests that the first of the new round of motion studies was made just north of the park at the Bay District Track, in which Stanford held stock.

Half a century afterward, a San Franciscan named Sherman Blake who had become a successful businessman wrote to a Muybridge scholar, "I take pleasure in informing you that I was the boy employed by the late Geo. D. Morse, photographer, 417 Montgomery Str., who carried a part of the equipment and assisted Mr. Muybridge in photographing Governor Stanford's horses at the old Bay District Track, and not at Palo Alto. There were no dry plates or films, as is now used, in Mr. Muybridge's time. The process being wet, sensitized plates, which were first dipped in collodion, and then in the nitrate of silver bath, and placed in plate holders, and used as quickly as was possible in the matter of exposure. It was necessary to improvise a temporary dark room out at the Bay District Track, and we took along with us in an express wagon, a heavy orange and red cloth tent, and an improvised ruby light containing a lit candle. I carried six buckets of water (the old fashioned wooden buckets) into the dark room, and when the horses sprang the instantaneous shutter, by means of the thread across the track, Mr. Muybridge immediately took the plate holder from the camera, went into the dark room, and developed same. Being a boy, between 16 and 17 years old (I am now 65 years), I distinctly recall the joy and pleasure when Mr. Muybridge called from the dark room, 'I've got the pictures of the horses jumping from the ground.'" It is the most exuberant moment on record in Muybridge's life, and it may be the pivotal one, the moment in which he finally unlocked the door of instantaneous photography and all it would lead to.

The result of the 1877 experiments was apparently a single image that was shown around San Francisco at the beginning of August 1877, in the midst of the anti-Chinese riots and shortly after the release of the first panorama. The *Alta* reported on August 3, "Mr. Muybridge sends us a copy of an instantaneous photograph of 'Occident,' taken when he was trotting at a speed of 35 feet per second, or a mile in 2 minutes and 27 seconds. The negative was exposed to the light less than one-thousandth part of a second, so brief a time that the horse did not move a quarter of an inch. The photographer had made many experiments to secure the highest sensitiveness and the briefest possible exposure, and the result was a novelty in photographic art, and a delineation of speed which the eye cannot catch. At 2:27 the spokes of a sulky are invisible to the eye, as they spin around so fast that, taken separately, they are not distinguishable. The photograph shows each plainly, without blur. The negative was retouched before the photograph was printed; but we are assured that the outlines are unchanged." As in 1873, the photograph was widely attacked as a fraud, both because so many were claiming to have achieved instantaneous photography at the time and because there was something decidely unphotographic about the appearance of the image. Muybridge explained in his letter to the newspaper, "This picture has been retouched, as is customary at this time with all first-class photographic work." In fact, it was more than retouched. It was a photograph of a painting of the photograph, as far as anyone has been able to determine, and the original painting is in the Stanford Museum (only the face of the driver was an actual photograph patched in). It seems that Muybridge had again managed an instantaneous photograph, and again it wasn't much to look at, so its information was translated into another medium. There were a number of attacks, but Stanford and Muybridge knew they were onto something, and the following year they expanded the operation.

The card on which the photograph of Occident was mounted announced that it was an "automatic electro-photograph." If Sherman Blake and the rest of the evidence can be believed, it wasn't quite so automatic and electric yet. There were three great breakthroughs in Muybridge's motion studies. The first was the achievement of a photographic process fast enough to capture bodies in motion. The second was the creation of successive images that, mounted together, reconstituted a whole cycle of motion rather than isolating a single moment. And the third was their reanimation as a moving picture. In 1877 he had only achieved the first, which required breakthroughs in photochemistry and the development of a very fast shutter—Muybridge may have overestimated the speed of his exposures, but they were dozens, even hundreds, of times faster than what anybody else was doing. Many were achieving instantaneous photographs, but in the era of wet-plate photography only he did it methodically, reliably, repeatably. The second and third breakthroughs were to come in 1878 and 1879.

He understood that the next stage would be to make rapid sequences of photographs of motion. Muybridge ordered a dozen superb lenses from the English firm of Dallmeyer, and Stanford directed the Central Pacific Railroad's chief engineer, S. S. Montague, to provide whatever assistance Muybridge required. What he required was a better way to trigger his shutters. His "guillotine" shutters each consisted of two wooden bars held in place by what he decorously called a spring but appears to be a powerful rubber band. He had tried taking a pin out of these shutters with limited success, and he had already set up the shutters triggered by a thread across the track the horse broke (if it was running) or wires the sulky wheels contacted (if it was trotting)—but he needed them to be faster yet, and smoother. Early that August of 1877, Muybridge visited Montague at the railroad's headquarters in San Francisco, and Montague sent him across the bay to the Oakland workshops. There superintendent of bridges and buildings Arthur Brown gave an order to make up some shutters according to Muybridge's specifications and set a young draftsman with a knack for invention named John D. Isaacs to work on a device to operate them. Brown went off to take care of some railroad business on the Colorado River, and Isaacs put his sketches in his pocket and went home for the weekend.

He brought them out that Sunday to discuss with a friend, recalling later, "I discussed this business with him, and we came to the conclusion that no mechanical contrivance of sufficient delicacy and rapidity to accomplish the purpose could be devised. We did not believe it could be done. And we had just about concluded our conversation on the subject and I think Mr. Palmer was about to change the subject when I said 'I have got it sir; it is electricity,' and the details of the whole thing just flashed into my mind in an instant, I thought of putting a magnet on the outside of the apparatus to pull out a catch, connecting that magnet with a battery on one side and with a wire which should reach over the track with the other; also connecting the battery with another wire which should run over the track and lie parallel with the first wire." *Electricity* was a magical word then, one that evoked speed, modernity, vital force, mystery, and power. It was used primarily for telegraphy and for the electrical time service that kept multiple clocks in multiple locations telling the same time.

One of the spectacles at the 1876 Philadelphia Centennial Exposition had been such an electrically linked collection of clocks, and a few years later *Scientific American* enthused over New York City's electric time service. That city, like many others, had a time ball that dropped at noon, triggered by a system from the National Observatory in the nation's capital. But, *Scientific American* asserted, "to reap the full benefit of the time ball, a great number of people must watch for its fall; that takes time, and time is money." Thus the electrical time service supplanted it and kept time "within a few hundredths of a second. The reader must not be incredulous; it is possible to measure, nay more, to record, the hundredth part of a second." Electricity, lightning harnessed, was a resonant word at the time, linked to simultaneity and to the accurate measure of tiny intervals of time. The same article noted that "where once men were satisfied to know the hour, they had recently begun to specify the time down to the nearest second." A new awareness of minute increments of time had arisen, and it was in this context that Muybridge began to make exposures of a thousandth of a second.

The electrical triggers helped. According to Muybridge scholar Phillip Prodger, their main merit was that they combined strength and smoothness; they did not jar the instrument in the act of releasing the shutter. The electrical current caused a magnet to move the catch that held the shutter, and the speed of electricity made the elapsed time between the wire contact and the shutter moving almost nothing. The California newspapers later linked this use of electricity to the moment in 1869 when Stanford hammered the last electrically wired spike to generate a simultaneous experience across the nation. It was the instantaneousness of the moment, the electrical transcendence of human limits, that seemed to link the two events, that and their expense. Stanford's costs for salaries, equipment, and supplies at the end of the two years of motion studies at Palo Alto were estimated at about $20,000.

Two carpenters constructed the electrical device that triggered Muybridge's shutter, and one of them, Charles Knowles, recalled afterward how Muybridge came to the shop to "see how we were getting along." A conversation arose, and Knowles said, "'It was a very happy thought of Isaacs in suggesting electricity for working this apparatus for getting instantaneous pictures by having a series of shutters or slides to work up and down as the horse passes in front.'

"And he remarked: 'Yes, it was a very bright thought.' And he said, 'Moreover it is going to revolutionize photography.'"

Various Animals, Deer, Running, plate 86 from *The Attitudes of Animals in Motion,* 1881.

Here Knowles may have shifted the emphasis from Muybridge's several inventions to Isaacs's single invention, for it was the combination of the triggers, the shutters, the photochemistry, and their orchestration with the horses on the whitened track that made the instantaneous photographs of 1878 possible. Muybridge was to make photographs with both mechanically and electrically operated shutters. He also used another invention, and it is not clear whether Stanford's engineers helped (though if they had, they surely would have mentioned it). It was a revolving cylinder reminiscent of those in of music boxes: "For recording the successive attitudes of animals not under control, an apparatus is used, comprising a cylinder, around which are spirally arranged a number of pins; upon the cylinder being set in motion . . . these pins are consecutively brought into contact with a corresponding number of metal springs; a succession of electrical currents is thereby created," which again triggered the shutter releases. It was used for animals "not under direct control"—for virtually everything except horses. The electrical devices only worked with movements that could trigger them at regular intervals. The cylinder was autonomous, but it was hard to calibrate to the movements of horses, and this is why the electrical triggers were valuable.

Though he used the railroad's resources, Muybridge was himself an inventor, as the skyshade had shown long ago, and in the summer of 1878 he took out patents on an "Improvement in the Method and Apparatus for Photographing Objects in Motion" (and in the early 1880s took out two other patents related to motion-studies inventions). He also invented a strange pneumatic clockwork apparatus himself, in which a series of pumps attached to the master clock control the motion of slave clocks, a device performing the same function as the electrical time delivery systems allowing clocks to be synchronized. After playing with time in so many ways, Muybridge had arrived at the central icon and device for the control of time and the metaphor for a mechanical universe.

Knowles recalled the rest of the conversation with the photographer-inventor: "I said: 'Can you take other objects aside from horses? Could you take a steamboat moving or a vessel sailing?'

"'Yes, take anything even of a flag flying—'

"I said: 'The trouble heretofore has been for instance if a person moves it mars the picture.'

"And he said, 'Yes but this won't do it. I know it is going to be successful in everything that moves. It is going to make a thorough revolutionizing in photography.'"

REVOLUTIONIZING PHOTOGRAPHY

"We began our experiments the next May," wrote Muybridge, and in June they released the results. He had often worked with assistants, but with the motion studies he had grooms and trainers handling the horses and up to eight men helping him. The motion studies already resembled film in that they were a collaborative project far more than almost any previous photography. Stanford functioned as the producer who put up the money and oversaw the project; Muybridge, as the director who made the key technical and aesthetic decisions; the aides for both horses and instruments, as gaffers and grips. The horses, riders, other animals and, by 1879, gymnasts were the actors before the cameras. And as with a film, there were arguments over credit—but that came afterward.

It's easy to see why the magnificent mammoth-plate panorama was never publicized or released commercially. Muybridge had once again overshadowed one achievement with another. During the winter between the 1877 large-plate panorama and single-image motion study and the grander panorama and sequential motion studies of 1878, he seems to have done little else but propose using photography to copy thousands of documents for the city of San Jose. His bid to photograph all the records one-sixth size, a sort of precursor of microfilm, was rejected only because he wanted the payment up front, whereas a hand copyist could be paid slowly over the years it took to do the work. That San Jose was to become the capital of Silicon Valley, whose central achievement includes compacting and mechanizing information, is a sidelong irony. And that Muybridge was again rethinking the capacities and functions of photography is indicative.

A laboratory for motion arose at Stanford's stables. Alongside the private racetrack a white wall was built with the distance marked off with lines and numbers at intervals of twenty-one inches. The set—for it was a stage set—was as blank as a sheet of paper; with its numbers, the wall looked like a colossal ruler; and everything in front of it looked toylike. The movement of figures in motion could be measured by it, and to do the measuring a row of cameras—at first twelve, later twenty-four—were set up along a ledge on the white trackside shed that served as Muybridge's studio. Thus each camera faced its subject directly and was triggered by the passing of its subject. Though the numbers make it clear that the horses are in motion, they always appear at the center of the frame. Visible at the edge of some of the photographs is the Palo Alto estate, a classic coastal California landscape of grasslands studded with handsome spreading oaks in which the paddocks and stables of the rancho are set. Leland Stanford Jr.'s pony was kept there, and Muybridge made a motion study of the boy riding while an attendant trailed him. The boy took up photography seriously enough to have his own mounts made, like a professional photographer's, and as illustration for the cover of an album of these photographs, he drew himself hunched under the darkcloth of a camera and tripod. He must have been impressed by the man whose work enthralled his father. Muybridge had moved to Palo Alto at some point, as he became more and more absorbed in the motion studies experiments. After more than twenty years as an independent man, he had been drawn into Stanford's orbit, though not quite as an employee.

One who was an employee, Stanford's young secretary Frank Shay, recalled, "He was living at the Palo Alto Ranch. He had a room outside of the McLane Boardinghouse, next door to it . . . . And all of his expenses there and also in town when he came to town were paid by Governor Stanford. . . . Governor Stanford was in the habit of going to the the ranch when he was in the state, Friday afternoon and staying there until Monday morning and sometimes Tuesday morning. And during that time he took great personal interest in the matter, and was at Mr. Muybridge's shed watching the photographs and directing the motions of the men, naming the horses he desired to be taken. . . . Mr. Muybridge used to call at his house down here after dark, and they would sit together sometimes for several hours. . . . The agreement was that the compensation should be such as the Governor might see fit to make it but Mr. Muybridge's chief compensation was to come from, I might call it, fame that he expected from this work. He said that he would rather have the fame that was to come from the taking of those photographs than any money that might be given."

The fame soon arrived. With the new technologies, Muybridge did what photographers had aspired to do for decades, and did it reliably and repeatedly. He captured motion photographically. The local newspapers filled up with stories, especially after Muybridge staged a demonstration for a group of reporters who came down to Palo Alto on the morning train on June 15. The show began with Abe Edgington, another champion trotter, who came by prematurely the first time; but the second time, the wheels of the sulky (a two-wheeled racing cart) made a sound "like that made by the wings of a woodcock, as the wheel touches the other wires, and in a trifle over a half a second the twelve pictures are registered." The small glass negatives were developed on the spot, and the reporter went on to describe the results coming out of the darkroom, "There is a feeling of awe in the mind of the beholder, as he looks at the glass plate which is held before the yellow curtain, and he sees the miniature of the flying horse so perfect that it startles him. Reduced in size until it would do for the scarf-pin of a lady, and yet in the weird opal-tinted light it is as distinct as if cut on a gem. The eye runs rapidly over the series, and there are positions which could never be explained by any hypothesis, but which cannot be questioned by those who have witnessed the operation."

The image survives as one of the six cards of Stanford's horses in motion that Morse's Gallery published soon afterward (and sold for $2.50 apiece or all six for $15, high prices for the times). It shows twelve images of the horse with the big-wheeled sulky close behind, and each image

Detail: *Abe Edgington*, one of six cards of *The Horse in Motion*, 1878, showing the horse trotting with all four feet in the air.

looks so similar that only the numbers above its head and the position of its legs tell that they are a sequence, not a repetition. They are small and nearly silhouettes, but they achieve their purposes. The other five cards showed Edgington trotting more slowly; walking; Mahomet cantering; Sallie Gardner galloping; and Occident trotting. For contemporary viewers, the positions of the horses' legs at a trot, canter, and gallop were startlingly, shockingly, and in some cases unbelievably unlike their expectations. Both San Francisco's *Illustrated Wasp* and Britain's *Punch* published parodies in which the horse's legs paddle wildly in impossibly entertaining positions. Running horses had almost always been represented in the "flying gallop," with both fore and hind legs stretched symmetrically wide like those of a leaping horse or a child's rocking horse. Trotters had moved so mysteriously that, before Muybridge, no one was certain whether they ever had all four feet off the ground at once. Even details of the walk had defied the observation of the most dedicated artists. The reverse of each card gave intricate details of the gait.

For those with equestrian interests, the motion studies were gripping, as they were for artists and scientists. The Victorian equivalent of a media blitz ensued, no doubt encouraged by Muybridge and Morse. Muybridge was becoming an international celebrity and a showman. In July he began giving magic-lantern lectures, rounding out his series of images of horses in motion with images of Central America and with, by the time he took his show to Sacramento, views "illustrating the geology of the Sierras, the latter of which will be explained by Mr. J. M. Hutchings," the former Yosemite promoter. The images of horses were projected near life size, and the shows were enormously successful. Muybridge had joined the ranks of scientists, philosophers, suffragists, soldiers, and spiritualists on the lecture circuit that was so central a part of nineteenth-century American amusement and education in those days when the two were so entwined. By late summer, debates and discussions were going on in the photographic publications, and a note had appeared in *Scientific American*—which that October put engravings based on the motion studies on the cover and devoted an article to them, as did France's scientific journal *La Nature* in December. Though the series convinced many who doubted the veracity of the single image of 1877, there were still detractors. That summer of 1878, Rulofson wrote in to the *Philadelphia Photographer* to denounce the motion studies as "bosh." The two men must have had a falling-out, though whether it had anything to do with Muybridge's move from Bradley and Rulofson's gallery to Morse's is unknown. Bradley had gone bankrupt in 1877, and the gallery had fallen on hard times after so many years of regional preeminence. But most of the attention to the motion studies was wildly enthusiastic.

Each of the six initial motion studies was arranged in a grid. The photographs could literally be read: the action unfolded from left to right and top to bottom, so the twelve images of Abe Edgington trotting were like twelve words in a sentence. They were the bare essence of a narrative, of a story: over time, something changed, something happened. The first sound recorded was Edison's voice reciting "Mary Had a Little Lamb," and the first voice transmitted by wire was Bell's request for his assistant to come over. The content was most often trivial, but the devices promised far more, and the motion studies augured much even for those indifferent to the gaits of racehorses. Photography had always shown approximately what the human eye could see; its use lay in its ability to hold onto that sight. With Muybridge's breakthrough, it became something that could see more than the eye and thereby extend vision into a new realm. Even the individual images provided utterly new information. The sequences did more.

Muybridge had long been photographing sequences, though they had earlier taken the form of panoramas and of series—stereoscope and large-plate images that were physically independent though meant to be seen together. As photohistorian Martha Sandweiss pointed out long ago, nineteenth-century western photographers had been telling stories all along, and their images were for the most part made to be seen in series rather than as single-image masterpieces or what the twentieth-century photographer Henri Cartier-Bresson would call "decisive moments." Muybridge had reduced the narrative to its most basic element: the unfolding of motions in space and time. Most of his sequences depicted the events of a few seconds or less, and he boasted that the individual exposures were as brief as one two-thousandth of a second. By imposing stillness on its subjects, photography had represented the world as a world of objects. But now, in Muybridge's work, it was a world of processes again, for one picture showed a horse, but six pictures showed an act, a motion, an event. The subject of the pictures was not the images per se but the change from one to another, the change that represented time and motion more vividly, more urgently, than the slow motion of parades passing and buildings rising. It was a fundamental change in the nature of photography and of what could be represented.

When photography itself was invented, Edgar Allan Poe declared, "All experience, in matters of philosophical discovery, teaches us that, in such discovery, it is the unforeseen upon which we must calculate most largely." In hindsight, these horse photographs are called the genesis of cinema, but in 1878 it looked like a breakthrough for photography and for the study of rapid motion, and the latter seemed of most significance for painters, physiologists, and equestrians. Though cinema would in the end devote itself primarily to entertaining fictions, the intermediate medium seemed at the time like a shift toward science. As a sideline, Muybridge had often produced work whose function was documentary—photographs of architectural plans, works of art, documents—but his central work had always been pictorial representation of place. Though even his landscapes had conveyed essential information, they had always corresponded to conventional aesthetics. They had been cousins of painting, conveyers of pictorial pleasure. The motion studies were not made for a visual pleasure akin to painting but for the extraction of information, though aesthetic considerations were never absent, and their grids of motions now look strangely beautiful.

Muybridge had given up place without motion for motion without place, and mountain ranges had been replaced by a gridded white wall, a grid within the grid, the one behind the figures in motion (which in the Palo Alto work was mostly a series of vertical lines on pale ground but would in the Philadelphia work of the mid-1880s become a regular grid of white lines on dark ground). The grid was everywhere in nineteenth-century America. Thomas Jefferson's great land survey of 1785 had imposed an imaginary grid spreading west from the Appalachians, and nearly all the towns and farms of the west were regulated by this grid, all the way to San Francisco, where lines traveled straight over even the steepest hills. The grid had been the mental and governmental logic that allowed Americans to proceed into the terra incognita of the West, and the alternating sections given to the transcontinental railroad make some of that terrain look like a checkerboard on maps. The grid meant rationality in its regularity and democracy in its equal apportionment of space. It was also a resonant emblem of science in the nineteenth century, of a science that like settlement was trying to manage the wild abundance of the natural world. Specimen collections, the pigeonholes of a desk, charts, the graphs of account books, and cartographers' surveys all reproduced this pattern.

Charles Willson Peale painted himself in 1822 surrounded by two walls of shelves divided into the perfect squares that held his natural history collections. Muybridge made each photograph a metaphorical museum case holding a single phase of motion; he had collected motions themselves as specimens, and in so doing had performed the alchemical feat of transforming energy into matter, motions into still pictures. Those who paid the fifteen dollars for the six cards could hold in their hand the canter, the gallop, the walk, could hold a handful of time, live as snakes, caged in the grid. The grid was also a familiar artist's device to enlarge or transfer drawings: the grid on paper mapped a figure much as it mapped a mountain range—a famous engraving by Albrecht Dürer shows a man drawing a supine woman through a gridded screen. Each of the frames of the earliest motion study sequences has rounded corners and floats on a black background, but the later ones were perfect rectangles with thinner divisions between them, making a more perfect grid. The grid gave the works the aesthetic of science—dispassionate, orderly, coherent. And science responded.

TIME DOES NOT STAND STILL

The December 28, 1878, issue of *La Nature* published a letter from the eminent Parisian physiologist Etienne-Jules Marey asking, "I am impressed with Mr. Muybridge's photographs published in the issue before last of *La Nature*. Could you put me in touch with the author? I would like his assistance in the solution of certain problems of physiology too difficult to resolve by other methods." Marey was born the same spring of 1830 and was fated to die the same year as Muybridge, but he had been on a steady and well-supported path while Muybridge wandered in the wilderness of a new medium and a new country. But both men were innovators. Since graduating from medical school, Marey had dedicated himself to studying the movements of the body, not as a doctor might have, but as an engineer or physicist. He began with the circulation of the blood and quickly distinguished himself by the invention of sophisticated instruments to chart these hitherto imperceptible processes. By the 1870s he had turned his attention to external motion. His book *La Machine animale* had been published in 1873 in French and appeared in an English translation the following year (Stanford eagerly read it). He had, with elaborate mechanical devices attached directly to the bodies of horses, men, and birds, derived more accurate information than anyone before him. The equestrian expert Lieutenant Colonel Emile Duhousset had translated the instruments' information into drawings showing the horse's positions in various gaits and published his own book, *Le Cheval,* in 1874.

It is hard to recover the resonance such information had, because what is known is quickly taken for granted, because horses are now so remote from everyday life for most people, and because accuracy is no longer so important a goal for painting. Indeed, at the time there was a conflict in French painting between the scrupulous realism of the established painters and the experiments of the Impressionists, who were pursuing a different kind of realism, the realism of what things look like rather than what they are. The sculptor Auguste Rodin took the side of appearances, declaring, "It is the artist who tells the truth and photography that lies. For in reality, time does not stand still." Muybridge created a crisis of representation for realist painters: they had always insisted that they represented their subjects with maximum accuracy, but that accuracy had always been based on the observations of the eye. Truth and appearance had been reconcilable, and like the artists in Yosemite, the artists painting horses could consider art and science as aligned in their investigation of nature. The American painter Thomas Eakins, for example, incorporated the study of anatomy, dissection, and the nude into his curriculum at the Pennsylvania Academy of the Fine Arts and was captivated by the early motion studies (he sometimes relied on photographs for his own paintings and eventually made his own motion studies). Upon first seeing the motion studies, he immediately wrote Muybridge, incorporated them into his classes, and began a picture of four carriage horses whose positions were based on information gleaned from Muybridge. The painting was later criticized because the horses' legs were portrayed as sharply as they would appear in a high-speed photograph but the spokes of the wheels blurred as they would to the eye or a slow exposure. Even Eakins was confused by the new information. Only artists such as Claude Monet, whose images of the same subject transformed by time of day or season were akin to the motion studies, were at ease with Muybridge's revelations. Edgar Degas made a number of drawings based on the equestrian photographs.

What a high-speed photograph showed and what the eye saw were in conflict, but the evidence of the camera was incontrovertible to those who had dedicated themselves to realism. The eminent academic painter Jean-Louis-Ernest Meissonier suffered most. Stanford visited him in Paris in 1879 and used the motion-study photographs to dazzle and eventually depress the painter, who specialized in battlefields, historical subjects and genre scenes and particularly prided himself on his representation of horses. Meissonier at first thought that the pictures had been edited, eliminating one position of the gallop, the position he had often painted. When he realized the sequences were complete, he declared, "All these years my eyes had deceived me." Stanford reportedly replied, "The machine cannot lie," and gave him a tutorial on horses' gaits, which ended with the painter exclaiming in despair, "After thirty years of absorbing and concentrated study, I find I have been wrong. Never again shall I touch a brush!" He had gone to enormous lengths to draw horses accurately, even building a miniature railway track on his estate so that he could travel alongside a horse in motion to observe it closely (pushed on a sofa with wheels, according to one source). Each of the horses in his paintings had derived from extensive studies and sketches from life, or from life as it appeared to the human eye. The photographs precipitated a crisis. "His commitment to the veracity of his representations forced him to ignore what he could see in favor of what he could not," writes the art historian Marc Gotlieb, "but Meissonier remained faithful to a standard of truth unavailable to human perception, a standard that nullified his project. From this perspective, Meissonier's choice could be said to have brought the tradition of French Salon painting to its terminus." Meissonier repainted the legs of a horse in one of his most famous paintings to accord with the facts supplied by

Muybridge, but the entire mission of painting had changed. He wryly acknowledged this when he painted Stanford sitting in front of a table laden with books. One of the books is open, revealing a few panels of a Muybridge motion study. The photographs lie in the painting like a virus in the body, a virus that would change the nature of the visible.

AFTER STANFORD

Stanford was interested in horses, but Muybridge was interested in photography. The treasurer of the Southern Pacific Railroad, who was frequently at the Palo Alto estate, recalled, "They first started in by taking pictures of horses, and then, at the suggestion of Mr. Muybridge they took pictures of other animals and of men and of birds in flight." The birds had been photographed at Marey's request, but the men must have been Muybridge's idea (though in 1892 he wrote of Jane Stanford's "desire to extend the investigation"). Early in August 1879 the superintendent of the Olympic Club, the club's boxing instructor, strongman, and several other athletes came down to Palo Alto to be photographed in motion. Muybridge made one sequence in which he appears greeting the athletes, looking modest in his baggy black suit beside their muscular forms. The resulting images are the only interruption of the dispassionate scientific aesthetic of the motion studies, as well as the only images in which the artist appears social and socially at ease. Muybridge had doubled the number of cameras at work to twenty-four, and he had begun to take photographs from various angles, rather than only from the side or, as he put it, "laterally." Sometimes, rather than portray several stages of a gesture, he portrayed several angles simultaneously, apparently prompted by a studio visit to an artist wrestling with the depiction of a galloping team of horses. He was exploring the variations.

That year he photographed himself running in two images and swinging a pick in a third, looking athletic and a little dangerous. This was the first of the hundreds of nudes he was to photograph, including several more series featuring himself. For a male artist to portray himself nude was a profound transgression of both propriety and the authority of the seer over the seen, but Muybridge did so blithely when he made himself the first of a long parade of nudes trooping through the motion studies. Like all of them, his self-portrait is both intimate and impersonal. Photography had always specialized in the specific and the particular, and photographs close up had always been intended to distinguish the individuality of the subject. Muybridge put photography to a contrary use. His human figures always remained anonymous, representative of a type, a gender, a feat. Their ancestors are the anatomical illustrations of such artists as Vesalius, elegant skeletons or networks of nerves or veins standing in a blankly classical landscape.

As for the Olympic Club athletes, the faithful *Chronicle* reported, "In order to display as completely as possible the movements of the muscles, the athletes wore only brief trunks while performing. Mr. Muybridge, the photographer, had every arrangement made at the racetrack for carrying out the work, and from ten o'clock in the morning until four o'clock in the afternoon boxing, wrestling, fencing, jumping, and tumbling followed in quick succession and all of their intricate movements were instantaneously and exactly pictured. The first experiment was in photographing Mr. Lawton while turning a back somersault. He stood in front of the camera motionless, and at a signal sprang into the air, turned backwards, and in a second was again in his original position, and in his very tracks. Short as was the time consumed in making the turn, fourteen negatives were clearly taken, showing him in as many different positions. The eye cannot follow the rapid motions of a man turning a somersault, nothing but a gracefully revolving figure being presented; but the various positions assumed, as faithfully portrayed by the lightning-like system of photography, show an

Summersault [sic], 1879, plate 106 from *The Attitudes of Animals in Motion*, 1881.

amusing succession of positions which should cause a revolution in the matter of circus-bill printing." The revolution in photography was well under way. The system was no longer limited to racehorses or even animals. It was a decisive shift, and a sign that Muybridge was moving out of Stanford's orbit to define the project and its meanings himself.

That fall of 1879 Muybridge also debuted his zoopraxiscope, or, as he originally called it, his zoogyroscope, for Stanford and his guests. In his December 1878 *La Nature* letter, Marey had added, "Then, what beautiful zootropes he could make. One could see all imaginable animals during their true movements; it would be animated zoology. So far as artists are concerned, it would create a revolution for them, since one could furnish them with true attitudes of movement; positions of the body during unstable balances in which a model would find it impossible to pose." *Scientific American* had also proposed the images be used in a zootrope, and the idea may already have occurred to Stanford and Muybridge. Marey and Eakins both made their own zootrope strips out of the early motion studies. But Muybridge was to do more, bringing together three visual technologies at once: photography, zootropes, and magic lanterns, the combination that would be the basis of cinema. Nothing demonstrates his genius as an inventor better than this.

The zootrope was one of those philosophical toys created in the 1820s and 1830s, an era of intense research into vision and visual technology of which photography was only one result. Researchers were fascinated with the phenomenon of "persistence of vision," whereby the mind retains an image for a moment after it has disappeared. One of the first toys to exploit this was the Thaumatrope of 1825, in which a disk with an image on either side was spun so that the images merged: the bird into the cage, the rider onto the horse. That year, an English mathematician, Peter Mark Roget, watched an early railroad train pass behind a fence and noticed that the intervening bars of the fence radically altered the appearance of the spokes of the wheels, which appeared to be motionless or moving backward. The illusions produced by interrupted sight held many possibilities. The physicist Michael Faraday produced his Faraday wheel, two slotted wheels on the same axis that when spun in opposite directions produced further illusions of movement by the same principle as the fence and the railroad wheels. The Belgian scientist Joseph Plateau and the Viennese Simon Ritter von Stampfer each independently improved upon the Faraday wheel in

1832 with what Plateau called the Phenakistoscope, a slotted disk with images printed on one side. Spun with the images facing a mirror so that they were seen through the slots, they appeared to move. Plateau's first disk contained sixteen images of a man in successive stages of a dance; when set into motion, these seemed to be a single dancing man.

"The illusion," writes one historian of cinema's precursors, "was easily explained: if several pictures, regularly separated and differing gradually from each other in shape and position, are shown successively to the eye at very close intervals, the successive impressions which they produce in the brain . . . become connected without merging. As a result one believes that one sees a single object gradually changing shape and position." The Phenakistoscope was a huge success, and "in the years 1833–1840, 'magic wheels' span rapidly before enchanted eyes in a great many homes: embracing couples twirled in an endless waltz, horses exhausted themselves leaping endlessly through hoops, gentlemen strugged not to fall off their fancy horses, snakes tried to escape from the disks, and shrewish wives never ceased battering their husbands. It was this kind of little animated drama which—for the time being—offered the only satisfaction for the frenetic desire of the viewer for the illusion of movement." The zootrope, or wheel of life, was the final step on this progression before Muybridge. Invented by William George Horner, it consisted of a drum pierced with slots; a band of images could be placed below the slots inside the drum, and when spun, it gave the same illusion of movement. Publicized and marketed in the mid-1860s, it remained a popular toy well into the twentieth century.

Another source of technology was the magic lantern, invented in the seventeenth century to project pictures painted on glass onto a wall or screen. Magic-lantern shows were popular enough to encourage a lot of innovations in the nineteenth century, including dissolving views that simulated motion, sequences that told a story, even a panoramic slide, as well as more powerful sources of light. By the end of the 1860s a device that combined the persistence-of-vision toys with the magic lantern, the Choreutoscope, was in circulation, and though it projected simulated motion, it never achieved widespread popularity. Photographic images had been used in magic lanterns since 1849, and making slides and giving presentations were a significant part of the photographers' trade. Muybridge had been giving magic-lantern lectures since his return from Central America. In one such show he had projected the motion studies life size and "in quick succession," probably beginning to simulate motion. But his zoopraxiscope, a combination of photographically derived images, zootrope motion simulation, and the magic lantern, was utterly new.

Muybridge used a powerful projector and sixteen-inch disks on which photographic images and painted images drawn from the photographs were revolved in one direction while a slotted disk revolved in the other to provide the intermittent visibility that persistence-of-vision illusions require—the technique of the Faraday wheel. He had found that setting the images in motion foreshortened them, and the manual reproduction of the images allowed him to elongate them to compensate (as well as to enhance the dark early images in which, Eakins complained, it was difficult to distinguish the horses' near and far legs). He did, however, use some photographic images in the zoopraxiscope, and the Stanford Museum owns a set of tiny glass positives whose angled scraps of black tape show that they had been pasted up into a circle. Others had invented more sophisticated motion-simulating projectors, but they had relied on drawings from the imagination to approximate motion or posed photographs that approximated a motion sequence. For example, Henry R. Heyl had in 1870 projected a sequence of six pictures of people posed as though waltzing, but Heyl's device was never more than a novelty without consequences. Muybridge's photographic sequences of motion were unique at the time, and so was their combination with zootropes and magic lanterns. Others around him were striving toward the same goals—the acceleration of photography, the capture and reproduction of sequences of motion. His success on these fronts was to start the next phase of research into the possibilities of photography and the capture of motion. When that phase was complete, it was cinema, film, movies, motion pictures, the first new artistic medium in millennia.

By May 1880 Muybridge was giving public presentations combining lantern slides of the photographs with zoopraxiscope projections of the disks. (The intricate zoopraxiscope had been designed so that it could show both slides and disks.) As dissection disassembled a body into something ungainly and unfamiliar, so the high-speed photographs had disassembled motion, but the zoopraxiscope reassembled it back into the familiar grace of bodies in motion. Audiences were enthralled, and it was this reassembly of the fragments that convinced the last doubters of Muybridge's epochal achievement. The *San Francisco Call* reported of a May 4

show at the San Francisco Art Association, "What attracted the most attention, in fact aroused a pronounced flutter of enthusiasm from the audience, was the representation by aid of the zoogyroscope of horses in
motion. While the previous views had shown their positions at different
stages of the motion, these placed upon the screen apparently [were] the
living, moving horse. Nothing was wanting but the clatter of the hoofs
upon the turf and an occasional breath of steam from the nostrils, to make
the spectator believe that he had before him genuine flesh-and-blood
steeds. In the views of hurdle leaping, the simulation was still more ad-
mirable, even to the motion of the tail as the animal gathered for the jump,
the raising of his head, all were there. Views of an ox trotting, a wild bull on
the charge, greyhounds and deer running, and birds flying in mid-air were
shown. The exhibition concluded with a number of fine, instantaneous
photographic views of athletes in various positions." Muybridge would
give variations of this show into the 1890s (and the animations he made
then now appear on many Web sites, where even to modern eyes their motion is impressively smooth and lifelike).

At the beginning of the 1880s Stanford had brought his old friend, the
forty-niner J. D. B. Stillman, to Palo Alto to work on a book drawn
from the project. Though Stillman was a medical doctor and an oft-
published writer, he knew nothing about the subject at hand and laboriously set about to teach himself. He ordered a horse's skeleton and had
Stanford's carpenters spend several weeks jointing it so that it could be
photographed in all the poses the live horses assumed (and nothing conveys the eccentricity and expense of the project better than this image of
carpenters toiling over a horse's bones). Muybridge could tell he was being
supplanted and was politely unhelpful; Stillman, the more rancorous of
the two, accused him of stealing a collection of photographs he was using,
apparently Muybridge's own photographs, and declared, "He lied to me,
and I think he behaved very shabbily, and he put me to great expense that I
could have avoided if he had given me the aid he ought to have." Despite
his reservations, Muybridge wrote an introduction for the book Stillman
was working on. Stillman suggested he ought to boil it down from thirty-
five to two pages. It was never used at all. Shay, Stanford's secretary, recalled that Muybridge didn't think the book "would be successful, because
Dr. Stillman was going to write it, but he was hoping that it would."

Stillman carped that the photographer "expected to be like the moon to the sun: the more light the sun shone, the more he would reflect." But Muybridge, who had once called himself Helios, had been used to being the sun himself. The last thing he photographed for Stanford was an eclipse of the sun on January 11, 1880. The resulting images he arranged in an elegant circle and published with Morse's Gallery, a motion study of the celestial bodies. In 1881 he created several handmade albums containing 203 motion studies he titled *The Attitudes of Animals in Motion. A Series illustrating the Consecutive Positions Assumed by Animals in Performing Various Movements executed at Palo Alto, California, in 1878 and 1879.* He gave a copy to Stanford, signed and dated May 15, 1881, though he may have made it to protect his authorship against his patron. The book opens with a view from a nearby hill, overlooking the vast equestrian area of the ranch at which he had worked with its traceries of paddock fences and tufts of oaks; then the whitened stretch of track with its cameras; the cameras and shutters themselves with the electrical device visible; and more details of the scene at which the photographs were made. These introductory photographs are curious because each is printed with a gorgeously cloudy sky, a different kind of cloud formation for each page. These clouds were clearly added in the darkroom, so that, even as Muybridge pursues scientific research, the delicate relationship between photographic truth and beauty arises again. Following the cloudscapes are page after page of horses, then a few dozen pages of men in motion, including several of himself, then more animals. It's a small book, unemphatic in its dimensions if not in its content.

Muybridge seems to have created the book in part to establish his authorship and his copyright as he wound up his work at the ranch, his nine-year association with Stanford, and his much longer residence in California. In July 1881 Stanford sold to him for the sum of one dollar "any and all photographic apparatus" and patents and copyrights pertaining to the motion studies project, officially closing down their long collaboration. That month, Muybridge advertised for sale in the *Photographic Times and American Photographer* "a number of Dallmeyer lenses forming part of the equipment of Mr. Muybridge, of San Francisco, who proposes to retire from the branch of the profession for which they are specially adapted." The list included more than thirty lenses. He was renouncing landscape and preparing to devote the rest of his life to bodies in motion, and he was renouncing California too. It was the end of the tumult of extraordinary creativity in which he had taken all his most significant photographs, taken a life, and begun and nearly perfected all his contributions to cinema. Everything he did afterward only refined and expanded upon these final California creations.

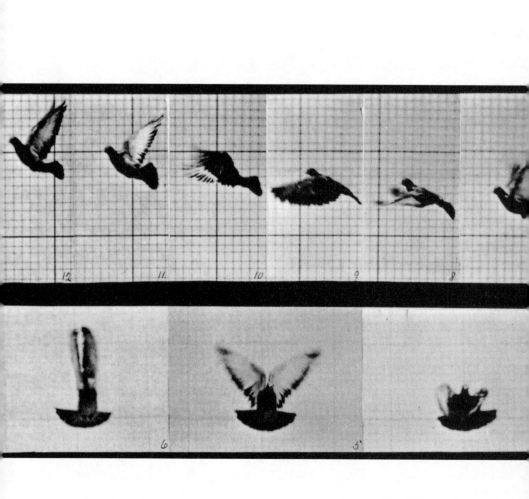

THE ARTIST IN MOTION
AND AT REST

Paris ▪ *London* ▪ *Philadelphia* ▪ *Orange* ▪
Chicago ▪ *Kingston*

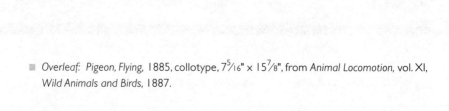

■ *Overleaf: Pigeon, Flying,* 1885, collotype, $7^5/_{16}$" × $15^7/_8$", from *Animal Locomotion,* vol. XI, *Wild Animals and Birds,* 1887.

PARIS

131 Boulevard Malsherbes, Paris, Saturday evening, November 26, 1881—
Muybridge's photographs may have thrown Meissonier into despair, but
the painter didn't hold it against the photographer. Instead, he invited to
his vast studio about two hundred of "the most eminent artists, scientists,
and literati of Paris" to see a zoopraxiscope exhibition and to meet Muybridge during his season in Paris. This and the salon Marey had held in his
honor two months earlier must have been culminating triumphs to Muybridge. The photographer who had spent so much time on the far edges of
the European world had arrived triumphantly in its very center. It is hard to
imagine him among the fashionable crowds on the new boulevards of
Paris that ran straight into the distance, this man who remembered watching an eagle soar across the Sierra Nevada on a morning of absolute stillness, but he came ready to resume the European identity he had shed long
before. At that time, most westerners came to Europe playing up their
buckskin and marksmanship. But Muybridge came having achieved a
technological breakthrough that had nothing to do with the picturesque
roughness of the frontier, though it might have had something to do with
its lack of limits. California had come unmoored from the past during the
gold rush, and it is this lack of templates, of precedents, that seems to have
made the place a capital of social and technical innovation ever since.

Among the guests at Marey's September salon at his house in the
Trocadero had been many eminent scientists, including Hermann von
Helmholz, who thirty years before had explained the first law of thermo-
dynamics. Also present was the flamboyant portrait photographer Nadar,
whose career had many parallels with that of Muybridge. A decade older
than Muybridge, he had assumed the nom de plume Nadar upon becoming a photographer in the 1850s and in 1860 had distinguished himself by

photographing the skeleton-filled catacombs underneath Paris by electric light. Subsequently he became an aeronautical enthusiast who photographed from hot-air balloons and advocated research into mechanical flight. Thus like Muybridge he was a showman, an experimentalist, and a technophile. But he had another side, as a bohemian radical and a friend, before their untimely deaths, of the extraordinary poets Gérard de Nerval and Charles Baudelaire. Both photographers came from lost worlds—the one from the labyrinthine medieval Paris of the romantics buried under two revolutions and a massive overhaul of the city, the other from the remoteness of the Far West undone by the transcontinental railroad, the defeat of the Indian nations, and the spread of settlement.

Muybridge's influence was profound. Meissonier was to change some of his paintings, and the very meaning of academic painting had diminished when the camera outstripped the eye in representing the body in motion. But Marey's work had expanded. He had been using complex instruments that, in direct contact with the body being measured, produced graphic information—lines on paper and the like, precursors of such medical devices as the cardiograph. "My enthusiasm is boundless," he had written of Muybridge's motion studies when he first saw them in *La Nature* in 1878. He asked Muybridge to train his cameras upon flying birds, for like Nadar he was fascinated by flight. When Muybridge arrived in person three years later, he brought the bird pictures, which Marey found disappointing because they were not sequences—but he may also have brought Marey ideas about photographic technique, for Marey's involvement with photography dates from this period and clearly draws from Muybridge. Over the winter, the physiologist adapted an existing "photographic gun" to his own need for precision. He had as his model the astronomer Jules César Janssen's 1874 photographic revolver, used to capture images of an eclipse on a rotating glass plate. The device's exposures were not fast, but it had the ability to create photographic sequences with a single camera and a single plate. It looked like a gun and was apparently inspired by a revolver's rotating cache of bullets.

Marey's new device took twelve photographs in a second, each according to his calculations an exposure of 1/720 of a second. A dozen images filled a disk, and the camera-gun could hold twenty-five disks. In many ways it was an improvement over Muybridge's battery of wet-plate cameras; it was comparatively simple, at least as fast, and far more precise in its timing. Marey was concerned with the exact measurement of time and space, and Muybridge's photographs triggered by the breaking of threads or wheel contact with wire would reflect whatever unevenness of speed the horse had. On the other hand, Muybridge's cameras worked like the modern tracking shot, so that the images maintained their position in relation to a horse covering dozens of feet per second. With a photographic revolver swiveling from a fixed position, the angle of sight would have changed radically. The differences in their devices have everything to do with the differences in their subjects and aspirations. Muybridge was "doing science," but he was for the most part doing it for artists and horsemen, who needed far less precision than a rigorous scientist like Marey.

A second Marey camera in use by July 1882 allowed multiple exposures to be made on a single plate. One athlete becomes a crowd as several moments of his movement appear simultaneously (it is these startling images that were the source for Marcel Duchamp's *Nude Descending a Staircase* and several Futurist paintings early in the twentieth century). A camera that could make quick successive exposures was a step toward the movie camera, but one that made multiple exposures on the same plate was a step away from cinema. Such an image could not be animated as Muybridge's images could—but Marey scholar Marta Braun points out that cinematic flow was irrelevant to the scientist: he wanted to deconstruct, not reconstruct, the mysterious motions of the everyday. Like Stanford, he was interested in what photography could reveal about bodies in motion, not in the medium itself.

Muybridge's motion studies are like an early life form from which wildly divergent species descend. The motion picture is the most linear of those descendants, or looks that way in retrospect, and for Muybridge the project was always about extending the capacity of photography. For Stanford, however, it was about extending the capacity of horses and our understanding of them. He expected the pictures to be useful in breeding and training horses, in managing them yet more precisely for yet faster results. Almost the first use of watches that recorded fractions of seconds was horse racing, and though racing was a sport, not an industry, it came to have many affinities with the development of industrial work in the late nineteenth century.

Early in the 1880s, Frederick Winslow Taylor began his own time studies in a Philadelphia steel manufactory, armed not with a camera but with a stopwatch. Taylor was endeavoring to generate more scientific ways of measuring and controlling industrial workers, and his hugely influential methods came to be known as Taylorism. He divided manufacturing tasks into brief, simple movements, attempted to eliminate the wasted time from the gestures, and used the results to dictate how and how fast a task should be done (resulting, in the words of one labor leader, in the elimination of "personality, intelligence, even the very desires of the workers," and in those of another, "the organization of exhaustion"). By 1886 Marey would use motion-study photographs modeled on Muybridge's approach to the same end, saying, "As we regulate the use of machines in order to obtain a useful result with the least exertion of work, so man can regulate his movements with the least fatigue possible." And in the early twentieth century, another American, Frank Gilbreth, would use motion-study photographic techniques and motion pictures proper to study and streamline industrial activities. Sometimes workers revolted against these methods, which denied the needs of the body, but the tendency to use new technologies to speed up industry never ceased. Its contemporary forms include both the acceleration of computer and network operations and the automatization of tasks once carried out by industrial workers—increases in, as Stanford called it, "the power of production." Long known as "the father of scientific management," Taylor is often credited or blamed for the systematization of much of modern life in the name of efficiency and economy. Muybridge's still photographs had considerable relationship to Stanford's, Marey's, and Taylor's interest in dissecting motion to understand and control it, to the mechanization of everyday life. But with the zoopraxiscope, he reassembled what had been dissected. This was an artistic rather than a scientific move, an impulse to reenchant what had been disenchanted, reanimate what had been frozen.

The Stanfords had left Paris the day of Meissonier's salon and seem to have had little to do with Muybridge's Paris triumph. The photographer still gave them copious credit when he spoke, but he was no longer in their orbit. He wrote to Stanford's secretary, Frank Shay, "I saw them off on the cars and much regret the state of the Gov's health left so much to be desired . . . but if the CP and SP can spare him, I believe he proposes to return next spring; by that time I shall hope to be in full operation, experimenting with new subjects, that will practically exhaust the scope of the investigations which will take place in France or England." He was also seeking a new patron to allow him to expand the motion studies. In Europe, perhaps direct from Marey, he had learned of the new dry-plate photography system which eclipsed the process in which Muybridge had always worked. Dry-plate photochemistry was not far removed from the black-and-white gelatin-silver processes in use today. The film was so stable it could be prepared in factories, and it could be developed long after being exposed. The era of the field darkroom, of mixing chemicals and coating and developing glass plates in the most discouraging circumstances, was over. And the new gelatin-silver dry-plate film was far, far faster than wet-plate photography. Instantaneous photography was no longer miraculous, and Muybridge's heroic achievement in high-speed wet-plate photography was obsolete. He wrote to Stillman that, as the doctor recalled later, "he had come to the knowledge of a new process of instantaneous photography, that it was twenty five times better than he used, and to delay the publication of my book until he could furnish a new set of pictures by this process."

In his next letter to Shay he wrote, "Mr. Meissonier exhibits the greatest interest in the work and through his commanding influences I have obtained a recognition here which is extremely gratifying and advantageous. Not withstanding the large prices obtained for his pictures, unfortunately Mr. Meissonier is far from rich; but his influence with wealthy people is immense; and one of his friends has expressed a desire to associate himself with Mr. Meissonier, Professor Marey and myself in the instituting of a new series of investigations which I intend shall throw all those executed at Palo Alto altogether into the shade. I have been experimenting a great deal and have no doubt of its successful accomplishment. . . . Using the photographs I propose to make next year as his text, Mr. Meissonier intends to edit and publish a book upon the attitudes of animals in motion as illustrated by both ancient and modern artists. He proposes it shall be a most elaborate work, and exhaustive of the subject. It is to be the joint production of Meissonier, Professor Marey, 'the capitalist' and myself, and be a standard work on art which as Meissonier says will hand the names of all four of us down to posterity. But he and I consider it appropriate to invite the Governor to join us if he is so disposed, which we have done by letters." The letters to Stanford have never been found, and neither has any trace of Meissonier's capitalist who was to fund this European expansion of the motion studies. It would have been a heady collaboration, these talented men from such different fields who found their common denominator in the study of motion, and it is further testimony to the intersection of art and science in the era. No doubt its threat of eclipsing the Palo Alto work was an annoyance to Stanford and Stillman. In London that March, Muybridge remained optimistic about the plan and wrote to the doctor again to invite him to join up, saying "I anticipate no difficulty in pursuing the investigation on a larger and more comprehensive scale than has yet been done and to an exhaustive conclusion, (and I think it probable my anxiety, and financial embarrassment, now of some years duration, is over). . . . I am promised every facility for work in Paris, but whether I shall commence there or in England I have not yet fully determined. The Prince of Wales takes a great interest in the matter."

LONDON

The Royal Institution, 21 Albemarle Street, London, Monday evening, March 13, 1882—"I should like to see your boxing pictures," the Prince of Wales told Muybridge, who replied, "I should be very happy to show them, your Royal Highness." Or so said one of the dozens of newspaper accounts of his presentation at the Royal Institution, a London research center founded in 1799. The Princess of Wales had also attended, along with her daughters Louise, Victoria, and Maude, as had the Duke of Edinburgh, the superintendent of the institution, physicist and glaciologist John Tyndall, evolutionist Thomas Henry Huxley, and poet laureate Afred Lord Tennyson. It was, said the *Photographic News,* his first public demonstration in his home country, "and throughout his lecture he was welcomed by a warmth that was as hearty as it was spontaneous." It was at this time he began spelling his name Eadweard, perhaps prompted by a return to his birthplace or a renewed sense of Englishness. It was the last of his name changes.

A picture in the *Illustrated London News* shows him looking grand and fierce with dramatic dark eyebrows and a foaming white beard, an Old Testament prophet in evening dress. He gave much the same lecture he had given before, would soon give at the Royal Academy of Arts and would continue giving for some years, first explaining the technology and showing slides of the racetrack setup and his equipment, then showing depictions of horses in motion throughout the ages, followed by his own still images of the positions of horses in motion and his moving pictures. "After

Mr. Muybridge had shown his audience the quaint and (apparently) impossible positions that the horse assumes in his different gaits, he then most ingeniously combined the pictures on the screen, showing them one after another so rapidly that the audience had before them the galloping horse, the trotting horse, &etc. A new world of sights and wonders was, indeed, opened by photography, which was not less astounding because it was truth itself." The premise of the lecture was that art had always attempted to progress to the most accurate depiction, and that these photographic revelations had finally made that goal possible. The Victorians vainly imagined that the people of every time and place aspired to their own state rather than that the goal was nearly as new as the arrival. Muybridge's achievement was remarkable, but it was the fruit of a very specific set of desires and notions of truth.

The question of truth came back to bite him. The Royal Society, perhaps the most distinguished scientific institution of the time, had invited Muybridge to present a monograph that would then be published in the society's proceedings. Three days before the date appointed for the public presentation, as Muybridge himself recounted a decade later, in a draft of a letter to Stanford probably never sent, "I received a note requesting my presence at the Rooms of the Society. Upon my arrival I was conducted to the Council Chamber, and was asked by the President in the presence of the assembled Council, if I knew anything about a book then on the table having on its title page, the following: 'The Horse in Motion, by JDB Stillman MD, Published under the auspices of Leland Stanford.'"

The book contained no mention of Muybridge until Stanford's introduction, where he appeared as the "very skillful photographer" Stanford employed to carry out his ideas about equine motion. Stillman and Stanford had ignored the motion studies depicting other animals and men, and they had translated the motion studies depicting horses into drawings that were turned into lithographs. *The Horse in Motion* was an expensive, old-fashioned tome with a gilded and embossed cover, and it never sold enough copies to justify the rancor it created. Muybridge's account continues, in his sprawling, boyish handwriting with many crossings out and insertions, "I was asked whether this book contained the results of the photographic investigation of which I had professed to be the author. That being admitted I was invited to explain to the Council how it was that my name did not appear on the title page, in accordance with my professions.

No explanation of mine could avail in the face of the evidence on the title page, and in the book before the Council, I had no proof to support my assertions. My monograph was refused a place on the records of the Royal Society until I could prove to the satisfaction of the Council my claim to be considered its original author. . . . The doors of the Royal Society were thus closed against me, and in consequence of this action, the invitations which had been extended to me were immediately cancelled, and my promising career in London was thus brought to a disastrous close. My available funds being exhausted I was compelled to sell the four original photographic copies of *The Horse in Motion* [he probably means *The Attitudes of Animals in Motion*] . . . and with the proceeds of their sale I returned to America."

The bitterness is unmistakable. At the height of his glory, Stanford and the resentful Stillman had brought him down, and if Stanford's gesture was not outright malicious, it was certainly callous. Muybridge had left all his motion-studies equipment but the zoopraxiscope in the United States, so he could not have argued his case by immediately making further motion studies. And the question of who was responsible for the motion studies has never been fully answered. It is clear that Muybridge was the guiding intelligence that coordinated all the elements and produced the results, the hand and eye present at every stage, the experienced photographer who extended photography into a new arena. It is less clear how far beyond patron and sounding board Stanford went. Stanford had supplied encouragement, racehorses, trainers, work space, the technical resources of the railroad workshops, and copious quantities of money, and these were crucial resources for the motion studies. He initiated the project when he approached Muybridge in 1872, but he was never a photographer, and he never understood the project's implications beyond its revelations about equine motion.

Toward the end of their collaboration, the photographer advanced the project into sequences and reconstructed their motion with the zoopraxiscope (and no one ever argued about his authorship of the latter device). But most collaborations are murky: ideas arise in conversation that might not have arisen otherwise, and even the most talented can benefit from the participation of interested others. When Muybridge brought suit against Stanford in 1883, the railroad baron did everything he could to diminish his achievement. "Muybridge has commenced a suit by attachment in

Phases of the Eclipse of the Sun, January 11, 1880.

Boston," Stanford wrote Stillman, "charging that I have, by the publication of the book, injured his professional reputation. He wants damages to the extent of $50,000, and claims that the idea of taking photographs of horses in motion, originated with him, and not with me, and that I set up that claim in the book. . . . I think there will be no difficulty in defeating his suit and showing that his merit such as it is, was in carrying out my suggestions." Defeating his suit consisted mostly of shifting the focus from the overall achievement to one minor aspect, John D. Isaacs's electrical trigger.

Those who testified for the defense were all former or current employees of Stanford or his railroads, as was everyone involved in the project besides Muybridge and Stanford's old friend Stillman. Hundreds of pages of testimony taken down in Stanford's lawyer's office in San Francisco all focused on the electrical trigger, the one aspect that was definitely not Muybridge's creation. Contracting out details or bringing in assistants is not an unusual aspect of invention or one usually considered to cancel out the main contribution, but Isaacs's inflated sense of his own contribution never died down. Half a century after the idea for the electrical trigger came to him in a flash, he modestly admitted that he was the designer of the movie camera that even Muybridge never achieved: "Godfather of Movies" and "Grand Dad of Movies," the newspapers called him, when he was an old man claiming even to have taken the pictures himself. It may be Isaacs who originated the tale of Stanford's bet, for it appears in these 1923 news stories, and Isaacs also was a key source for Terry Ramsaye's 1920s film history *A Million and One Nights,* which dimmed Muybridge's reputation for many decades.

Muybridge's life had three great crises, and they all ended up in court. The stagecoach accident changed his plans and his character, and he sued the stage company successfully. Flora's infidelity had devastated him, and he had reacted savagely and been exonerated. But it was folly to sue a man as wealthy and powerful as Stanford, even though he had suffered damage to his professional reputation, even though he had copyrighted the photographs in his own name, even though he had with Stanford's knowledge and apparent assent been universally acknowledged in San Francisco and in the magazines of many nations as their author. In an odd way it resembled the previous crisis, which had begun when he found out that he might not be Florado's father. This was another kind of paternity suit (and the men who have written about Muybridge have often called him "the father of the motion picture"), but this time he had confidence in his position. It was ill-placed, for Stanford and his railroad corporations had prevailed when they had committed far more criminal damage than this. Muybridge lost.

There is another way to look at it. Cinema can be imagined as a hybrid of railroad and photography, an outgrowth of those two definitive nineteenth-century inventions, the technologies Stanford and Muybridge represented, in which case fatherhood is too simple a metaphor for it. After all, zootropes, photography, and magic lanterns are also key aspects of it, and Muybridge only initiated and did not complete the invention of cinema. The railroad had in so many ways changed the real landscape and the human experience of it, had changed the perception of time and space and the nature of vision and embodiment. The sight out the railroad window had prepared viewers for the kinds of vision that cinema would make ordinary; it had adjusted people to a pure visual experience stripped of smell, sound, threat, tactility, and adjusted them to a new speed of encounter, the world rushing by the windows; had taken them farther into that world than they would have ever gone before, broadening many horizons at the same time it made the world itself a theater of sorts, a spectacle.

Photography had adjusted them to moving freely in time, to a past that was retrievable and a world in which even the things over the horizon were visible, to a world that had become vastly more accessible, but only as monochromatic images. And these images were not only the photographs in frames, albums, lockets, but the immersive mediums of the magic-lantern show and the stereoscope producing "a dream-like exaltation in which we seem to leave the body behind us and sail away into one strange scene after another, like disembodied spirits." Disembodiment was an aspect of both technologies, and it is interesting that most of the rest of Muybridge's work would be given over to documenting the human body and its most basic acts, a reconstruction of experiences become more remote. Cinema was a technology and a cultural phenomenon neither the railroad baron nor the photographer anticipated, though it would not have come into existence as it did without them. And Stanford and Muybridge prefigure cinema in another way; the medium at its most influential was to be the fruit of the meeting of huge monopolistic corporations and their fistful of dollars with dreamers and self-invented people, the marriage of business and art.

PHILADELPHIA

Muybridge's studio, University of Pennsylvania campus, Philadelphia, morning of October 16, 1885—In the outdoor studio in the veterinary department of the University of Pennsylvania, Blanche Epler, aged twenty, posed for eleven motion studies for Muybridge. She started with poses described as "varied" while she was "draped." In the nude she twice each underwent the motions of "lying down and rising," "kneeling and praying," and "pouring water from pitcher"; she also stooped for the camera, posed as Euphrosyne with, the notebook mentions, "6 wreath 6 goblet," and finished up "ascending stairs with lamp." The resulting series are numbered 1499 to 1509 in Muybridge's notebooks, for he had been at the task more than a year. This time around he had more sophisticated equipment and better methodology: he was often able to take thirty-six images, twelve each from three points of view, of a single act. The dry-plate technology gave him far better resolution of detail at high speeds, and he had developed a circuit breaker that made the business of triggering and timing sequences easier and more reliable. He had published a prospectus in March 1883 titled *The Attitudes of Man, the Horse and Other Animals in Motion,* notable for its nonchalant Darwinian listing of humans as among the animals as well as for its optimism. At the time, he had neither the funds nor the publisher to carry out such a venture, though he still hoped Marey and Meissonier would contribute. That August the University of Pennsylvania in Philadelphia began negotiations to sponsor the project. It was an auspicious new beginning. The university had professionals in all fields, from art to engineering to medicine, who took an interest in and sometimes contributed to the new motion studies. The town was a capital of photographic experimentation, the home of the country's leading photographic magazine; it had a substantial zoo whose wild beasts Muybridge would photograph as well; it had a Gentleman's Driving Park from which he obtained fine horses as subjects; and it had Thomas Eakins.

Eakins had written to Muybridge in 1878, urging him to improve the accuracy of the motion studies, but they had been good enough that the Philadelphia painter bought a set of the cards and immediately began to study them, make drawings from them, teach with them. Eakins had studied in Paris with Jean-Léon Gérôme, one of the Salon painters Muybridge had met at Meissonier's, and he shared the Salon painters' concern with anatomy and physiology, though his work had a fresh American informality far removed from the plodding French history and genre painting. By the time Muybridge arrived in Philadelphia, Eakins was the director of instruction at the Pennsylvania Academy, a prestigious position he was to lose in 1886 for removing a male model's loincloth before a mixed group of students. Sometimes frustrated by the limitations of Muybridge's method, Eakins was nevertheless a supporter who experimented with photography himself. In multiple exposures akin to Marey's, he photographed human beings, and this time around so did Muybridge mostly. Of the 781 published Philadelphia motion studies, 562 depicted human beings, and the many boatmen Muybridge photographed must have had something to do with Eakins's preoccupation with the sport of sculling.

Eakins was, like the French painters, an artist preoccupied with science as a standard of accuracy for painting and as a subject in paintings such as *The Gross Clinic,* which depicts a gory thigh operation conducted by an eminent surgeon. Muybridge was supposed to be working scientifically, though what science meant for the motion studies was never well defined. He was certainly doing science for artists, and the classical subject matter—wrestling men, women carrying vases—of many of his human motion studies seems geared toward the needs of painters (and countless artists still use his motion studies as aids). Muybridge had moved among painters since the 1850s, had been friends with the eminent California painter Charles Nahl, one of his first dealers, and with Bierstadt, had mentioned that the idea for the lateral studies came out of a California painter's request, had met the most celebrated painters of his day in Paris and now in Philadelphia. But he also began to work with doctors. The physician Francis X. Dercum befriended him and recalled him long afterward as "a rather remarkable man; an idealist with a thought for the future. He was not a scientifically trained man but he . . . was clear thinking and possessed marked executive ability." Muybridge made more than two dozen studies of patients drawn from the university clinics of three doctors, including Dercum. Most of them depicted in the act of walking men, women, and children with various disabilities ranging from curvature of the spine to missing limbs. Along with a sequence of a nude 340-pound woman laboriously getting up from the ground to stand, they are the most disturbing of the motion studies.

The three doctors were colleagues of Silas Weir Mitchell, one of the chief physicians involved in defining and treating the condition called neurasthenia. Neurasthenia had been most publicly diagnosed by another doctor, George Beard, in his 1881 book *American Nervousness*. Beard believed that "modern civilization," notably railroad travel, telegraphy, noisiness, the demands of punctuality, and the general rapidity of modern life—as well as "the mental activity of women"—were responsible for the nervous collapses he described. He used the metaphor of a steam engine or one of Edison's new electrical generating stations to describe the limited resources of the nervous system that when overtaxed produces "American nervousness." Beard was one of the long line who decried modern technology. "The perfection of clocks and the invention of watches have something to do with modern nervousness, since they compel us to be on time, and excite the habit of looking to see the exact moment, so as not to be late for trains or appointments. . . . We are under constant strain, mostly unconscious, to get somewhere or do something at some definite moment." In Philadelphia, Mitchell prescribed a rest cure for neurasthenia that confined women to bed and a rich diet and sent men into the rural outdoors to exercise. Though radically different in their assessment of the sexes' needs and wildly sexist by the standards of a century later, both prescriptions broke sufferers away from the industrial world's bustle.

Much has been written about the gender roles Muybridge assigned his male and female models. The men tended to carry out comparatively neutral sporting and working activities, from shoeing a horse to hitting a baseball, with considerable walking, running, jumping, throwing and other basic exercises. The women were more often engaged in domestic and social activities, dressing, pouring tea, sweeping, waltzing, though they too walk, climb stairs, jump, run, carry loads. The project, Muybridge said in one of his lectures, "embraced a large number of actions incidental to men and women in the course of their every-day life; we followed the farmer to his field and the blacksmith to his anvil, the athlete to his recreation ground, and the child to its nursery; the lady to her boudoir, and the laundress to her wash-tub. We have them running, jumping, wrestling, facing washing, sweeping, scrubbing, dancing." Photohistorian Jayne Morgan argues that the men and women are illustrating the medical treatment for the newly diagnosed illness of neurasthenia. It is an interesting notion, that these men and women performing before the array of electrically controlled cameras taking split-second pictures are enacting the cure for urgency, precision, speed, and information overload. But we do not experience the motion studies as fast, but as frozen. The figures seem to be moving in a dreamy, self-absorbed time in which the most basic gesture is stretched out into a series of images. A leap becomes permanent in all its stages; its form has been laid out on paper and can be examined at leisure. We have all eternity to contemplate Blanche Epler walking and pouring water from a pitcher on October 16, 1885. Some of the figures in drapes look like classical statues come to life; some of the nudes look as though they were photographed yesterday.

Marta Braun argues, "Muybridge was not using his camera as an analytical tool at all but was using it for narrative representation." One source of her conclusion is her discovery that many of his motion studies are not perfectly sequential. In part because not all the cameras produced usable results every time, Muybridge created what looked like tidy chronological sequences though part of a sequence would be missing or an image would be repeated to replace one that didn't work out. Often, however, the numbering makes it clear that only part of a sequence is present: no deception is intended. And a lot of the studies are intact enough in their sequences to be animatable, a key test. Other times Muybridge would simply compile a series of studies that was not chronological or put together several different views of the same moment. Braun's conclusion is that the disordered sequences and the many representations of women suggest that he was not making documents but telling stories, often erotic ones, and she suggests that he was already close to cinema as we know it: "Muybridge's concern, then, is with narration, not with movement. . . . Each sequence and each single image within the sequence invites us to transform the models into dramatis personae frozen into unaccustomed poses of beguiling attraction. We are not limited to a purely formal consideration of the contours of the body or the shape of any action but are impelled beyond, into the world of dramatic narrative and biography."

Some of the poses the women strike are familiar from pornography, already a thriving branch of photography. They take off a stocking, undress, recline invitingly; or two women interact in ways familiar from paintings of harems and odalesques. Directing the women in these sensual and transgressive acts must have provided the photographer with erotic pleasure of a cool, distanced sort, and the pictures hark back to the bare-breasted campesinas of Central America. But if Muybridge was making science for

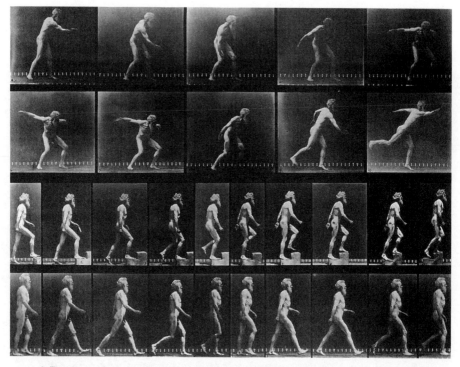

A: Throwing a Disk. B: Ascending a Step. C: Walking, plate 519 from *Animal Locomotion,* 1885–87.

artists, then his motion studies are not primarily about his own imagination but echo the way male and female bodies were already imagined: men toiled, rowed, wrestled; women lolled and posed and did domestic tasks. One could go beyond Braun in arguing not only that the individual sequences suggest narratives, but that whole stories are implied in the order in which he shot the motion studies of women. On the morning of October 16, Epler lies down and rises, kneels and prays, pours water from a pitcher, and ascends stairs with a lamp for the camera. It's a sequence that seems to begin with awakening and end with departing. Were these animated together they would present far more sophisticated narratives than, say, the first films of the Lumière brothers, which took a single action as their subject—a train arriving, workers leaving a factory, a baby being fed.

But in some ways Muybridge was far from film and theater: his models kept a kind of reserve even nude, even in the most intimate acts, that con-

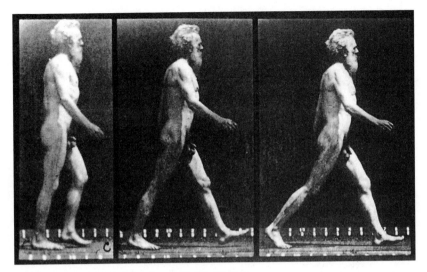

Detail: *Walking.*

nected them to his earlier photography. He photographed the impersonal, landscape, architecture, and groups engaged in action. He never made a portrait, and there was something curious in all his photographs of people, a sense of psychological distance, a failure to connect. The figures often seem abstracted, attuned neither to the photographer nor to each other. Pretty Blanche Epler with thick fair hair down to her waist was an immeasurable distance away in her own thoughts, more a body than a person, not as women are bodies in pornography but as people are bodies in anatomical and medical texts. Unlike an actress, she was not emoting or expressing for the camera; she offered it only the motions of her body.

Muybridge used himself several times in the motion studies, nude with utter unself-consciousness, even facing forward, genitals on view, walking on level ground, walking up and down a set of stairs, sitting, "stooping for cup and drinking," sprinkling water with a watering can, throwing a disk, and using a hammer and anvil, a hatchet, and a saw with apparent competence. Halfway through his fifties, he was still straight-backed and strong, though age is apparent in the whiteness of his beard and the strained skin of his neck as he raises a tool. In these pictures, he called himself "ex-athlete." This distancing was part of the legitimizing aesthetic of science necessary to carry on the extensive photography of nudes in prim Philadelphia in the 1880s, even if it was also part of his emotional limits. Every tool bears its maker's imagination, it is sometimes said, and one psychological aspect of cinema is already evident in this series with Blanche Epler: a substitute intimacy that is safe, distanced, and visual, a realm intense in its emotionality and drama and yet forever on the other side of an emotional partition that cannot be crossed, a substitute life that Muybridge seemed to live watching this young woman who looked like Flora carry out her domestic life and that now billions carry out with movies and television (and in this light it's noteworthy that one of the charges Flora brought against Muybridge in her divorce proceedings was that he peeped in at her as she lay sleeping).

Yet another aspect of the scrambled sequences worth considering is their relation to the great panoramas of 1877 and 1878, which also brought together a sequence of photographs to reprise a larger whole and suggest a passage in time and space. The first impression is that the panorama was a simultaneous seeing; the easy conclusion is that it constituted a pan of the city skyline in sequence; study reveals that it is several nonconsecutive pieces of time edited into a unity of experience, as films are edited. Muybridge seemed to be working out other concerns of his earlier life and work in the motion studies. Again and again both male and female nudes are shown pouring water. He had photographed Yosemite's waterfalls in long exposures that turned them into white blurs, into what Hollis Frampton called "a tesseract of water." In Philadelphia, with a bank of fast cameras, he could capture spilling water in elegant and startling shapes that had never been seen before: every droplet is visible, and the water retains its transparency as it billows into capes and cloaks and arcs of liquid, into serpentine lines and ceremonial arches that lasted less time than the eye can see. The plates look discontinuous, so dramatically does the body of water change shape in fractions of a second as it moves through the air. Sometimes the water seems like a second presence, a tall specter sharing the space with the model whose gesture has brought it to life. As dramatically as the pictures of horses galloping, the pictures of water showed something that had always been concealed from the human eye, fluid dynamics as sculpture of extraordinary ephemerality. Water splashed in 1885 can still be seen hovering in midair, and that is something remarkable about instantaneous photography and about Muybridge.

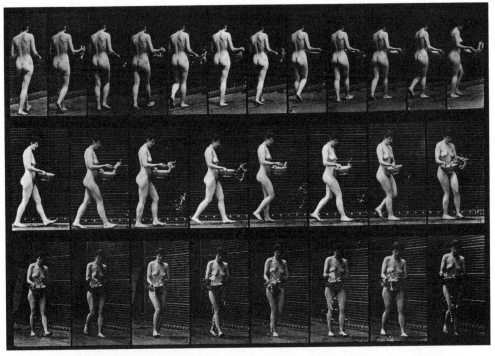

Walking, Sprinkling Water from a Basin and Turning Around, plate 43 from *Animal Locomotion,* 1887, vol. III, *Females (Nude).*

Detail: *Sprinkling Water from a Basin.*

ORANGE

Monday, February 27, 1888, laboratory of Thomas Edison, Orange, New Jersey—
Edison's meeting with Muybridge was important enough to the inventor
that he afterward denied what happened and tried to reshuffle the sequence of events. Muybridge had been on a speaking tour when he came
to West Orange with his zoopraxiscope on a Saturday night. The motion
studies in their entirety, 781 plates, each plate consisting of as many as thirty-
six images, with subjects ranging from tigers and vultures to toddlers and
wrestlers, had been published the year before to considerable acclaim, and
the subscribers included many of the best-known artists, scientists, and institutions of the day. Muybridge's great dictionary of motion and gesture
was finished, and there was nothing left for him to do but circulate it. His
talk at Orange to a crowd of six hundred was the usual mix of education
and entertainment. It featured a parade of images of lions, elephants,
camels, rhinoceroses, buffaloes, tigers, deer, elks, kangaroos, dogs, hogs,
and other creatures. His show concluded with zoopraxiscope animations
of boxing and dancing, and at least one viewer was not amused. In a letter
to a local newspaper, this man objected to the emphasis on the "sporting
world" of boxing and racing as well as to "the propriety of exhibiting semi-
nude figures to a promiscuous assembly. . . . Among savages such exhibitions are natural and expected, but in civilized society they are shocking to
the moral sentiment, indecent and demoralizing."

The following Monday, undoubtedly by invitation, Muybridge visited
Edison's West Orange laboratory, a research and design studio in which
several others with engineering and inventing ability toiled alongside
the man who, as the author of significant telegraphic innovations and
the phonograph, was already famous. (Edison also had a knack for self-
promotion; he, for example, only improved the lightbulb but was happy to
be regarded as its creator, and he would claim to be the inventor of cinema
too.) A few months later, a journalist from the *New York World* visited Edison and reported on the substance of the meeting: "Mr. Edison said that
Prof. Muybridge, the instantaneous photographer, had visited him lately
and had proposed to him a scheme which, if carried to completion, will afford an almost endless field of instruction and amusement. The photographer said that he was conducting a series of experiments recently and had
almost perfected a photographic appliance by which he would be enabled

to accurately reproduce the gestures and the facial expression of, for instance, Mr. Blain in the act of making a speech. . . . He proposed to Mr. Edison that the phonograph should be used in connection with this invention, and that photographs of Edwin Booth as Hamlet, Lillian Russell in some of her songs, and other artists of note should be experimented with. Mr. Edison, he said, could produce with his instrument the tones of the voice while he would furnish the gestures and facial expression. This scheme met with the approval of Mr. Edison and he intended to perfect it at his leisure."

The passage suggests that Muybridge already imagined the direction cinema would take, toward theater, toward celebrity, toward the synthesis of reproduced sound and image, toward what Edison himself soon after proposed, "that grand opera can be given at the Metropolitan Opera House at New York . . . with artists and musicians long since dead." There's irony in Muybridge's realization that his invention might well move into the realm of theater, since his trial lawyer had long ago said of his marriage, "He permitted her to go to the theaters and elsewhere and to enjoy herself in ways which had no attraction for him." He himself had come down from the mountains and battlefields to the social world and become something of a theatrical performer himself. He would not live to see "the talkies" or Hollywood's manufacture of movie stars, but he would see movies become a huge industry, providing dramas and comedies by the yard for audiences around the world.

Edison seems to have taken up Muybridge's idea of combining images and sound, though he later claimed in error or evasiveness that he began work on motion pictures in 1887, the year before their meeting, and denied such discussions took place. But the work didn't begin until the fall of 1888, after the spring meeting had been followed up by purchase of motion studies from and correspondence with Muybridge, and Edison didn't do that work himself. A talented young employee, William Kennedy-Laurie Dickson, did, and his first assignment was to coordinate moving pictures with the phonograph. The initial idea seems preposterous now. A rotating cylinder akin to the cylinders of the early phonograph was to be covered with "pin-head photographs" that would be viewed through a microscope. Edison first saw cinema as an augmentation of his phonograph; only later did Dickson pursue it as an independent medium; and four more decades passed before recorded sound and image were securely wed. The

Edison laboratory was starting from scratch on photographic processes, and it took them time to get up to speed with photographs fast enough to simulate motion. Sometime in 1889 they abandoned the microphotographic apparatus and began experimenting with other approaches. Spurring them on were the Muybridge motion studies that had been, according to another assistant, "mounted on boards and set up in the library for Mr. Edison's inspection and they were there for some months. It was these pictures which again started him working on the development of the moving picture machine."

Another intervention was necessary to bring this machine into being, and it came in August 1889, when Marey guided the visiting Edison through the Paris Exposition Universelle. A cinema historian reports that in the photography section, "more than 300 participants exhibited their works and equipment, among them Eugène Pirou, a future cinema entrepreneur, Nadar with his photographic enlargements on Eastman paper, the Lumière brothers with their gelatino-bromide plates, Janssen with his astronomical photographs, and [Albert] Londe with his pictures of the Salpêtrière hospital." Marey himself had chronophotographs on display and showed them and his cameras to Edison. He had begun using the new paper roll film invented by George Eastman to make strips of motion studies that could be reanimated without reassembly—a huge breakthrough. Muybridge had persevered heroically with technologies that had been supplanted, first with the wet-plate process all through the Palo Alto studies and then with glass-plate negatives all through the Philadelphia years. As long as he was making his pictures with multiple cameras and printing them on glass to project them, he was limited in what he could do: the number of frames in a sequence was limited to the number of cameras, and the circular format of the zoopraxiscope disks limited the number of frames that could be projected without interruption. His zoopraxiscope plates could contain only a finite eternal return of motion. Motion studies on film strips were literally linear time arrived for the camera, and Marey seems to have made them first.

Eastman's celluloid film in long strips was the crucial breakthrough. Marey would use it by 1891, and Edison came back from Paris with the ideas that are his most important contributions to cinema: perforated film and an effective drive mechanism to move the film forward. Motion pictures ever since have been the same size, with the same spacing of the perforations, that Edison employed. By May 20, 1891, the Edison laboratory was able to display to a visiting delegation from the Federation of Women's Clubs a primitive motion picture that showed Dickson bowing, smiling, and doffing his hat. It was a peepshow picture, seen by peering into a box that contained the loop of film, the projecting device, and other mechanisms, paid for with a penny or nickel in the slot. By 1895 the dozens of subjects they filmed included dancers, athletes, a scene in a barbershop and another in a dentist's office, several members of Buffalo Bill's Wild West show, and snippets of history played by actors.

Edison's kinetoscope boxes would not be commercially manufactured and distributed until 1894. And in 1895 the Lumière brothers came up with something far better, motion pictures proper, projected as Muybridge's zoopraxiscope images were. Their ideas came from several sources: from Marey's former assistant Georges Demeny, from Marey himself, and from an 1894 encounter with the kinetoscope in Paris—and all these had their initial inspiration in Muybridge. By 1895 they had a camera and projector using perforated film and a tooth-and-claw mechanism to create the intermittent motion necessary to project pictures. They called their device the Cinematographe and the new medium cinema. On March 22 of that year they gave their first film show. On December 28 they gave their first public screening. They had all but finished the project Muybridge had launched twenty-three years earlier. "The importance of this development in the history of communications cannot be overrated," a film historian declares. "Transcending differences of language and national custom, Lumière's Cinematographe suddenly made the world a smaller and more ordinary place: the invention of faster forms of transport and of the radio—Marconi invented wireless telegraphy in 1895 and the Wright Brothers first took flight in 1903—were never to have the same shocking, elating effect."

CHICAGO

Chicago, April 1893—Muybridge was sixty-three when the World's Columbian Exposition opened in Chicago. His beard was bushier and whiter than ever, and after so many years of restless innovation, his work had ground to a halt. Though he supplied others with new ideas, he never borrowed theirs to advance his own work, and thus he seems to have ignored the celluloid strips that the Lumières and Dickson put to such effective use. He had paid out of his own pocket for the construction of the Zoopraxigraphical Hall on the midway of the fair, next to the Street in Cairo, across from the Moorish Palace, and close to the huge Ferris wheel that became the fair's emblem as the Eiffel Tower had during the Paris Exposition Universelle of 1889. World's fairs were hugely popular during the century after Britain's Crystal Palace invented the genre; they were an encyclopedia come to life, a carnival of information, a suggestion that the whole world could be cataloged and collected, and perhaps that it had become "a smaller and more ordinary place." This fair had cavernous halls devoted to machinery, electricity, transportation, and art, but the midway was a less earnest region whose attractions included "a panorama of the Bernese Alps, giving the views across the Grindelwald and Lauterbrunnen Valleys from the Maennlichen peak; an electric scenic theater, depicting in a realistic way every change of Nature from dawn till night in the Swiss Alps; a panorama of the Kilauea volcano; the Barre sliding railway; an ice railway; a pavilion where cider was made in the French way from apples brought from France; an electro-photographic tachyschope, which depicted with bewildering accuracy the real movements of animals; a zoopraxigraphical hall; stereopticon views of Pompeii; a beauty show of women from more than forty countries; a camera obscura where views of the World's Fair grounds were obtained; an exhibition of submarine diving; a Colorado mining camp, where the modern method of gold mining was shown; a California ostrich farm."

The midway included a huge variety of old and new visual technologies, from the ancient camera obscura through various panoramas and stereographical exhibitions to photographer Ottomar Anschutz's Electrical Tachyschope, a successful adaptation of Muybridge's motion-study and zoopraxiscope techniques (Anschutz's main innovations were the use of a far larger wheel of images and of electrical light flashes that created the necessary intermittent vision). Elsewhere were photographs galore, as science, as art, and as documentation of the participating nations—there were forty-two displays in the Mexican section alone. Londe's studies of the expressions of the mentally ill and of bodies in motion in the French exhibition were, like Anschutz's Tachyscope, evidence of Muybridge's influence; the Frenchman had begun in 1882, the Prussian in 1883. The Edison workshop tried but failed to prepare a kinetoscope to show at the fair. One Muybridge scholar has proposed his exhibit as the first movie theater, but that gives it more credit than it deserves. Muybridge himself was still undecided about whether he was an entertainer or a high-minded researcher, and the unwieldy term "Zoopraxigraphical Hall" inscribed across the pillared cube of his showplace offered poor competition for the belly dancer in the adjacent Street of Cairo. He offered fifty different paper disks of the motion studies for sale, five dollars for the whole set or individual disks for sale as "zoopraxiscopic fans." Modeled after the Phenakistoscope Joseph Plateau had invented in 1832, they were a retreat to a simpler simulation of motion. He also apparently gave illustrated lectures as he had for the past fifteen years. But like many other concessions in the slow first weeks of the fair, his was a financial failure, and it was replaced by a painted panorama of Pompeii by the "the celebrated Neapolitan painter Count Antonio Coppola," which was a tremendous success.

The Chicago world's fair, wrote Clarence King's old friend Henry Adams, who spent two weeks scrutinizing it, "asked in 1893 for the first time the question whether the American people knew where they were driving." The answer was probably negative, for as Poe had noted half a century before, it is the unimaginable that technology brings next, and cinema and the private automobile were only two of the most dramatic technologies poised to alter life in the industrialized world. Four centuries earlier a befuddled Columbus had landed in the Caribbean and, at least in the paintings of the event, planted a flag like a golden spike to link the two hemispheres. The exposition commemorated the anniversary of this event that had become schoolchild mythology. Its jumble of ethnography, technology, and culture seemed to take stock of the Columbian project of exploration and conquest, conflating once again technological and geographical achievement. Many tribal peoples were on display, and much of the message of the exposition was that the world was now accessible in its remotest reaches, full of differences but reigned over by a dominant worldview of science, reason, and industry. Writing of the Columbian Exposition in the magazine *Century,* architect Henry Van Brunt urged that it should "bring together evidences of the amazing material productiveness which, within the century, has effected a complete transformation in the external aspects of life."

At the beginning of the nineteenth century, European settlement had been spread thinly along the eastern coasts, and clocks were the only machines that played a role in ordinary life. Roads were few and rough, and transport and communication moved at the same pace as they had for centuries. At midcentury, the country had contained 9,000 miles of railroad, all of it east of the Mississippi; by the end of the century it would have 175,000 miles of track, along with thousands of miles of telegraph and telephone wire, electrical generating stations for the electrically lit cities, highly mechanized factories, and the first tens of thousands of automobiles. In 1883, after a grand international conference, time had been standardized throughout much of the world, and so the hands of clocks everywhere ticked in alignment with each other like battalions marching with their backs turned to the sun. The year of the exposition, an American railroad engineer succeeeded in going 112.5 miles an hour; three years earlier the journalist Nellie Bly had won a race around the world with a time of seventy-two days, six hours, and eleven minutes; three years later the Lumières would dispatch crews to Egypt, Japan, Australia, and Russia to film and screen movies. The world had shrunk, and the human place in it towered like the Ferris wheel, casting an enormous shadow across what had not very long before been a truly natural landscape.

A little farther down the midway from the Zoopraxical Hall was the American Indian Village, whose exhibits one old account enumerates as "Sitting Bull's original cabin . . . brought from the Standing Rock agency in North Dakota, with the arms used in the arrest and killing of that chief, an oil painting of him, and his buckskin shirt, trimmed with porcupine quills and human scalps. There was a collection of arms and guns found on the battle ground where General Custer fell; also a large variety of Indian work and curios. Pretty Face, niece of Sitting Bull, who is the best bead worker in the Sioux Nation, exhibited her handiwork, and Chief Rain-in-the-Face, who was with Sitting Bull at the Custer massacre, was on exhibition." Sitting Bull, who sat down in the face of history in 1872, who had defeated Custer and fled the United States in 1876, who denounced the Northern Pacific Railroad in 1883, who joined up with Buffalo Bill's Wild West show in 1885, had returned to the reservation afterward. Late in the 1880s, he tried to prevent the great expanse of land the Lakota had been given from being broken up and partly taken away, and in 1890 he became interested in the Ghost Dance religion that was spreading across the West from Nevada. The Ghost Dance preached by the Paiute prophet Wovoka was in its beliefs and its rituals much the same religion that the Modoc had taken up in 1872, and it offered the same hope to people who found hope nowhere else. The reservation administrators saw the Ghost Dance as insurrection and Sitting Bull as a leader, and they wanted him arrested. On December 15, 1890, the reservation police woke up Sitting Bull to take him away. While he was getting dressed, his small house was surrounded by his supporters, and in the shootout that followed he was fatally wounded. But the white horse Buffalo Bill had given him was trained to perform at the sound of gunfire, and for a moment that fused entertainment, spirituality, and confusion, everything stopped when it seemed that the horse was dancing the Ghost Dance.

In 1893 Sitting Bull was dead and most of the Indian wars were over. Clarence King had gone mad in Central Park that year and been institutionalized, a far cry from his glory days as the charismatic young director of the U.S. Geological Survey who had asked Muybridge to photograph glacial traces. Carleton Watkins had fallen upon hard times and was losing his eyesight, and though he was to live more than two decades more, those years were increasingly dark for him in every sense. Timothy O'Sullivan, whose work suggested a photographic vision nearly as complex as Muybridge's, had died of tuberculosis in 1882, and the writer Helen Hunt Jackson died of cancer in 1885. But John Muir had risen in the world since he was a young glacier-drunk guide and laborer in Yosemite Valley, becoming an influential writer and activist. With his participation, his beloved Yosemite had become a national park with vastly expanded boundaries in 1890, and the year before the Chicago exposition, he had cofounded a mountaineering organization called the Sierra Club. Many of the characters of Muybridge's California life—Rulofson, Flora, Captain Jack, Emperor Norton—were dead, and Stanford was dying. But Muybridge's influence, like Muir's, had spread. So had Stanford's.

Stanford came to the exposition in April 1893, but it is not known whether he met Muybridge there. The photographer had spent some time in San Francisco the previous year, planning a lecture tour to Asia that never transpired, writing letters to Stanford he never sent and to the president of Stanford's new university that were apparently never answered. Nothing had been the same for the Stanfords since their son had died. Leland Jr. had contracted typhoid fever in Greece and died of it in Florence in March 1884. The night the boy died, his father had a visionary dream in which Leland Jr. told him, "You have a great deal to live for; life for humanity," or in another of the several versions of the vision, "Father, do not spend your life in a vain sorrow. Do something for humanity. Build a university for the education of poor young men." By the time the devastated parents returned from their European tour, they had decided to build a university to commemorate him. When they docked in New York that May, they began visiting the major universities of the East. Commemorating their son became the center of the Stanfords' lives, though grief did not blunt Stanford's ambition. In an 1885 double-cross comparable to the publication of *The Horse in Motion* without Muybridge's name, he suddenly decided to run for senator of California against the Central Pacific's own anointed candidate, a bid by which he won both national office and his longtime partner Huntington's undying enmity. As a senator he worked for the railroads' interest as he had as governor, but he was often absent because of his deteriorating health and because of the immense project inspired by his son's death.

Theirs was not to be an ordinary university. Stanford, who called much of the classical curriculum "millinery," was taken with the emphasis on science and practical arts at Cornell and the Massachusetts Institute of Technology. In a speech, he asserted, "It will be our aim in the college to give a practical education, to cultivate manual dexterity, to open the range of inquiry and make the scholar rely on his own resources. I have already fitted up some machine shops and hope that the college will in some measure fill the gap opened in our systems of industry by the difficulty that besets a boy who wishes to learn a mechanical art. Still that is not, by any means, the extent of our aims." Unlike his many political projects, the university was very nearly an equal collaboration with Jane Stanford, who steered it prudently and devotedly during the decade she outlived him. It may have been her influence that made it coeducational, and the women at Leland Stanford Jr. University were free to be athletes and scientists to a degree unusual for the time. It was also initially a low-cost school that attracted poor, rural, and working students from around the state and the West. The Stanfords hired David Starr Jordan, the athletic ichthyologist president of Indiana University, to head their instutition, and they began to build it on the Palo Alto estate. So strong was Jordan's belief in "blood" that some of his comments made the school sound like an extension of the stud farm. Like many of the old-immigrant Anglo-Saxons of the day, he buttressed his ethnocentrism with doses of Darwinism to denigrate immigrants, Europeans of non-Anglo-Saxon origin, and nonwhite peoples. "An aristocracy of brains is the final purpose of democracy," he asserted.

Though Stanford had taken an anti-Chinese stance when it was expedient, he never indulged in Jordan's eugenicist ideas. But he did share with his university president the idea that California was a unique and heroic place that the university could encourage and refine in its pursuit of greatness. The dying tycoon effused, "Nowhere are the conditions of life happier and better, no place on the globe contains so fully the resources necessary for the physical and intellectual improvements of mankind. The faculty for advantageously using the resources of nature, which is only bounded by the almost illimitable range of human conception, is all that is needed to place this State in the position it is possible for her to occupy—the land of the highest development of human comfort and intellectuality." Jordan effused, "Life in California is a little fresher, a little freer, a good deal richer, in its physical aspects, and for all these reasons more intensely and characteristically American."

KINGSTON

Kingston-upon-Thames, May 8, 1904—Two months after his visit to Chicago, not quite two years after the opening of his university, Stanford died in his sleep at home in Palo Alto, California. Like many of the other millionaires who founded the first big corporations—Rockefeller, Carnegie—and were afterward known as the robber barons, he had late in life tried to improve his legacy. Though the Southern Pacific never went away, Stanford University for its first decades provided affordable education to many westerners and has all along produced research—but the content of that research is another story. Huntington's money went to his nephew Henry Edwards Huntington, who founded the Huntington Library, Art Collections, and Botanical Gardens in southern California, a major site for scholarship; Crocker's home in Sacramento eventually became an art museum; and Hopkins's house became the headquarters of the San Francisco Art Association, which generated two major arts organizations.

Muybridge returned to his family in Kingston-upon-Thames to live out his final years. His cousins must have been somewhat surprised to find that the ambitious, eccentric boy who had left nearly forty years before had become a white-bearded celebrity who wished to become part of the family again. "Edward Muggeridge has come to Kingston from Japan and is lodging in Mr. Gennett's house in High St.," one of his cousins wrote, unaware that he had never boarded the Asia-bound ship in San Francisco in 1892. "He has been to Tom's, and Florrie likes him." He eventually settled in with his unmarried cousin Kate Smith and her stepbrother. During a brief final visit to the United States, he told a reporter at the *Photographic Times* that he felt "as young as he did twenty years ago" and took a ten-mile walk every Sunday. He continued to lecture a little and put together some books. *Descriptive Zoopraxography* came out in 1893 and did better than its title might augur, and *Animals in Motion* and *The Human Figure in Motion* followed in 1899 and 1901 and went through several printings each (they are in print still and have sold steadily over the past half century). Little else is known about his last years. A much-repeated story has it that he built a scale model of the Great Lakes in his garden, an odd pursuit, since he seems to have seen little of the upper Midwest aside from his Chicago stint. He had not forgotten California. In 1903 he wrote to the University of California at Berkeley to offer copies of his recent books, saying that he would be "much pleased to donate a copy of either or each of them for use in your Reference Department," and signed the letter, "faithfully yours, Eadweard Muybridge." He died of prostate cancer on May 8, 1904, and his cremated remains were buried under a brown marble slab that misspelled his name as "Maybridge." His effects were valued at 2,919 pounds, 3 shillings, and 7 pence, but like Stanford he had long before set into motion legacies that would extend, for better or worse, far beyond his lifetime and all the way around the world.

FROM THE CENTER OF THE WORLD TO THE FINAL FRONTIER

Flora's Grave ▪ *Captain Jack in Plato's Cave* ▪
Muybridge's Birthplace

■ *Overleaf: Captain Jack's Cave in the Lava Beds,* from the series *The Modoc War,* 1873.

FLORA'S GRAVE

I remember sitting in the darkness of movie theaters, a space that to a child seemed almost religious: so many people gathered together hushed to share the same thing, something more vivid than anything but life and more dramatic than ordinary life. In those days it usually seemed to be western movies: horses galloping across deserts and wagon trains circling up on prairies. Every so often I would look up to watch the beam of light through the darkness above instead of the story on the screen. The light flickered, broke into several beams that corresponded to the action on the screen, and made it clear that the movie wasn't only a story but a medium, a roiling stream of light in the darkness. Up above in the projection booth would have been a stream of celluloid rushing by at the rate of a foot a second, making one of those western movies a trail of photographs miles long. The river of light and shadow and the trail of film had an origin, a source in those galloping horses and western landscapes, and it came back to that place, though the place was transformed. My city is Muybridge's city, and the places he haunted during his crucial years I often walk, and at night I see in the windows I pass by that same strange flickering light, this time the blue light of television in dim rooms.

When I went looking for Muybridge, I found him everywhere. A lot of artists have paid explicit homage to him, and he is visible in their work as a source of both specific images and general ideas. He is there in equestrian drawings by Edgar Degas; in photographs and paintings by Thomas Eakins; in many paintings of his motion-study figures by the British artist Francis Bacon; in the photographic work *Muybridge II* by the minimalist Sol LeWitt, who for more than four decades has been exploring serial imagery, a subject initially inspired by the motion studies; in Philip Glass's opera *The Photographer,* which dramatizes incidents from Muybridge's life and turns the motion studies into choreography; in the San Francisco panorama of Mark Klett, made by rephotographing the earlier artist's vista, and in Klett's subsequent panoramas showing what he learned there; in the *Vegetable Locomotion* series of photographs that are Hollis Frampton's and Marion Faller's fond parodies of the motion studies. Motion-study sequences are a standard mode of depicting an event now, from the famous images of the first atomic bomb detonating to champion golfers demonstrating their swing in sports magazines. Web sites and advertisements have of late appropriated and paid homage to the motion studies, and the science-fiction movie *The Matrix* modeled its fight sequences after the stop-start action of the motion studies, using multiple cameras to achieve what is now a standard special-effects technique.

But if Muybridge was at the root, the zero point, the dawn of moving pictures, then he is everywhere as the ghost at the end of those trails of photographs rushing by, beamed across the world as television, dreamed across the world as the shared content of contemporary life, present not only as specific images but as several media. Muybridge is often called the "father" of something, the father of motion pictures usually, and Jane and Leland Stanford said the children of California would become their children. Here parentage works as a metaphor, for children become things their parents cannot imagine and can at best claim partial credit for, and yet they go into the unknown carrying the indelible traces of their parentage. A history streams forward from the events of the 1870s, one that sometimes seems like a relay race, a torch-passing, a game of telephone: something is transmitted, but it changes with every transmission, every carrier. The places themselves seem to tell the story best.

Flora Muybridge is buried behind the United Artists Multiplex Cinema in Colma, California. In many California coastal Indian theologies, souls travel west over the Pacific after death, and west of nineteenth-century San Francisco was a quartet of large cemeteries, a city of the dead. Flora was among the San Franciscans who were buried there from the 1860s until the turn of the twentieth century, when the expanding city decided there was no longer room for its past and banned burials. A few decades later, city workers began to exhume the bodies so that the graveyards, which had grown wild and weedy, could be recycled into real estate. The dead were sent a dozen or so miles south to Colma, the cemetery city that is now also a city of big-box stores on the San Francisco peninsula, and their tombstones were recycled as landfill and building material. The exact location of Flora's remains is inked in an old ledger book at the Greenlawn Cemetery, but she is buried with hundreds of others in a scruffy field behind United Artists marked only by a single marble monument rising from the weeds. Surrounded by chain-link fence, the plot is bordered on its other sides by the better-tended graves of those who were actually buried there when they died, by a hulking Home Depot store, and by a road across which chain stores and fast-food restaurants stand. San Francisco had done what it could to erase its Ohlone Indian past, to wipe out some of its hills and bays, to cannibalize itself as building succeeded building even before the 1906 earthquake and fire took out most of the central city. It has been a transient place whose identity keeps shifting, though it always kept alive a certain kind of freedom, a certain kind of experimentalism, the freedom and the greed of the gold rush and the people who kept coming here to become something else, a freedom that sometimes seems to depend on the ability to erase and reinscribe meaning at will.

In 1872 the writer Helen Hunt Jackson came to California, where she admired little but the landscape and Muybridge's photographs of it. Later that decade she heard some Omaha and Ponca Indians from the plains on a speaking tour talk about the injustice they had experienced, and after years of dabbling and scepticism she found her calling. In 1881 she wrote a scathing report on Indian policy that failed to rock the world. Georgia O'Keeffe once said she painted her flowers big so that people would look at them, and Jackson rewrote her history melodramatically so that people would read it. She returned to California, and she set *Ramona,* her 1884 novel of racial injustice, in the southern part of the state, where the Spanish influence still could be seen in ruined missions and vast ranchos. She built *Ramona* out of vivid evocations of real places and accounts of real brutalities by Yankees against the native population. Smitten as so many would be by the romantic ruin of the Franciscan missions, she left out their domineering intolerance and focused on the way the romance of Ramona and Alessandro is blighted by the greedy cruelty of the Yankees: the couple loses successive homes and a child, and finally Alessandro loses his mind. The book became a huge best-seller, though it seemed to lead not to reform but to nostalgia, for in its celebration of Spanish California it gave the southern part of the state the identity it had sought as it grew into an empire. *Ramona* became southern California's false memory, a backward glance touched with a sunset glow that softened the contrary and contrived details.

In 1905, a year after Muybridge died, two decades after Jackson published her best-seller, an actor who called himself Lawrence Griffith came to Los Angeles playing Alessandro in a stage version of *Ramona,* and there he too fell in love with the ruinous missions and romantic atmosphere. His acting career was never a distinguished one, and not long after his tour he stooped to acting in films at the Edison Studios in the Bronx, in those early days when stage actors regarded the movies as shameful. Movies were then short, simple, and silent flickers at the Nickelodeon, sought out mostly by the poor. Edison had gone into motion pictures, and though he was uninterested in the artistic possibilities and kept a tight hold on the budgets, his former chief cameraman, Edwin S. Porter, had already revolutionized the medium with *The Great Train Robbery,* the movie that told a more complex story with more sophisticated techniques of representing time and simultaneous events. The young Griffith moved from acting to directing, since it was both more lucrative and more anonymous, and he directed hundreds of films for the Biograph Company in New York in those days when movies were made in a day or a few days and New York and Chicago were the capitals of moviemaking.

But in the winter of 1910 Griffith brought his troupe of about thirty actors and technicians to southern California. A few other companies had already tried California, which had three great advantages. One was the golden light that never seemed to run out, day after day, month after month. Another was the landscape, or rather the landscapes. Within a few hours of the city of Los Angeles were deserts, grasslands, forests, mountains, seasides, orange groves, and farms, as well as architecture of every imaginable type: southern California looked like everywhere and anywhere for the movies. A third was proximity to Mexico and distance from the Motion Pictures Patent Company, which attempted to control the entire industry with patents on cameras, control of film stock, and detectives and thugs to enforce their powers. In a pinch, a film company could cross the border, and southern California became the capital of independent moviemaking. Cheap land helped, and so did, less directly, the lack of an established society. In New York the movies were theater's illegitimate child; in California they became Hollywood, an aristocracy of glamour that conquered the world.

By the time he settled in California, the director was using his real name, D. W. Griffith, and he was making the new medium of film supple, subtle, and evocative as it had never been before. A technical and formal prodigy, he had new ideas about lighting, about close-ups and distance shots, about staging and special effects, and especially about editing—intercutting, cutting to details or pulling away, dissolves and fadeouts. He almost singlehandedly established the vocabulary of filmmaking. But all this was in the service of storytelling, and he told stories visually as no one ever had before. The first film he shot in California was *The Thread of Destiny,* a romantic tale about an orphan girl raised at one of the missions that had captivated him years before. The second to last on that first excursion to the West was *Ramona,* with Mary Pickford in the title role.

The relay race became a boomerang: the Sephardic Jew David Belasco was the great impresario of the San Francisco theater from the 1860s until his migration to New York in the 1890s, where he became a national figure, but his protégé Cecil B. De Mille came out to California in 1913 and began making westerns and overwrought epics that served cinema as Belasco had served theater. "Hollywood," the minor place that became shorthand for the global phenomenon of American movies, was hatched. Almost from the beginning, from Porter, from Griffith, from De Mille, the movies were obsessed with the West, that fiction of authenticity, that fantasy of gritty reality. The fluidity of identity that had always been a hallmark of the American West finally came home to roost and to feather its nest in Hollywood, for the medium of cinema encouraged it as nothing else had. The West was both the location of an industry and the subject of the fantasies it distributed around the world, fantasies about cowboys and pure heroines, Indian raids and charging cavalry, an improved national past as *Ramona* was a regional past. Hollywood was the capital of an industry as Chicago was of meatpacking, Detroit of automobiles, New York of clothes, but the product was imagination, dreams, fantasies. Later, the two world wars sapped the strength of the European film industry and gave Hollywood the economic preeminence it still holds today.

In 1907 an estimated two million people a day attended the nickelodeons that had sprung up by the thousand in cities and towns, sitting in the darkness where they were transported to the somewhere else that within a decade would almost always be southern California in one guise or another. Later, movie houses became more luxurious and larger; they were called palaces, dream palaces, dreamland, movieland; they were island republics in which people sat alone together in the dark and let the visions enter them, became possessed by movies, lived somewhere they could never otherwise visit: the past, the future, places more glamorous, dramatic, dangerous than everyday life. The whole world dwelt in Hollywood, and Hollywood was the whole world and no place at all. D. W. Griffith was able to re-create the Civil War in southern California for his epochal 1915 masterpiece, *Birth of a Nation*, and then to build Babylon on Sunset Boulevard for *Intolerance*, his attempt to exculpate himself from the rank racism of *Birth of a Nation*, a racism that justified itself with a fantastic rewriting of history. Babylon crumbled on that thoroughfare for years.

"Hollywood is afflicted with total amnesia," one of its writers declared, "a complete group blackout and loss of recall when it comes to anything that happened more than twenty-four hours ago." And the movies themselves made fictions out of history, made up a South and a West that never existed, specialized at various junctures in westerns that turned a place into a genre that could be made anywhere, that prompted the sense of self of generations of American men, even politicians, that even generated a president who remembered as reality things that had only happened in movies. And from movies women learned how to look, how to love, how important looking and loving were. A lot of the early movies were lost forever when they were recycled for the silver nitrate in the film stock or left to decay, for the nitrate film was flammable and prone to disintegration. The people too were invented and erased quickly, stars burned out, directors were eclipsed, scandals ended careers, everyone changed their names so that the Ellis Island richness of the place was smoothed over into something reeking of the *Mayflower*. But the movies themselves made and remade history. *Birth of a Nation* fostered a resurgence of the Klan and its racial terrorism. And Hollywood movies became a huge industry themselves, grossing $8 billion in the second year of the new millennium. (That the actual locale named Hollywood has, in Mike Davis's words, "gone from picturesque dilapidation to hyperviolent slum" in recent decades means only that this place name still corresponds to a region and an industry, but not to an actual place.)

In 1919 Griffith joined forces with Hollywood's biggest stars, Mary Pickford, Douglas Fairbanks, and Charlie Chaplin, to form an independent distribution company, United Artists. Mary Pickford was the first movie star, and the stars became hybrid beings, an amalgam of the characters they played and the carefully controlled public images they maintained. Pickford, "America's Sweetheart" with her sausage curls, was really the smart businesswoman Gladys Smith; Chaplin was an English vaudeville comic who had, while touring Los Angeles, been recruited to movies by Mack Sennett, another early director there; Fairbanks, who reigned with Pickford as Hollywood's first royalty, had started out as Douglas E. Ulman. "The lunatics have taken charge of the asylum," said one film executive in a condemnation so lively it later became the refrain of a pop song, but United Artists thrived. A railroad administrator, Oscar Price, became the company's first president, and UA produced some of Hollywood's best movies even after the Transamerica Corporation bought it in 1967, the year UA released the trio of spaghetti westerns that made Clint Eastwood a major star.

Transamerica, a financial services corporation, was headquartered in San Francisco, and the year after it acquired United Artists, it began constructing, on the site where the Monkey Block had been, the pyramidical Transamerica Building, the most recognizable landmark on the downtown city skyline. The Monkey Block was the first four-story building west of the Mississippi when it was built in 1852. As a financial center it dominated Montgomery Street for years and had been part of Muybridge's commercial milieu, but by the twentieth century it had become artists' studios before it was demolished. The site was reborn as a financial center: business and bohemia have always switched off like that in San Francisco. United Artists still thrives as a subsidiary of MGM, and the Transamerica Building now belongs to a Dutch conglomerate. Flora was originally buried near where the big Coronet single-screen movie theater now stands on Geary Boulevard. Had she lived seventy years instead of twenty-four, she could have seen the slightly seedy thespian milieu she celebrated in her photograph album and loved through Larkyns hybridize with her husband's innovations into a multimillion-dollar industry that ruled the world, or at least its dreams and desires, the industry that plays nightly next door to her unmarked grave.

Somewhere in Colma not far from Flora are the remains of Wyatt Earp, who was alternately a lawman and outlaw in his Arizona youth, the youth that Henry Fonda, Ronald Reagan, James Garner, and Kevin Costner romanticized in the movies. Earp himself lived long enough to become a movie consultant after he married a San Francisco actress, for there was no real gap between the Wild West and its cinematic representation. Movies had to come back west, because no place else had the fluidity and freedom they needed to evolve, to dominate, to become that light that flickers everywhere like a new celestial body, the starlight of Hollywood. One western is still waiting to be made: the movie about an Englishman who became a rugged outdoorsman, an explorer, a murderer, an inventor, and the fastest photographer in the West, the western movie that would have been about the genesis of both medium and genre in the strangely malleable moments of the 1870s.

In the 1970s and 1980s, European and Eastern cultural theorists—Umberto Eco, Jean Baudrillard, Fredric Jameson—invaded California, which they described as the capital of postmodernism, as the place where the future had arrived. Had they spent as much time reading the region's history as they did staring out car windows and watching TV, they would have found that theme parks and drive-by shootings, rogue cops and actor politicians, amnesia and fluidly changing identities, were nothing new. They were western heritage. The West was a place where latent possibilities emerged like mutations, where Muggeridge became Muybridge and Stanford became a grand thief and patron and Norton an emperor and Griffith a genius and Pickford America's Sweetheart, the place where the dead lie unmarked behind the movie theater.

CAPTAIN JACK IN PLATO'S CAVE

One brisk spring day, I went to the Lava Beds and was surprised that nothing I'd read evoked the terrain around it, too open for forest though it was scattered with pines, too lush for desert, too sparse for grassland, a meeting of many regions, many forces. The Lava Beds, the starkly stony area within this terrain, became Lava Beds National Monument in 1925; Captain Jack was right that nobody would want the land for practical purposes. The Park Service sells a walking-tour map of the Lava Beds that lets viewers wind through the labyrinth and the events of 1873 there according to the numbers. I was a modern tourist that day, I drove a car that let me traverse great distances in comfort and solitude and seventy miles an hour, I carried recorded music to, as we say, pass the time, a laptop computer to sort out and record my thoughts, I had the electronic money of a credit card to take care of whatever needs arose. On my way to the Lava Beds, I looked at Schonchin Ridge and the site where Captain Jack killed General Canby, and I walked the long loop through the Lava Beds trying to imagine the war and the strangeness of being stranded in the center of your world, within sight of the lake, the creation story, and the snowy cone of Mount Shasta. I tried to imagine a vanished sense of time and place that must have made this region utterly different for the Modocs who fought to stay here. More profound even than the changes in the landscape are the changes in our relation to it.

Tule Lake has been mostly drained for rice fields, and what remains of it is a rectilinear body of water that doesn't suggest much of this place from which the creator first hauled mud to make the world. The center of the world that used to be a peninsula jutting into the water now stands in a dry agricultural landscape, up a road that passes the cylindrical metal silos of the Newlands Grain Collective, a new fortress of agribusiness facing off the old lava fortress. The outcropping with its petroglyphs and swallows seems lost in its new surroundings, for its meaning came from a context that has been erased, but the petroglyphs still stand enigmatic and evocative above the dust that used to be water. I saw the Lava Beds, I saw the center of the world, I looked at my watch and saw that there was a lot of daylight left. Looking at my atlas, I saw that the Tule Lake Internment Camp was just down the road and decided to go. There was something irresistibly perplexing about these landmarks lined up in a row: battlefield, birthplace, prison, the first for a local war, the last for a world war. I turned off the main highway and drove past the small hamlet looking for a ghost town like the camps I'd visited before, but the road rolled by under my wheels, and there was nothing but agricultural land out the window. Coming back, I realized I hadn't accepted the evidence of my eyes: the high ranch gate and barbed wire around the hamlet, which was a portion of the camp.

The prison built to hold the Japanese Americans who wouldn't swear loyalty to the United States during the Second World War was still inhabited, though it was debatable what kind of prisoners were within. More than a dozen of the original wooden barracks were still there in the same grid formation, painted pink, green, brown, augmented by trailers, wrecked cars, and toys in the dust. Someone had put up barbed wire around the petroglyphs, but no one had taken down the barbed wire around the camp. I drove up and down, frightened that this place I had expected to be part of the past was in the present, wondering what poverty keeps a prison without guards inhabited, seeing no sign of life that weekday afternoon until I noticed two little girls in bright clothes, a blond one in pink, a brown-haired one in red, in front of a doorway. The back road was named Captain Jack, as though the history of Japanese internment and modern poverty were truly linked to the last stand of the Modocs, and when I turned off Captain Jack to drive back up one of the side roads, I saw a figure holding a broom come out of the house where the girls were playing in the dust. Up close she looked to be in her midteens but also looked pregnant under her big T-shirt. I stopped my car and asked her to confirm that I was in Tule Lake Internment Camp. It was obvious that it was, but I was dumbfounded. And I couldn't ask her what it's like to live in a prison, so I asked her what it was like living in this place. "It's nice," she said wanly, her small features still blank. The little girls waved as I left. Later, the photographer Masumi Hayashi, who was born in another of these camps and has made panoramic portraits of all of them, told me that a former prisoner from Tule Lake told her that Shasta's resemblance to Japan's celebrated Mount Fuji was all that made the place tolerable. What had been the center of the Modoc world had been the bitter edge of it for the internees, but what it was for the current inhabitants I could not guess.

I drove away stunned and stopped a few miles up the road at a Forest Service office. I wanted someone to tell me how the lake could have vanished, how the prison could be inhabited, what this landscape meant. The garrulous older woman behind the desk was glad to see me, but she didn't want to talk about what I wanted to talk about. There was a monument to the camp back there, but I'd missed it, she said, and she didn't seem to think there was anything peculiar about the fully inhabited but unguarded historic prison. What she really wanted to talk about was the fact that Lieutenant Sulu in *Star Trek* was born there and came back with a group to visit a few years ago. She hadn't actually seen him, she volunteered, as though that was too much to expect, he didn't come into the office, but he came to the camp. And that was what the place meant to her. It didn't seem shameful that he—or rather the actor George Takei, who was actually born in East L.A.— spent years of his childhood there, just dazzling that a celebrity was linked to the site. For the woman in the Forest Service, it seemed, Lieutenant Sulu was more real than the people down the road.

It took exactly a century, 1867 to 1967, to go from Muybridge's return to California as a photographer to *Star Trek*'s launch as a television series. You could call it the journey from Captain Jack's cave to Plato's cave. Captain

Jack's cave is a real place. It was the center of my exploration of the land-scape of Modoc County, an angled pit of lava in which the Modoc leader also known as Kientpoos, his two wives, and his children lived during the siege of 1873. It could not have been a comfortable home, though it was warmer and dryer than what lay outside, and it seems fitting that Jack's attachment to the earth ended with him living in the earth itself, a womb, a grave, an ancient exhalation of molten stone become home. In Muybridge's photographs it looks like the mouth or the eye of the land, a pit full of dark awareness.

Plato's allegory of the cave has often been used to describe cinema and television. "Imagine an underground chamber like a cave, with a long entrance open to the daylight and as wide as the cave. In this chamber are men who have been prisoners there since they were children," it begins. "Some way off, behind and higher up, a fire is burning, and between the fire and the prisoners and above them runs a road in front of which a curtain-wall has been built, like the screen at puppet shows." The prisoners of the cave see nothing of what takes place outside the cave, know nothing of the light, color, and dimensionality of the outside world. They see shadows on a screen, and Socrates, who is Plato's own shadow-self, asks, "Would they not assume that the shadows they saw were the real things?" Plato assumes that when they, like Dorothy in *The Wizard of Oz*, see what is behind the curtain, they will grow disillusioned with it, find representation limited as sensory experience and as truth.

He was wrong, for watchers in the cave of representation are free to come and go, and they keep coming back; they fill the multiplexes and keep in business the dozens of television stations beaming from satellites and the thousands of video-rental stores around the country. The Modocs had stories, stories that sprang from the land and brought them back to it, but the Ghost Dance they danced to defeat time always seems cinematic to me, a movie run backward, the dead revived. They wanted to escape from time, but only so they could stay in place. Plato objected to the cave dwellers because they relied on the false testimony of the senses, but life in the cave seems disturbing now because it is disembodied, disconnected, a realm of two-dimensional shadows in the dark. Rather than being too reliant on the world of the senses, it is not reliant enough. Not absolute truth—after all, there is the Weather Channel—but engagement is missing.

Enterprise, that catchword of Victorian capitalism, has become a spaceship. If the premise of the *Star Trek* series resembles anything, it resembles the geological surveys of the nineteenth century, which were military missions seeking to know rather than to fight, missions with scientists, information gatherers, and faith in the rationality of their culture, missions that understood that knowledge is power. *Star Trek* takes place on a "final frontier" that links the show to the frontier of the American West, though the otherness of Native and Chinese westerners is supplied by genuine extraterrestrials. Earth has been left far behind, and time itself has become almost optional, for there is instantaneous spatial travel—"beam me up, Scotty"—of individual bodies and "warp speed" travel through outermost space and even, in one of the *Star Trek* movies, travel back in time. The darkness of outer space suggests that Plato's dark cave now fills the universe, that the annihilation of time and space is complete, both in the premise of the show and in the desires of the watchers sitting at home watching electrons and image fragments turn into a transporting story.

The western movies themselves were always anchored in a sense of place and a passion for it, a passion that was more the filmmakers' than the protagonists, as the camera panned riders across deserts, zoomed in on houses swallowed up in the prairie, followed herds across rivers. The desire for the real lives on, if nowhere else, in representations in which Web sites and cell phones are marketed with pictures of rock climbers and shepherds with their flocks. Another way to think of Plato's cave is as a condition in which people live entirely in representation and interior space, in a universe constructed by humans, ultimately inside the imaginations of those who came before, an operation that suggests nesting Russian dolls and a certain crampedness of the imagination after a few generations. Muybridge's work teetered between these two conditions, between the noplace of the whited-out Palo Alto racetrack and the black-walled Philadelphia studio and the brilliant description of place in all his other work, from Guatemala to Alaska. He gave up place for the laboratory of motion, and it is from this relinquishment that he produced the bare bones of cinema. We are still teetering too, between Captain Jack's cave and Plato's cave.

MUYBRIDGE'S BIRTHPLACE

The house in which Muybridge was born and raised also hosted his parents' grain and coal business, a holdover from the preindustrial order of things when work and home were seldom separate. One of his biographers who went to visit it in 1971 found that the building on High Street still sold "sea-borne house coal." But when I went there at the beginning of the twenty-first century, it was a computer store. That is to say, Muybridge's English birthplace is now an outpost of Silicon Valley, where silicon chips and the cheap, compact computers they make possible were conceived, where the acceleration and dematerialization of everyday life took a huge leap forward, the Silicon Valley that sprang, so to speak, from the loins of Stanford University, which itself came out of those eight thousand acres and the Stanfords' bereavement and their vision of what California could be and what the world should be. Muybridge's birthplace so far away is now a shell stuffed with California, and for that matter this book was written on a computer created by one set of Stanford University spinoffs headquartered in that place, printed out on a printer manufactured by another, and researched in part via a search engine made by a third. If the world is Hollywood and Hollywood is the world in terms of the pervasive presence of its entertainment in the global imagination, then in another even more pervasive sense, the world is Silicon Valley, the source of much of the electronics and communications technology that have changed the pace, expectations, and practices of everyday life.

This time the transmissions seem less like a game of telephone or a relay race than a list of begats, a great chain of patriarchs spreading out into the world, the Abrahams who are fathers of multitudes of programmers, engineers, hackers, Web site designers, and on and on, an industry of millions, and like the Biblical begats it is a list of fathers and sons, unless you count Jane Stanford in as the Eve to Stanford's technocratic Adam in the oak-shaded Eden of the Palo Alto estate. For Stanford hired Jordan, and Jordan hired Lewis Terman (the eugenicist who created the Stanford-Binet test to quantify intelligence), and Terman's son Frederick took a degree in chemistry at Stanford, studied further in the East, but came back to run a laboratory in the new field of radio communications on campus, the field that became electronics. And though this Terman did not beget David Packard or William Hewlett, he begat Hewlett-Packard when he brought his two former students back to Palo Alto to start their own electronics firm. Walt Disney, a young entertainment entrepreneur who'd worked with United Artists, placed the first order with Hewlett-Packard, for audio oscillators to use on the animated film *Fantasia,* and soon after they were servicing the war industry. The products of Silicon Valley would be used by the public, by the entertainment industry, and by the military, making a sort of military-industrial-entertainment complex evident in the location of Lockheed and other high-technology war makers in the valley as well as the ever more technologically sophisticated special effects of Hollywood and those new hybrid genres such as video games (and war American-style is a lot like video games, while Top Gun, a ride named after a movie about military technology, is one of the main attractions in the Silicon Valley amusement park Paramount's Great America). Silicon Valley makes entertainment and war seem like one enterprise designed to control populations via the channeling of electrons through circuits, however divergent the details of their deployment.

The university and commercial technology kept feeding each other. In 1951, the Stanford Industrial Park opened, and Hewlett-Packard and a branch of Eastman Kodak moved in (and when French prime minister Charles de Gaulle visited California a decade later, he asked to see two sites: Disneyland and Stanford Research Park). Hewlett-Packard's founders gave more than $300 million to Stanford University, much of it plowed back into engineering programs that generated yet more technical prodigies who founded many more companies in the place that in 1971 became known as Silicon Valley. From this university at the center of this valley have come further generations of entrepreneurial technocrats who struck it stunningly rich, among them former Stanford professor Jim Clark of Silicon Valley Graphics and Netscape and former Stanford students Jerry Yang and David Filo who started Yahoo! to navigate the burgeoning chaos of the Internet. Sometime in the 1990s, the computer itself as a tool stopped being the unit of the annihilation of time and space. It was replaced by the networks that computers link up to, a wired world that extended the globalization of the railroad and the instantaneity of the telegraph into every first-world home, into portable devices, into the everywhere that more and more becomes nowhere.

It's a remarkable landscape, an explosion of Stanford and Muybridge's ambitions far beyond their comprehension. Only a barn remains of the stable and racetrack complex where Muybridge made the motion studies, but Stock Farm Road is now a side road onto campus from Sand Hill Road, and Sand Hill Road, which winds through a classic California landscape of rolling hills and oaks, has two notable features. On the south side of this road that runs past campus from the back freeway, Highway 280, is the Stanford Linear Accelerator, a sort of white-painted tunnel three miles long through which electrons and positrons are hurtled close to the speed of light for research into the structure of matter and the forces between these elemental particles. This strange sight has stood there since 1962, the white tube of the accelerator like a racetrack for basic matter. In the early 1970s the founders of Apple Computer emerged from a club of computer amateurs who met regularly in the accelerator's auditorium.

The other side of Sand Hill Road looks far more familiar, though what happens there is at least as strange. On this north side is a long series of nondescript office buildings with mansard roofs and a lot of glass, created when the manager of Stanford University's land developments decided to strike out on his own. Around the time that the place was named Silicon Valley, the first venture-capital offices went in, and this side of Sand Hill Road is the capital of technologically focused venture capitalism, the men who bankroll the acceleration of everyday life and new technologies, the Montgomery Block of its day. The film critic David Denby ventured afield to investigate the new technologies that were being bankrolled by Sand Hill's venture capitalists and concluded, "The revolution will end by changing the nature of time itself, thereby altering the way we live, work, seek pleasure, and gather together. We shall achieve simultaneity, ending the gap between desire and fulfillment; we shall no longer *wait*." Denby does not embrace this future in which those who are not hooked up to the accelerating technologies become irrelevancies and points out that the utopian visions of the valley are undermined by how unlivable it is, with its manic work schedules, gridlocked traffic, astronomical housing costs, pervasive social problems. The premise of the efficiency and convenience of every technology is that it will save time, though as Stanford himself remarked, "if you could limit man's wants it might be called 'labor saving,' but as there are no limits to his wants, the machinery really increases the power of production." That production is now dematerialized too. Because machines streamline the production of material goods from apples to automobiles, more and more first-world labor is concentrated in the production and management of information, the virtual substance running through all those satellites and cables. This is the promise behind the windows of Muybridge's birthplace, with their displays of software and hardware.

The Modoc center of the world was the center of a world a few hundred miles across, and just as the world once had an infinite number of local times, so it had countless centers—what we mean by a world rather than the world. Greenwich Time, the prime meridian down the river from Muybridge's birthplace, was the first attempt to make a world into the whole earth, though it was an abstruse effort noticed mostly by astronomers, nautical navigators, and the makers of schedules. California is the first center of the world that is coextensive with the planet, but it is the center of displacement, distraction, and a kind of transcendental disembodiment, as well as endless images of bodies, from Hollywood and even from the capital of the porn industry a few dozen miles north in the San Fernando Valley (and the huge online porn market). Which means that most of us do not live at the center of the world but look toward it, a center that, as Pascal once remarked, is everywhere and nowhere.

Now when I walk in downtown San Francisco, where Muybridge walked and photographed, it sometimes seems that all the tourists are videotaping and all the locals are talking on cell phones. That is to say, the tourists will only experience the place later; the locals have entered a disembodied private space in public, a space they share with those who are not there and that shuts out those who are. The stores that line the streets are, with every passing year, more and more likely to be outlets of international chains, so that this place becomes more and more indistinguishable from countless others. The pace at which people walk is unchanged, but signs, lights, music, machines, all turn the street into a dazzle of distractions. At the end of the twentieth century, Silicon Valley invaded San Francisco. South Park, where the Muybridges lived early in their marriage and Flora met Harry Larkyns, was nicknamed Multimedia Gulch as it changed from a quiet Filipino community to a buzzing, upscale center of networking, dot-com offices, and of the magazine *Wired,* which preaches the gospel of salvation through gadgets and accelerations. The whole South of Market area where Muybridge had long resided became the global capital of this new industry of online information and commerce, financed more often than not by the venture capitalists down the peninsula. But the venture capitalists there had financed other technologies too.

Mission Bay at the south end of South of Market was a real bay that had in the nineteenth century become a landfill and on the cusp of the twentieth the Southern Pacific train yard. At the end of the twentieth century ground was broken, ground that had been water, to build a huge biotechnology facility, for Stanford and Silicon Valley and Venture Capital Row had involved themselves with the microcosm of genes as well as the macrocosm of communications networks. The Catellus Corporation, a spinoff of Southern Pacific, is the real estate agency managing the transformation. It also represents SP's transformation from the nineteenth-century transmission of people and materials to the present-day transmission and manipulation of the microcosmic, of electrons and genes. The Central Pacific and the Southern Pacific were always about reach, about extending technology into new arenas to gain wealth and power, and genetic engineering extends the human reach into the genetic code of all life. The multimedia explosion, like Silicon Valley, was compared again and again to the gold rush, for the frenzy, the rush into the unknown, the uncertainty with which the daring could become billionaires or flops, the generation of huge new supplies of wealth and a brave new world to spend it in. Sometimes those who made the comparison remembered the dark side of the gold rush, the extermination of the Indians and the evisceration of the motherlode landscape, the greed and the stampedes. A bust followed the boom, but the changes are here to stay. The world seems run from Silicon Valley now, run by engineers whose decisions affect all of us, those engineers whose constant question is never why, but only how.

Not all the stories are so unsettling, though. Mark Hopkins's Nob Hill house, from which Muybridge photographed his great 360-degree panoramas, was given by his heir to the San Francisco Art Association, which had been headquartered on Pine Street when Muybridge was a member and sometimes a resident. (Up there where the Big Four once dwelt in splendor, the site of Hopkins's house is now the Mark Hopkins Hotel, next to the Stanford Arms Hotel, the Huntington Intercontinental Hotel, and the Crocker Parking Garage.) Out of the Hopkins-housed Art Association grew two institutions, the San Francisco Museum of Modern Art and the San Francisco Art Institute. The two institutions, one the second museum of modern art and the other for a while one of the preeminent art schools in the country, did much to foster a continuing cultural life on the West Coast. San Francisco was the center of several significant art movements from the 1940s on, but it never stopped being the capital of photography: the pictorialist movement that was soft-focus both literally and intellectually only really came to an end with the founding of the f64 group in San Francisco in 1932 by Imogen Cunningham, Edward Weston, Ansel Adams, and a few others, and Adams taught for years at the Art Institute. By then it was housed not on Nob but on Russian Hill, the other high point of San Francisco's central saddleback, a few blocks from where Philo T. Farnsworth invented television with the help of a loan from Crocker Bank, another Big Four spinoff.

In the 1970s the Art Institute's president found, behind the couch in the school library, a number of Muybridge's Yosemite mammoth plates, doubtless a legacy of the Hopkins era, and he sold them to buy the school's first video cameras for what became the influential Performance/Video department. Many students emerged from that department to make a mark, but two pieces by the professors who have been there almost from the beginning stick in my mind: Douglas Hall's *The Terrible Uncertainty of the Thing Described,* which with a Tesla coil throwing bolts of lightning and several video monitors replicates the disturbing sublimity of violent weather, and Paul Kos's *Chartres Bleu,* in which a tall stack of video monitors in the approximate form of a window in that Gothic cathedral display in accelerated time the changing light pouring through the stained glass, a piece that is like Hall's both ironic and iconic about the old world behind us, the pace and power of celestial forces we feel more seldom now. It is a study of the motion of the sun akin in some way to the panorama's study of the movement of light across the city, a test of whether the luminous spirituality of another age can come to us through electronic media. It suggests too that the technologies that surround us can be yoked to the service of the slow, the contemplative, the beautiful, as well as to the usual jumble of advertisement and information; it is the window one would want in Plato's Cave.

Muybridge pursued the transformation of bodies and places into representations, representations that in some ways fed that unslaked desire for landscape, geography, beauty, embodiment, and the life of the senses, but Stanford, who hammered the Golden Spike, pursued the annihilation of time and space without mercy, without misgivings, without deference to what might be lost, and this might be the difference between Hollywood and Silicon Valley. Hollywood would become the center of the world of movies, while Silicon Valley is the center of the world of information technology, and in the way these two institutions dominate the world one can say California is the center of the contemporary world, but of a world in which time and space have been annihilated, a world that is in some obscure way so disembodied, dislocated, and dematerialized that the very idea of a center is perplexing.

Muybridge and Stanford died far too soon to have any inkling of the high-speed world of electronic communication and information process-ing, but their own pursuits and desires prefigured it and laid some of the groundwork. This too is inscribed in the landscape. Stanford pursued speed in its most evident nineteenth-century forms: railroads and race-horses. Muybridge refined speed from a material to a visual phenomenon with the most high-speed photographs of his time. His birthplace, the house that is now a computer store, once dealt in grain grown locally and brought in on horse-drawn carts; his grandfather in the same town had moved at a predictable pace through a world in which human beings and their voices and knowledge were no faster than the animals and water and wind that surrounded them. There are infinite ways to measure what has been gained and what has been lost, and only one clear thing: the world is utterly changed.

■   ■   ■

CHRONOLOGY

(WITH EMPHASIS ON MUYBRIDGE'S CALIFORNIA YEARS)

1824

Leland Stanford born March 9.

1830

Muybridge born April 9.

1836

Younger brother, Thomas Muggeridge, born.

1843

March 5: Muybridge's father, John Muggeridge, buried.

1847

October 19: Muybridge's older brother John Muggeridge Jr. buried at the age of twenty.

1852

Possible date of Muybridge's emigration to the eastern United States.

Stanford emigrates to California.

1855

Muybridge arrives in San Francisco and enters the book business, remaining a bookseller until 1860.

1857

June 5: Muybridge advertises for sale illustrated editions of Shakespeare and a history of the United States, or rather offers to "complete the above works," published serially, by arrangement with the publishers.

September 11: *San Francisco Daily Bulletin* lists Robert Vance and Silas Selleck's photographs, and Muybridge's "large case of splendid books" at the Mechanic's Fair.

October 8: Muybridge advertises a pamphlet on the *Great Eastern* steamship being built in London.

1858

August 31: Muybridge shows steel engravings and illustrated books at Mechanics' Fair.

September 30: Muybridge advertises a *History of the Indian Mutiny and the Chinese Empire, the Chinese book in 40 parts, 50 cents per part, four engravings per part.*

December 13: Muybridge is selling "Baster's oil pictures" (prints).

1859

November 3: Muybridge elected a director of the Mercantile Library, which has 10,066 books.

December 27: Muybridge advertises "For Sale—AN AUSTRALIAN BLOOD HOUND and four PUPS. E. J. M. 163 Clay."

1860

February 1: News item says Muybridge at 115 Battery Street has some of Audubon's *Birds of America* plates; "Mr Muygridge is now receiving subscriptions for this new edition."

March 16: At 115 Battery Muybridge offers "money to loan in sums to suit."

May 15: Ad says he sold business and is leaving for Europe June 5.

June 12: Muybridge, apparently intending to return to San Francisco before long, advertises that he "shall feel happy in receiving any commissions my friends may entrust me with for the PURCHASE OF BOOKS ENGRAVINGS OR WORKS OF ART."

July 2: Muybridge departs on Butterfield Overland stage, with seven other passengers.

July 22: Apparent date of accident, in the cross timbers, due north of Fort Worth.

1861

San Francisco directory lists "Edw. and Thomas Muygridge" at 423 Washington, Thomas as agent of London Publishing Company.

Muybridge returns to New York City to pursue lawsuit against Butterfield Overland Mail Stage Company.

1866

Muybridge apparently returns to San Francisco and joins Silas Selleck in photo business. No listing in directory.

1867

San Francisco directory gives Muybridge's address as 415 Montgomery (gallery).

Muybridge photographs in Yosemite; the *Mariposa Gazette* of November 2 reports him as still there (as A. M. Maybridge).

1868

San Francisco directory: "Muybridge, Edward J., landscape photographer, 415 Montgomery, resides Oakland."

February 15: *Call* announces "20 Yosemite Views, $20, at Cosmopolitan Gallery of Photographic Art, 415 Montgomery Street."

April: *Philadelphia Photographer* reports of Muybridge's Yosemite photographs, "That this Society takes great pleasure in attesting their high appreciation of the artistic skill in the selection of these views, and the eminent talent evinced in their photographic reproduction."

May 14: Muybridge presents Yosemite prints to Mercantile Library.

July 29: General Halleck and staff set sail for Alaska in the steamship *Pacific*.

October 9: *Bulletin* reports, "Watkins lately photographed the mountain and river scenery of Oregon and Washington; and now Muygridge brings us Alaska in a portfolio of sun pictures that give a very favorable opinion of Greeley's 'Walrussia.'"

October 13: Muybridge's Alaska pictures are officially accepted by General Halleck. The general writes, "I have to acknowledge the receipt of copies of your photographs of forts and public buildings at Sitka and other military posts taken for use of War Department and also views of scenery in Alaska."

October 28: *Alta* reports, "Muybridge, the photographic artist who uses the pseudonym of Helios in his work, has published several photographic pictures of some of the worst injured buildings, which show the effects of the late earthquake [October 21] in this city."

November 19: *Bulletin* describes Muybridge's "excellent photographs of the Pacific Steamship *Colorado*."

December 5: *Bulletin:* Muybridge is selling his "views" at Ewing, 138 Montgomery Street, "opposite the Occidental Hotel."

1869

San Francisco directory: "Muybridge, Edward J., landscape photographer, 121 Montgomery, res. San Jose."

May: Muybridge publishes "A New Sky Shade" in *Philadelphia Photographer.*

Muybridge photographs Alcatraz Island, Black Point, the Cliff House, and Fort Point, around the bay and coast of San Francisco, according to John Martini.

1870

San Francisco directory: "Muybridge, Edward J., landscape photographer, 121 Montgomery."

January 31: *Bulletin* ad: "HELIOS'S FLYING STUDIO.—Private residences, ranches, animals, ships, warehouses, interiors, etc., photographed in a style hitherto unequaled on this coast for artistic treatment. Having the most complete apparatus in the United States, lenses adapted to every strength of light or variety of subject, and a wagon constructed for open air work, perfectly satisfaction is guaranteed. MUYBRIDGE, Nahl Brothers, 121 Montgomery St."

Muybridge photographs Goat Island (now Yerba Buena Island), halfway between Oakland and San Francisco, and submits prints to the army, where they are stamped "rec'd Mar. 5 1870."

May 25: *Bulletin* reports the cornerstone of the Mint laid; "a photographer with his flying studio was on hand."

May 30: Muybridge advertises Mint photos for sale in *Bulletin.*

September 1: *Bulletin* announces stereocards of Woodward's Gardens.

1871

San Francisco directory lists Muybridge at 12 Montgomery (gallery address) and "Stone, Flora Mrs. dwl. 6 Montgomery."

January 13: Muybridge proposes to photograph the lighthouses of the Pacific Coast. Letter to Colonel R. S. Williamson from Muybridge, proposing a salary of twenty dollars a day "during my absence from San Francisco upon any expedition connected with the objects required. I will agree to furnish you with two photographic prints, views of all the light houses upon this coast, and such other views as you may direct of other subjects, without extra charge."

January 26: William Henry Pettee and other members of the California Geological Survey visit Muybridge at lunchtime and find that his work "invites comparison with Watkins (or anybody else) in all respects excepting size of picture." Pettee writes to Whitney the next day, proposing Muybridge as part of a High Sierra photographic survey.

May 4: Muybridge's photographs of Point Reyes lighthouse sent to lighthouse board, according to John Martini.

May 20: Muybridge marries Flora Stone.

July 4: Muybridge photographs San Francisco's parade of the miners of '49 (two small prints, Bancroft library).

December 11: Muybridge may be in Arizona; the evidence is a photograph of the participants in a murder trial in possession of the Arizona Historical Society of Tucson, stamped "Edw. J. Muybridge, Photographic View Artist, 12 Montgomery St, San Francisco, Calif."

1872

San Francisco directory: "Muybridge, Edward J., landscape photographer, 12 Montgomery, dwl. 32 Fourth."

January 17: *Bulletin* reports that Albert Bierstadt on the 16th goes to a reception for the Art Association; "Also at the reception was the celebrated photographer Eadweard Muybridge," who exhibited there "some very effective views in the Russian River Valley."

February 22: Muybridge photographs the laying of the city hall cornerstone, and his photograph of the plans for the building is enclosed in the cornerstone.

April: Muybridge makes twenty-three glass negatives of Stanford Sacramento home, apparently at this time. As the Brandenburg album and glass plates show, he also photographed Occident and Stanford's horses at the racetrack, also apparently at this time.

April 26: *Sacramento Union* reports, "We had an opportunity of looking last evening at some very fine large-sized photographic negatives representing some of the most picturesque views of Yosemite Valley and other portions of our coast. They are the production of Mr. Edward J. Muybridge. . . . He is now in Sacramento." "Large-sized" must mean full-plate; Muybridge had not yet reentered Yosemite Valley to make his mammoth-plate pictures there.

May: Prospectus from Nahl's gallery says, "At the suggestion of several artists and patrons of Art, I propose devoting the approaching season to the production of a series of large-size photographic negatives, illustrating Yosemite and other grand picturesque portions of our coast." Subscribers include the eight directors of the San Francisco Art Association, Bierstadt, Nahl, Bradley and Rulofson, Crocker, and Thomas Bell.

June 19 or 20: Helen Hunt Jackson meets Muybridge and his mule train coming into the valley.

July 20: "Edw. Muybridge" and "Wm. Towne" sign in at Casa Nevada Hotel register in Little Yosemite Valley as "photographic artists" in same hand.

September: Probable time of Muybridge's meeting with King and Bierstadt in the high country.

September 8: Muybridge writes to L. Prang (chromolithographer in San Francisco), "I regret not having the pleasure of seeing you during your visit to the valley; upon my return from an excursion this morning Mr. Hutchings informed of your having left[?] for Sacramento. I believe it is within your knowledge I am now engaged in making a series of large size negatives at the instance and for the use of the San Francisco Art Association, Central and Union Pac RRs, and to which also about 150 gentlemen in San F have subscribed $100 each."

1873

San Francisco directory: "Muybridge, Edward J., 429 Montgomery, dw. 550 Howard."

April 7: *Alta* and *Bulletin* both announce the Yosemite pictures and the Occident photographs, the latter exclaiming, "E. J. Muybridge has completed a series of pictures of Yosemite, most of which are taken from points of view not heretofore used. The views were taken last year, the artist spending several months in the valley, and climbering [*sic*] to the best points of sight with his camera, often with great difficulty and danger. He has a series of eight hundred pictures, some of which present effects beyond any heretofore taken."

April 23: Muybridge passes through Sacramento en route to Lava Beds.

April 29: *Chronicle* reports that Muybridge has gone to the front.

May 8: *Yreka Union* reports, "Mr. Muybridge has taken, in all, some fifty remarkable views of the 'beds' and their vicinity, which will be given to the San Francisco public in a few days through the house of Bradley and Rulofson."

May 10: According to the *Chronicle,* "Captain Lydecker, of the topographical engineers, with his assistants, Mr. Muybridge, the celebrated photographer, and J. W. Ward, topographical draughtsman, will start for San Francisco today."

September: Muybridge photographs at Point Bonita on the north side of the Golden Gate, including views of the stranded ship *Costa Rica,* which went aground at Point Diablo here in September 1873. He seems to have photographed San Quentin Prison at this time as well.

Muybridge's and Timothy O'Sullivan's work shown at the Vienna Exposition, each receiving the Medal of Progress.

1874

San Francisco directory gives Muybridge's address as 112 Fourth.

April 16: Florado Helios Muybridge born.

April 19: Susannah Smith Muggeridge dies, leaving fifty pounds to Edward, twenty to a niece, and the remainder to Thomas Smith Muggeridge of Walla Walla.

May: The *Berkeleyan* reports, "Muybridge spent a couple of days recently taking pictures of the University buildings, and the various rooms in them."

June: According to the *Daily Post*, "In June 1874, as Muybridge contemplated a professional tour through Central America, he sent his wife to Portland, Oregon, to visit an aunt and uncle. Muybridge was delayed in starting on his intended trip."

October 17: Muybridge murders Larkyns. *Sacramento Record* (October 20) reports, "In June last Mr. Muybridge's photographic business made a long tour in the interior necessary. He gave his wife the choice of accompanying him or going to Mrs. Stump, an aunt living in Portland, Oregon" (where, the story adds, she received Larkyns's letters from Calistoga).

December 14: Flora files for divorce on the grounds of extreme cruelty, and alimony is requested.

December 21: *Chronicle* publishes extensive interview with Muybridge.

1875

No entry in directory.

February 6: Muybridge found not guilty.

February 19: Muybridge sets sail for Central America, "sponsored" by the Pacific Mail Steamship Company (Hendricks says February 27).

March 16: *Panama Star:* "We are pleased to welcome to this city Mr. Muybridge, who is well known in the art world for the celebrated photographs he has taken of almost every place in California."

May 1: Muybridge goes to Guatemala.

May 1: *Chronicle* headline: "Flora Muybridge Again She Sues for Divorce on Stronger Grounds."

July 18: Flora Muybridge dies.

November 11: Muybridge photographs the San Francisco Assessors Building under construction, according to date on print in San Francisco Public Library.

1876

San Francisco directory: "Muybridge, Edward J. Photographer, dwl. 613 Pine."

February: *Philadelphia Photographer*, reporting on meeting of January 7, 1876: "A recess was then taken of the Photographic Art Society of the Pacific, during which a number of Panama, Alaska, Yosemite and other views were exhibited by means of an oxyhydrogen lantern, which produced an effect at once beautiful and surprising. The delicacy of tone and the fineness of finish being remarkable considering the number of times the views were magnified. The plates were of two kinds—the handsomest being those taken by the 'dry tannin' process. Those made by wet collodion were darker and not so clear in outline." Rulofson and his assistant, Mr. Jones, showed these slides, which are clearly Muybridge's; the article continues, "The Secretary was instructed to send an invitation to Mr. Muybridge to attend next meeting."

May: *Anthony's Photographic Bulletin:* "Muybridge's Catalogue of American and South America Views were duly acknowledged."

May 25: Muybridge writes to Mrs. W. W. Pendegast of Napa, "Your kind note afforded me much happiness in its perusal, although I feel I am entirely undeserving of the thanks you so kindly proffer me. It is I who should and do thank you for permitting me to offer you so slight an acknowledgement of my lasting appreciation of the noble and disinterested generosity shown me by your late husband when I was bowed down by grief and crushed with broken pride. . . . yours Faithfully, Edw Muybridge."

August 23: *Bulletin* on the Mechanics' Institute Fair: "An exhibit, labelled 'Muybridge, official photographer of the U.S. Government (to the San Francisco Industrial Exposition),' contains thirty-two photographic illustrations of Central American scenery."

September 16: Florado Muybridge entered in the Protestant Orphan Asylum, according to July 24, 1961, letter from California State Library to Gordon Hendricks; "upon application of his father," says the original record there.

December: Muybridge inscribes a dedication to Mrs. Pendegast on his photographic album *Pacific Coast of Central America and Mexico; the Isthmus of Panama; Guatemala; and the Cultivation of Coffee.*

"In 1876 and early 1877 Muybridge put his skill in this line at the service of the painter Norton Bush, copying the twenty-one paintings Bush had produced from sketches made in Peru in 1875."

1877

San Francisco directory: "Muybridge, Edward J. landscape photographer office 626 Clay."

June–July: Muybridge makes his first 360-degree panoramas from the Hopkins turret.

August 13: *Bulletin* announces "Panorama of San Francisco."

August 2: *Alta* announces the "Key to the Panorama of San Francisco," published by Morse. "The key is in itself a good picture of the city, though far inferior in clearness to the original panoramic picture, and the two together . . . will be a valuable record for the future of the architecture of San Francisco in 1875."

August 3: *Alta* headline, "'Occident' Photographed at Full Speed." The *San Francisco Daily Evening News* reports, "Mr Muybridge, the well known photographic artist, has executed a feat in his art which has never before been attempted. He succeeded last July in taking Occident while trotting at the rate of a mile in 2 minutes and 27 seconds. The negative was exposed for less than one-thousandth part of a second, yet the positive printed form is perfect."

August 22: *Bulletin* "Mosaics" column declares, "THAT MARVELOUS PANORAMA which Muybridge has taken, is creating a great furore among visitors. It is the most comprehensive and beautiful picture of San Francisco ever taken. Morse has it, at 417 Montgomery Street." On the 25th the *Bulletin* again praises "the great whirling, driving, bustling city of San Francisco" that "may now be had at Morse's."

November: Muybridge proposes microfilming San Jose's records.

1878

San Francisco directory: Muybridge, Edward J. landscape and animal photographer, G. D. Morse, dwl. SW cor Cal and Mont."

April 10: Muybridge photographs the new California Street Railroad (aka the cable car, built by Stanford, picture in Oakland Museum).

May 18: *Bulletin* reports that "this evening E. J. Muybridge will give a second exhibition of illuminated photographs of the Mexican Coast, Central America and the Isthmus of Panama, at the rooms of the Art Association Exhibition [and elsewhere]. They are enlarged by the magic lantern to about sixteen feet square and are very striking representations of some of the most notable scenery. Next to an actual visit to these countries, these representations will be the most satisfactory."

June 17: Muybridge applies for a patent on his "method and apparatus for photographing objects in motion."

July 9: *Chronicle:* "Mr. Muybridge gave yesterday evening at the Art Association rooms the first of a series of lectures, illustrating by instantaneous photography the stride of a horse. The attendance was not as large as might have been expected, considering the unique manner in which the subject was treated and the ability with which the illustrations were described."

July 18: *Call:* "In the rooms of the Art Association, last evening, Mr. Muybridge entertained a large audience of ladies and gentlemen several hours with photographic views. He first exhibited the different positions of walking, trotting, cantering, galloping, and running horses. . . . After an elaborate exhibition of his 'horse pictures,' Mr. Muybridge gave some very interesting views taken in Central and South America."

August 3: *Alta* and *Bulletin* both report on the Stanford-Muybridge motion-studies project.

August 28: *Bulletin* reports that Muybridge is exhibiting the slides at the Mechanics' Institute Fair.

September 18: *Sacramento Bee* and *Record Union* report that Muybridge is in town to show "by the aid of the steropticon and oxy-calcium light sixty illuminated photographs of life size, showing the action of the horse and his various gaits."

October 19: *Scientific American* article on motion studies.

December 14: *La Nature* (Paris) publishes article on motion studies.

1879

March 4: Muybridge applies for two patents.

March 21: *Watsonville Transcript* reports, "The celebrated photographer Muybridge, who probably stands at the head of his profession in the world, was in town this week. He came here to make views of James M. Rodgers' residence and yesterday he made some views of the town from the Watsonville water company's tank, of the schoolhouses and some other buildings. Mr. Muybridge was for years the government photographer of the United States."

April 14: Muybridge to the Mechanics' Institute: "As I am about sending the negatives to Europe; and in consequence of the great expense attending their production, there being little probability of any other series ever being made, I thought it advisable to renew my offer, with the proviso that instead of $200 cash the price of the entire series—I will accept $100—and a life membership. . . . Edw. Muybridge."

August: Muybridge begins photographing humans in motion, perhaps prompted by Eakins.

1880

January 11: Muybridge photographs eclipse.

January 16: Muybridge lectures in Stanford Ballroom.

March 27: *California Spirit of the Times* reports on Stanford's stables and Muybridge's "zoogyroscope."

May: Muybridge's motion-picture exhibitions in San Francisco.

May 8: *California Spirit of the Times* article on zoopraxiscope states, "The grand discovery of an eye which would catch and a plate which would register the most evanescent of movements, has enabled us to discover what was concealed before, and if we fail to avail ourselves of the teachings of this superhuman professor, it will be a confession of willful perversity and an avowal of stupid, mulish ignorance."

May 15: Muybridge delivers album of animals in motion to Stanford.

June 5: *Scientific American* article on Muybridge.

July: Muybridge files a patent for "Picture-Feeding Device for Magic Lanterns"; August, files for "Method of and Apparatus for Photographing Changing or Moving Object"; September, applies for reissue of "Method and Apparatus."

1881

May: *The Attitudes of Animals in Motion* copyrighted.

May 30: Muybridge signs a receipt for $2,000 from Stanford.

August: Muybridge offers for sale more than thirty lenses, and travels to Europe.

September 26: Exhibition at Marey's house.

November 26: Exhibition at Meissonier's house.

1882

February: Muybridge leaves for London.

March 13: Muybridge lectures to Royal Institution; following night Muybridge lectures to Royal Academy.

April 20: *La Nature* publishes Stillman review.

May 30: Muybridge writes to Marey, asking for his collaboration.

June: Muybridge returns to United States.

September 14: Muybridge files suit against Stanford.

1883

August: Muybridge files suit against *Horse in Motion* publishers.

September 3: Muybridge to William Pepper, Provost, University of Pennsylvania, "I received your kind letter of the 9th Aug. yesterday only, it having been delayed in New York in consequence of the absence of Mr Bradford and finally reached here during my absence in Maine. I will now merely thank you for having consummated the arrangements for the advance of the $5000 I estimate as necessary to complete the photographic investigations of the 'Attitudes of Animals in Motion' and will reserve for a more fitting opportunity my acknowledgement of your appreciation of the value of the proposed work. . . . Eadweard Muybridge."

1884

Muybridge begins University of Pennsylvania work, making about 30,000 photographs by 1886.

1885

Suit against Stanford dismissed.

1887

November 11: Muybridge writes, "My Dear Sir, It affords me great pleasure to inform you that the investigation of the consecutive phases of animal movements which for four years I have been conducting at the University of Pennsylvania is completed; the printing plates are in the hands of the printer, and the work, under the title of *Animal Locomotion,* is in process of publication."

1888

February 25: Muybridge lectures in Orange, New Jersey.

February 27: Muybridge visits Edison.

1892

February 11: Muybridge writes to President Jordan of Stanford on University of Pennsylvania letterhead inscribed *Eadweard Muybridge,* "I have recovered the position—at least in

reputation—from which I was displaced by the publication of 'the Horse in Motion by J D B Stillman'; and have completed under the auspices of this university a comparatively exhaustive investigation of animal movements, and I avail myself of the opportunity to send you two pamphlets on the subject. . . . I have recently seen both Mr. and Mrs. Stanford."

April 5: Palace Hotel, San Francisco, letterhead, Muybridge to Jordan, "A conversation which I this morning had with one of the Trustees of your University has led me to question the advisability of my coming to Palo Alto prepared to give a Lecture. . . . Dr. Harkness has done me the honor to invite me to lecture at the Academy of Sciences, which I have accepted with the understanding that your university has the prior claim."

1893
Muybridge at World's Columbian Exposition, Chicago.

1894
Muybridge returns to England.

1904
May 8: Muybridge dies in Kingston.

NOTES

ABBREVIATIONS

Alta = *Alta California,* San Francisco newspaper.

Bradley and Rulofson Catalog = Eadweard Muybridge, *Catalogue of Photographic Views Illustrating the Yosemite, Mammoth Trees, Geyser Springs, and Other Remarkable and Interesting Scenery of the Far West* (San Francisco: Bradley and Rulofson Gallery of Portrait and Landscape Photographic Art, 1873). Original and microfilm in Bancroft Library.

Bulletin = *San Francisco Daily Evening Bulletin.*

Chronicle = *San Francisco Chronicle.*

CHSQ = *California Historical Society Quarterly.*

Examiner = *San Francisco Examiner.*

Haas = Robert Barlett Haas, *Muybridge: Man in Motion* (Berkeley and Los Angeles: University of California Press, 1976).

Haas Papers = Robert Bartlett Haas's papers on Muybridge, Kingston-upon-Thames Local History Room, Surrey, England.

Hendricks = Gordon Hendricks, *Eadweard Muybridge: Father of the Motion Picture* (New York: Viking, 1975).

Huntington Papers = Reels 11 and 12 of Collis P. Huntington Papers, Syracuse University, consisting of material from Muybridge's lawsuit against Stanford, primarily statements for the defense by Stanford's and the railroad's employees. Used by permission.

Kingston Scrapbook = Muybridge's large scrapbook of clippings and publicity material from the late 1860s on, now at the Local History Room, Kingston-upon-Thames. A microfilm copy is at Bancroft Library, Berkeley.

Lone Mountain Albums = Extensive albums at Bancroft Library that were likely Muybridge's own, containing the majority of his stereoscope images and many full- and half-plate images from 1867 to the mid-1870s.

Mozley = Anita Ventura Mozley, with Robert Haas and Francoise Forster-Hahn, *Eadweard Muybridge: The Stanford Years, 1872–1882* (Stanford, Calif.: Stanford University Museum of Art, 1972).

1. THE ANNIHILATION OF TIME AND SPACE

page 3. Edward James Muybridge: Early on, someone asserted that Muybridge changed his name all at once upon emigrating in the 1850s, and this fiction has routinely been repeated since. Robert Haas and Gordon Hendricks correctly point out that Muggeridge became Muygridge in the 1850s, and only in the 1860s Muybridge, but for unknown reasons they subscribe to the notion that he became Eadweard at the same time he became Muygridge (sometimes even putting "sic" next to a plethora of documents that give the photographer's name as Edward). Court documents, newspaper and magazine articles, Muybridge's own applications for patents, and letters in his own hand through the end of the 1870s refer to him as Edward, Edw., or E. J.; in Central America in 1875 he called himself, with his usual flourish, Eduardo Santiago Muybridge. Neither in signatures nor in advertisements and court documents does Eadweard appear until after 1881. He often chose to go by his surname alone—and having made it up himself, it was a sufficient distinction. Only Anita Ventura Mozley notes, in her introduction to the Dover *Muybridge's Complete Human and Animal Locomotion,* that Muybridge did not deploy the name Eadweard until then; she pinpoints it to his March 1882 presentation before the Prince of Wales in London. But in his 1883 lawsuit against Stanford and an 1883 patent he is still Edward, though the Anglo-Saxon spelling of the name crops up regularly thereafter and appears on his letterhead by the end of the decade and his later publications. For a certainty, he was an Edward while he was a Californian, and he was likely an Eadweard by the time he was a Pennsylvanian.

page 4. "time lost or spent": Tarkovsky, in Ian Christie, *The Last Machine: Cinema and the Birth of the Modern World* (London: BBC Educational Developments, 1994), 12.

page 6. like a bullet shot through a book: This is a metaphor drawn from another photographer, Richard Misrach, whose Playboys series of photographs shows *Playboy* magazines used for target practice in the desert. Misrach has commented that in shooting at the women on the covers, the gunman or -men pierced the entire culture: his pictures show punctured landscapes, male celebrities, and more women.

page 7. An ancient market town: Kingston details based on visit to the sites, Haas and Hendricks accounts, and information from Kingston-upon-Thames Local History Room.

page 7. Muybridge's father, John Muggeridge: Family details from letters from Norma Selfe in New South Wales to Robert Haas in the 1960s, now at the Kingston-upon-Thames Local History Room with the rest of Haas's extant Muybridge papers. Much of Selfe's correspondence consists of her hand-copied extracts from documents by Muybridge's cousin Maybanke Susannah Anderson.

page 8. "drove in his gig to London": Anderson, in manuscript copied out by Selfe.

page 9. "The engine . . . set off": Frances Ann Kemble, *Records of a Girlhood* (New York: Henry Holt, 1879), 283.

page 9. Passengers found the landscape out the train windows blurred: Much of the background on the transformative experience of the railroad comes from Wolfgang Schivelbusch's brilliant *The Railway Journey: The Industrialization of Time and Space in the Nineteenth Century* (Berkeley and Los Angeles: University of California Press, 1986).

page 9. "We traveled at least": Ulysses S. Grant, in Stephen Ambrose, *Nothing Like It in the World: The Men Who Built the Transcontinental Railroad* (New York: Simon and Schuster, 2000), 85.

page 9. "frightened to death": Kemble, *Records of a Girlhood,* 298.

page 10. "the first mesh": Ibid., 278.

page 10. "Not only is distance": Emerson in John F. Kasson, *Civilizing the Machine* (New York: Grossman, 1976), 120.

page 11. "the annihilation of time and space": See Leo Marx, *The Machine in the Garden* (New York: Oxford University Press, 1964), 194: "No stock phrase in the entire lexicon of progress appears more often than the 'annihilation of space and time,' borrowed from one of Pope's relatively obscure poems ('Ye Gods! annihilate but space and time, / And make two lovers happy')."

page 12. "I felt as if": Kemble, *Records of a Girlhood,* 284.

page 13. "The periods which to our narrow": Scrope, in Claude C. Albritten Jr., *The Abyss of Time* (San Francisco: Freeman, Cooper, 1980), 153.

page 16. "Objects moving": Morse, in Michel Frizot, *A New History of Photography* (Cologne: Koneman, 1998), 28.

page 17. "Capital must on the one side": Karl Marx, *Grundrisse: Foundations of the Critique of Political Economy* (New York: Penguin, 1973), 539–40.

page 19. "The Nightingale": Hans Christian Andersen, translated by Zui Har'El, found at http://HCA.gilead.org.il/nighting.html.

page 20. "The Celestial Railroad": In Marx, *Machine in the Garden,* 27.

page 21. Paris's July Revolution of 1830: Walter Benjamin, "Theses on the Philosophy of History," in *Illuminations* (New York: Schocken, 1968), 262.

page 21. "Ingenious philosophers": George Eliot, *Adam Bede* (New York: Penguin, 1980), 557.

page 21. "Form is henceforth divorced": Holmes, in "The Stereoscope and the Stereograph," *Atlantic Monthly,* June 1859, 747.

2. THE MAN WITH THE CLOUDY SKIES

page 27. "My mother's sister": Maybanke Susannah Anderson, 1915, transcribed by Norma Selfe, Haas papers.

page 27. "while living in New Orleans": Letter to the *Standard* (an English newspaper), March 28, 1902, in Kingston Scrapbook.

page 28. "The attention of the writer was first directed to the soaring of birds": Muybridge, *Animals in Motion* (1898; reprint, New York: Dover, 1957), 69.

page 28. Silas Selleck recalled: *Sacramento Union,* Feb. 5, 1875. Selleck "knew Muybridge for 26 or 27 years, knew him in New York City; met in California in the Autumn of 1855; was intimate until his departure for Europe in 1860."

page 28. an athletic young man with hooded eyes: Photograph reproduced in Haas, facing page 1.

page 30. In 1851 Yosemite Valley was invaded: This subject is dealt with at great length in my book *Savage Dreams: A Journey into the Landscape Wars of the American West* (San Francisco: Sierra Club Books, 1994), which is itself based to a considerable extent on Lafayette Bunnell's firsthand account of that invasion, *The Discovery of the Yosemite and the Indian War of 1851 that Led to that Event.*

page 30. By 1856 the brand-new city had forty bookstores. Figures on bookstores from Nancy S. Peters, *Literary San Francisco* (New York: Harper and Row, 1980); other material from J. S. Hittell, *History of San Francisco and Incidentally of the State of California* (San Francisco: A. L. Bancroft, 1878).

page 30. saloons (537 by 1853, in one count): Doris Muscatine, *Old San Francisco: The Biography of a City from Early Days to the Earthquake* (New York: Putnam, 1975), 340.

page 30. "In California, Catholic and Protestant": Muscatine, *Old San Francisco,* 344, quoting B. E. Lloyd's *Lights and Shades in San Francisco,* published in 1876.

page 33. "brilliantly illuminated Railroad Saloon": *Daily Evening Bulletin,* June 22, 1856, describes the saloon, "with Nahl's great gallery of paintings and ice cream, strawberries and cream, at 12 cents per plate."

page 33. "Oh, what was your name in the States?": Carey McWilliams, *California: The Great Exception* (1949; reprint, Berkeley and Los Angeles: University of California Press, 1999), 72.

page 34. officially relocated the foothills of the Sierra Nevada: See David Haward Bain, *Empire Express* (New York: Viking, 1999), 136–37. Re naming, see the *Sacramento Daily Record,* June 5, 1872, writing with the era's characteristic ebullient exaggeration about Stanford: "Slow and fast horses are named after him, the Big Trees echo his name to the peaks of the Nevadas; hot, cold, mineral and mud springs bubble it up. . . . His name is the 'great Whangdoodle' to many newspapers and politicians; dogs, cats, saloons and hotels bear it, and we hardly know how the gentleman retains any part of his name, it has been so often used."

page 34. "represented as a great hero": Carson, *Kit Carson's Autobiography,* ed. Milo Milten Quaife (Lincoln: University of Nebraska Press, 1966), 135.

page 35. "Emmet Dalton, the last surviving member of the Dalton Gang": Christopher Frayling, *Spaghetti Westerns* (New York: Routledge and Kegan Paul, 1981), 74.

page 36. In the photograph Muybridge made of Norton: Lone Mountain Albums.

page 36. recycled into greenhouse plates: The information on Rulofson and Joaquin Miller is given in Robert Bartlett Haas, "William Herman Rulofson: Pioneer Daguerreotypist and Photographic Educator," *CHSQ,* Dec. 1955. In the *Bulletin,* May 14, 1869, the San Francisco photographer and photodealer William Shew announced that he was going to destroy 25,000 negatives in inventory and invited the public to come and get their portraits by July 1, before he did so. Of course negatives were often destroyed by accident— burned by fire, broken in transit. . . .

page 37. *Vernon Gallery of British Art:* In ad from the *Bulletin,* July 21, 1859.

page 37. "a gentleman well qualified": *Bulletin,* April 28, 1856.

page 37. elected a director of the Mercantile Library: *Bulletin,* Nov. 3, 1859. He advertised wolfhound puppies for sale in the *Bulletin* on Dec. 27, 1859, and money to lend on March 1, 1860.

page 38. "The stage left Mountain Station": *Bulletin,* Aug. 7, 1860.

page 38. "I left California July, 1860": *Daily Evening Post,* Feb. 6, 1875; *Napa Valley Register,* Feb. 5, 1875, reports that a Mr. Gray, a music dealer and friend of Muybridge's, took over his store. The discrepancy—the *Bulletin* reported one person killed, Muybridge two—may signify a death that was not immediate.

page 38. "physician named Gull": William Gull came to attention for two other things: he was the first to diagnose and name anorexia nervosa, and he is sometimes suspected of having been Jack the Ripper. The first is fact; the second is a stretchy bit of speculation explored most extensively in Melvyn Fairclough, *The Ripper and the Royals* (London: Duckworth, 1991).

page 39. a strong case that Muybridge suffered injury: Arthur Shimamura writes, in an unpublished manuscript, "Muybridge's head injury likely contributed to his profound emotional outbursts. His failure to regulate and control his emotions strongly suggests orbitofrontal damage. As such, it is probable that Muybridge's emotional instability contributed to the act of murdering Harry Larkyns. Of course, not all patients with orbitofrontal damage resort to such drastic actions. However, aggressive behavior and impulsivity are common symptoms. Third, it is interesting to speculate that Muybridge's risk-taking behavior, a symptom of orbitofrontal damage, led him to accept certain assignments (e.g., Central America, Alaska) or take photographs in precarious situations that may have seemed quite risky to others. Fourth, another symptom associated with orbitofrontal abnormality is obsessive-compulsive disorder. . . . It is interesting to speculate whether his injury actually enhanced his creative abilities." In *Woman: An Intimate Geography* (New York: Random House, 1999), 282, Natalie Angier recounts the history of "Rebecca," who four years after a severe head injury "began experiencing seizures, blackouts, and episodes of déjà vu. She turned irritable and hypergraphic, writing lengthy poems and philosophical musings." She also became violent. Also see "Damaged Brains and the Death Penalty," *New York Times,* July 21, 2001: "No one suggests that abuse or brain damage makes a murderer, but Dr. Lewis says that while most damaged people do not turn into killers, almost every killer is a damaged person. She concludes that most murderers are shaped by the combination of damage to the brain, particularly to the frontal lobes, which control aggression and impulsiveness, and the even more complex damage visited by repeated, violent child abuse."

page 39. according to the testimony of Muybridge's friends: *Napa Daily Register,* Feb. 5, 1875.

page 39. "on business that may detain me some months": letter of Aug. 17, 1861, quoted by Norma C. Selfe to Robert Haas, Haas, 10.

page 39. printing device and a proposal for a washing machine: Haas, 10 (British patent 2,352 of 1860: "An improved method of and apparatus for plate printing," and British patent 1,914 of 1861: "Machinery or apparatus for washing clothes and other textile articles").

page 40. Whether or not photography was an art: This debate continues to this day, most notably in the art historian Rosalind Krauss's essay, "Photography's Discursive Spaces," in *The Originality of the Avant-Garde and Other Modernist Myths* (Cambridge: MIT Press, 1986). Krauss objects to the recontextualization as art of the USGS photographers' work made as scientific documentation. She doesn't mention Muybridge or Watkins, who were clearly asserting at least their large photographs as art, shown in galleries and expositions, sold for display in the home or for collection in parlor albums. But the boundaries between art, science, education, and entertainment were blurry in that era of commercial speaking tours, chautauquas, popular reading in the sciences, celebrity preachers, and so on.

page 40. "Helios's Flying Studio": For example, *Bulletin,* April 22, 1868, ad read, "HELIOS is prepared to photograph private residences, animals, or views in the city or any part of the coast."

page 41. twenty-by-twenty-four-inch glass-plate negatives: According to the prospectus issued from Nahl's Gallery in May 1872, "The size of my proposed negatives will be 20 x 24 inches, and the prints about 18 x 22" (quoted in Mozley, 40). In both the Yosemite mammoth plates and the 1878 panorama, cropping the edge of the image may have allowed him to refine the composition and, in the panorama, ensure that the images meshed smoothly.

page 41. "The shutting out of surrounding objects": Oliver Wendell Holmes, "Sun-Painting and Sun-Sculptures," *Atlantic Monthly,* July 1861, 15.

page 42. "balustrades of new designs": Ad in the *Photographic Times,* 1870s.

page 42. photograph of Emperor Norton: Muybridge photographed Norton as part of the city's distinguishing landmarks. In Bradley and Rulofson's 56-page catalog of Muybridge's work in 1873, "Norton, Emperor of the United States" is stereoscopic view #676, between "Mission Hills, from the City Gardens" and "Military Exercises on Goat Island."

page 42. Lawrence and Houseworth was advertising over a thousand stereoscope views; see Nov. 1866 ad reproduced in Peter Palmquist, *Lawrence & Houseworth/Thomas Houseworth & Co.: A Unique View of the West, 1860–1886* (Columbus, Ohio: National Stereoscope Association, 1980).

page 44. "refinement of thought": Beecher and Stowe, *The American Woman's Home* (New York, 1869), 91.

page 44. Two hundred and forty tourists: Statistics in Hittell, *Yosemite: Its Wonders and Its Beauties* (San Francisco: H. H. Bancroft, 1868), 36.

page 45. "the first body of work to systematically present": Weston J. Naef, *Era of Exploration: The Rise of Landscape Photography in the American West, 1860–1885* (Buffalo, N.Y.: Albright-Knox Art Gallery, 1975), 79.

page 46. He began with 100 half-plate: Muybridge's half-plate Yosemite pictures of 1867 are rare; the largest collection is probably the *Sun Pictures of the Yosemite* album at Eastman House in Rochester, a scrapbook of images by Muybridge and Weed, mingled indiscriminately.

page 46. "A. M. Maybridge of San Francisco is taking photographs of Yo Semite Valley": *Mariposa Gazette,* Nov. 2, 1867.

page 46. "views of our world-renowned": Flyer in Kingston Scrapbook, dated February 1868 and issued from Selleck's Cosmopolitan Gallery at 415 Montgomery Street. The announcement goes on to mention some of the photographers buying sets and mentions the price: $20 for the set of twenty. A later advertisement mentions one hundred of the large-plate prints; the set of twenty may have been only a selection.

page 47. "just such cloud effects as we see in nature": *San Francisco Call,* Feb. 17, 1868.

page 47. "Mr. Muybridge's pictures": Helen Hunt (later Helen Hunt Jackson, the name she is principally known under), page 8 of Kingston Scrapbook, hand-inscribed "originally published in a Boston newspaper in 1872." Later published in shortened version as *Bits of Travel.* Though she wrote as Muybridge was on the verge of revisiting Yosemite, it was the 1867 work she saw and described.

page 47. "tolerated more darkness": Palmquist in conversation with the author, January 2002; Palmquist also explained technical details and pointed out the abundance of clouds in the engravings Muybridge would have been familiar with.

page 49. "sky shade": Muybridge's technical account of the workings of the sky shade appears in the May 1869 edition of the *Philadelphia Photographer* and is reproduced in Mozley. In the *Philadelphia Photographer,* he also gave a description of his darkcloth for draping himself in while looking at the camera's ground glass, and it is a good example of his ingenuity and constant desire to improve the technology: "I prefer," he wrote, "a draw-shutter to my plate-holder that comes entirely out, and before adopting my present cloth, was frequently troubled with lite-struck plates. It is large, of course, covering the camera with about three feet drop from the bottom all around, and covered with white cotton outside. On one side (the right) I have an attachment like the sleeve to a coat, so fashioned, with an opening at the bottom large enough to insert the hand; the cloth being fastened under the camera, I draw out the plate-holder as it may be called, and let it hang down out of the way until the exposure is complete; you will readily see the light has no chance of getting to the plate while the shutter is being withdrawn. The white covering is a great protection, keeping both the head and camera cool."

page 52. a commission to go to Alaska with General Henry W. Halleck: An unpublished 2001 report by John Martini for the Golden Gate National Recreation Area of the National Park Service discusses Muybridge's government work in detail: "As part of this study, the author searched the National Archives for any special authorizations, letters, or contracts granting Muybridge admission to these posts. Special attention was paid to the records of the Adjutant General's Office (AGO), the records of Quartermaster General's office (OQMC), the records of the Office of the Chief of Engineers (OCE), and correspondence of the Department of California. If the military granted Muybridge any special clearances or favors, the documentation has not survived. It appears instead that Muybridge used his reputation following the Alaska expedition—and possibly his personal relationship with General Henry Halleck—as an informal carte blanche to photograph the various posts. Based upon copyright dates printed on stereograph cards, many of the photographs were taken shortly after the Alaska expedition when Muybridge's credibility with the Army would have been at its height."

page 52. "These views": Halleck, Oct. 1868, in Martini report.

3. LESSONS OF THE GOLDEN SPIKE

page 57. The photograph by A. J. Russell: This picture and its sister photographs are reproduced in Bain, *Empire Express,* Naef, *Age of Exploration,* and many other books. *CSHQ,* June and Sept. 1957, reports that the Chinese workers were grading the site, laying the rails, driving the spikes, and bolting the fishplates at 10:30 A.M., leaving only the last spike to be driven. Since the rails were fully functional without this one bolt, an alternate history could have anonymous Chinese men linking the rails that would connect Atlantic and Pacific. The event had been scheduled for May 8, but UP labor trouble delayed it two days.

page 58. sledgehammer . . . that had been wired: The sledgehammer become telegraph key is described in Michael O'Malley, *Keeping Watch: A History of American Time* (New York: Viking, 1990); Bain, *Empire Express;* and J. N. Bowman, "Driving the Last Spike," *CHSQ,* June and Sept. 1957, among other places. A popular story has it that Stanford ineptly missed his mark and the telegraphers had to patch through the signal, but even his most amusing detractor, Oscar Lewis in *The Big Four* (1938; reprint, New York: Ballantine, 1971), mentions that Stanford had spent much of his youth chopping wood—at one point his father got a contract with the railroad for 2,600 cords of wood and put his sons to work providing it (116, Comstock Edition). A man who had chopped so much wood could probably manage to hit a golden spike. The *CHSQ* account says that both Stanford and Durant missed their first strokes but succeeded afterward.

page 58. first live national media event: Details of the national reach of the celebration are from Bain, *Empire Express,* and O'Malley, *Keeping Watch.*

page 58. "a triumph bloodless, deathless": Oscar Lewis, *This Was San Francisco* (New York: David McKay, 1962), 165.

page 60. "Time exactly obtained and kept": Samuel Langley, "The Electric Time Service," *Harper's New Monthly Magazine,* April 1878, 665. O'Malley gives details of his time service, and O'Malley and Derek Howe, in *Greenwich Time and the Discovery of the Longitude* (New York: Oxford University Press, 1980), give information on Charles Ferdinand Dowd's proposal for standardized time.

page 61. John Smith and his clocks: Maybelle Anderson, Haas files.

page 61. "I watch the passage": Thoreau, *Walden* (New York: Penguin, 1983), 162–63

page 62. a stray party of soldiers seeking a Paiute: Bain, *Empire Express;* the 1863 Treaty of Ruby Valley is reproduced in many places, including the Western Shoshone Defense Project Web site.

page 62. "Claiming to own most, if not all, of the Territory": Bureau of Indian Affairs, *Annual Report,* 1872, 45.

page 62. "No interruption . . . will be tolerated": W. T. Sherman, in Bain, *Empire Express,* 361.

page 64. driven the Lakota south and west: The centuries of change in Lakota location and activity before the railroad are documented in Robert W. Lawson, *Red Cloud: Warrior-Statesman of the Lakota Sioux* (Norman: University of Oklahoma Press, 1997); Donald Worster, *Under Western Skies: Nature and History in the American Landscape* (New York: Oxford University Press, 1992); and Andrew C. Isenberg, *The Destruction of the Bison* (Cambridge: Cambridge University Press, 2000).

page 64. "If you have horses everything will be changed": Isenberg, *Destruction,* 41.

page 64. "The building of the Union Pacific Railroad has driven the buffalo": Ibid., 128

page 65. a train once ran for 120 miles: Angie Debo, *A History of the Indians of the United States* (Norman: University of Oklahoma Press, 1970), 213.

page 65. number of hides shipped east on the railroads: Isenberg, *Destruction,* 134, 136.

page 66. the biggest corporations of their time: See William G. Roy, *Socializing Capital: The Rise of the Large Industrial Corporation* (Princeton, N.J.: Princeton University Press, 1997), particularly the chapter "Railroads: The Corporation's Institutional Wellspring"; or Page Smith, *The Rise of Industrial America: A People's History of the Post-Reconstruction Era* (New York: McGraw-Hill, 1984), for example, ix: "When Charles Francis Adams returned to the United States in 1868 from his post as ambassador to the Court of St. James's, he had been away from the United States for seven years. . . . The most noticeable change of all, he wrote, 'is perhaps to be found in a greatly enlarged grasp of enterprise and increased facility of combination. The great operations of war, the handling of large masses of men, the influence of discipline, the lavish expenditures of unprecedented sums of money, the immense financial operations, the possibilities of effective cooperation were lessons not likely to be lost on men quick to receive and apply new ideas.'"

page 67. the federal government had given the railroads 204,688 square miles of land: Lloyd J. Mercer, *Railroads and Land Grant Policy* (New York: Academic Press, 1982), 7.

page 67. California Immigrant Union: Ads for the union appear in the *Resources of California,* a promotional published semiannually, then monthly, by a friend of Muybridge's. The union's president was W. T. Coleman, head of the Committee of Vigilance. Thus thicken plots.

page 67. "A detailed study of the finances of the whole Central Pacific network": Norman E. Tutorow, *Leland Stanford, Man of Many Careers* (Menlo Park, Calif.: Pacific Coast Publishers, 1971), 111, 113.

page 69. the seventh-richest man in the United States: Ibid., 250.

page 69. so many jewels she was said to have more than any royal family: Ibid., 283.

page 69. hundred-thousand-dollar diamond necklace: Oscar Lewis, *The Big Four,* 137.

page 70. "became interested in thoroughbred horses . . . through ill health": Mozley, 8.

page 70. Darwinian rhetoric of his university: See Kevin Starr, *Americans and the California Dream* (New York: Oxford University Press, 1973), 310–11, 341.

page 71. "an ass, a lunatic": Thornton Willis, *Nine Lives of Citizen Train* (New York: Greenberg, 1948), 196.

page 71. scheme for the Credit Mobilier: "In March 1864, Train and Durant bought control of an obscure Pennsylvania corporation called the Pennsylvania Fiscal Agency that had been chartered five years earlier to do damn near anything it wished. The company had not even organized until May 1863, and then it had transacted no business until March 3, 1864, when Durant and Train were made directors. . . . Greatly simplified, the process worked this way: The Union Pacific awarded construction contracts to dummy individuals, who in turn assigned them to the Credit Mobilier. . . . It didn't matter if the UP ever got up and running and made a profit, because the Credit Mobilier would make a big profit on it." Ambrose, *Nothing Like It in the World,* 93.

page 71. "I have lived fast": Willis, *Nine Lives of Citizen Train,* 281.

page 72. "as exactly regulated as a Leroy chronometer": "Phileas Fogg, who was not traveling, but only describing a circumference." Jules Verne, *Around the World in Eighty Days* (New York: Penguin, 1994), 14, 60.

page 72. "I want those roads stopped," "You cannot stop the locomotive": Alexander B. Adams, *Sitting Bull: An Epic of the Plains* (New York: Putnam, 1973), 158–59. Accounts of Sitting Bull's sit-down in Stanley Vestal, *Sitting Bull, Champion of the Sioux: A Biography* (Norman: University of Oklahoma Press, 1957); and Robert Marshall Utley, *The Lance and the Shield: The Life and Times of Sitting Bull* (New York: Henry Holt, 1993).

page 73. Jim Fisk's box at New York's Metropolitan Opera: Smith, *Rise of Industrial America,* 57.

4. STANDING ON THE BRINK

page 77. Agricultural Park track: *Sacramento Bee,* Feb. 21, 1872: "RACE TRACK.—The abominable weather has recently interfered with the commendable enterprise of Ex-Governor Leland Stanford in filling in and finely grading the Agricultural Park race track. The contemplated improvements . . . will make this track. . . . the very finest track in North America." "Stanford's Charley" in *Sacramento Daily Union,* May 2, 1872.

page 77. Born in Sacramento in 1863: Information on Occident in *Sunset Magazine,* Jan. 3, 1901.

page 78. "It was a hobby with him": Stillman testimony, *Muybridge v. Stanford,* 1883, Huntington Papers, Syracuse University.

page 78. Some of the East Coast's prominent horsemen: Haas, 46.

page 79. Muybridge always asserted: Here and elsewhere I have assumed that Muybridge began, as he so often asserted, the motion studies in the spring of 1872. He often specified May 1872, which is consistent with his presence there in late April. Since he was first whether his accomplishment was in 1872 or 1873, there was no reason for him to dissemble about the date, and though Muybridge was a great self-promoter he was never an outright liar. It is conceivable that Muybridge was first busy making his mammoth plates of Yosemite and the Sierra and then sequestered to print them and thus chose to wait to make the announcement, which coincided with the publication of the mammoth plates. In the Muybridge-Stanford lawsuit of 1883, Stanford testified, "that acting on the said conclusions and conceptions the Dft in 1872 or thereabouts, applid to the Plff whom he believed to be a skilful photographer and asked him to take a photograph of said horse Occident at full speed." It is generally accepted that Muybridge photographed the Stanford house in 1872, and it seems likely he photographed the carriage horses at the same time; since the latter were photographed at the racetrack, this is another thread linking the racetrack photographs of Occident to 1872.

page 79. often naming the month of May: He said this in introduction to *Animals in Motion,* 13.

page 79. "Each of the photographs made at this time": Ibid., 13

page 80. Fred MacCrellish: Haas; and H. C. Peterson, "The Birthplace of the Motion Picture," *Sunset Magazine,* Nov. 1915. Though neither source is entirely reliable, they seem to concur with Muybridge's own statements to the *Alta,* which MacCrellish owned and edited.

page 80. "Editors *Alta:* When you did me the honor": *Alta,* Aug. 3, 1877.

page 80. "Having devoted much attention in California": "Attitudes of Animals in Motion," 1883 lecture at Franklin Institute, published in its journal of April 1883, 262.

page 80. "HELIOS is prepared to photograph": *Bulletin,* April 22, 1868.

page 80. "a bold experiment": *Alta,* Aug. 7, 1877.

page 81. Talbot had experimented with instantaneous photography: *Philosophical Magazine and Journal of Science,* July 1851, 154.

page 81. "securing a picture in a tenth of a second of time": *Photographic News,* vol. 4, 1860, 13.

page 82. "exposures of from two to three seconds to thirty": *Philadelphia Photographer,* Nov. 1878.

page 82. "All the sheets in the neighborhood of the stable": *Alta,* April 7, 1873.

page 82. "This is probably the most wonderful success": Ibid. The San Francisco newspapers often said virtually the same thing about Muybridge in articles published the same day; the most likely explanation is that Muybridge was either in speech or in writing providing not only the information but the language of those articles.

page 82. "shadowy and indistinct": *Examiner,* Feb. 6, 1880.

page 84. *Helmet Dome and Little Yosemite Fall:* This depicts what is now known as Sugar Loaf and Bunnell Cascade at the east end of Little Yosemite Valley.

page 84. "long exposures which produce images of a strange, ghostly substance": Hollis Frampton, "Eadweard Muybridge: Fragments of a Tesseract," *Circles of Confusion: Film, Photography, Video, Texts* (Rochester, N.Y.: Visual Studies Workshop, 1983), 77.

page 85. went to locations that had never been photographed: Mary Jessup Hood and Robert Bartlett Haas, "Eadweard Muybridge's Yosemite Valley Photographs," *CHSQ,* March 1963; "first coverage of Four Mile Trail, Union Point, Cloud's Rest, Mt. Watkins and top of Upper Yosemite Fall."

page 86. He spent months in the region: This is based on shadow dating by Byron Wolfe and Mark Klett on-site, August 2001, comparing Muybridge's prints to the scene itself in the course of rephotographing many of these works with the author. Their conclusions suggest that Muybridge may have photographed the valley, returned to San Francisco, and then made a second foray, that he worked very slowly after arriving June 20, or that he engaged in some other process that prolonged the making of the mammoth plates.

page 87. "sparing no pains to get views": *Alta,* April 7, 1873. In a good deal of the California newspaper writing about Muybridge, he himself has some authorship, though it is not clear whether he wrote, dictated, or was interviewed. He clearly wrote the *San Francisco Examiner's* 1881 article, "Leland Stanford's Gift to Art and to Science," which was originally his contribution to the Stanford-sponsored volume on the motion studies Stillman excluded him from.

page 87. "an eagle from a peak of the Sierra Nevada mountains": "Records of Movements from Observation," in Muybridge, *Animals in Motion,* 69.

page 88. Chinese landscape paintings: Muybridge did, however, photograph Chinatown, a few blocks away from Montgomery Street, and may well have seen Chinese landscape painting in one form or another.

page 88. one or more small figures: Re the figure in the landscape, see Barbara Novak, *Nature and Culture: American Landscape and Painting, 1825–1875* (New York: Oxford University Press), 183–200. Though it could be argued that the figures in Muybridge's photographs are aimless because they are in between tasks, that Muybridge directed or allowed them to appear thus is nevertheless an aesthetic decision.

page 88. probably Muybridge's assistants and packers: In his Tuolumne Meadows stereograph there are four figures, and up to four figures can be found in his mammoth plates. Up close, they are rough-looking bearded figures, which may be the effect of outdoor living or may indicate that some are mulepackers or guides, not photographic assistants. His own statement mentions packers, and he became a rough-looking character himself that season. Some of his photographs in the high country seem to be of mountaineers with alpenstocks, which could mean he had come across Joseph LeConte's party from the University of California or that his own men were playing at mountaineer. That these photographs are pasted into the Brandenberg Album (see chapter six) may suggest that they were friends or acquaintances of the Muybridges.

page 89. "became nerve-shaken for the first time": Muir, *The Mountains of California* (San Francisco: Sierra Club, 1988), 52

page 91. "In none of these pictures do we see the least signs of man": Naef, *Era of Exploration*, 39.

page 92. Bierstadt did paint: See Nancy K. Anderson and Linda S. Ferber, *Albert Bierstadt: Art and Enterprise* (New York: Hudson Hills Press and the Brooklyn Museum, 1990), for a pair of bark huts painted direct from the photograph; and, in the the Oakland Museum's collection, Bierstadt's *California Indian Camp,* which lifts motifs from the photographs but adds figures and changes composition. A third painting, *Indians in Council,* shows not the view Muybridge photographed but the view Bierstadt would have seen when Muybridge photographed him.

page 94. it was news of glaciers that prompted his first small article: Muir, "Living Glaciers of California," *Overland Monthly,* Dec. 1872.

page 94. "a mere sheepherder, an ignoramus": Francis Farquhar, *History of the Sierra Nevada* (Berkeley and Los Angeles: University of California Press, 1965), 155.

page 94. "the eroding power": Ibid., 163: "The following year he returned to Mount Lyell, and with Galen Clark's assistance made measurements of the movement of the Lyell and Maclure glaciers. He was then satisfied to publish announcements of his findings. Professor LeConte went to Mount Lyell and observed the evidences and concurred that there was true glacial motion. But acceptance of Muir's discovery was not immediately unanimous. Whitney continued obdurate. 'It may be stated,' he says in his ultimate publication on the Sierra, 'that there are no glaciers at all in the Sierra Nevada,' and Clarence King gave what he considered a final verdict: 'In the dry season of 1864–'65 the writer examined many of the regions described by Mr. Muir in the Sierra Nevada, and in not a few cases his so-called glaciers had entirely melted away.'"

page 94. requested that Muybridge photograph Temple Peak: According to the *Alta,* April 7, 1873, Bierstadt "made several suggestions to Mr. Muybridge, while in the Valley, and is, in fact, a patron and advisor. The view of Temple Peak, in Monastery Valley, is twenty miles from Yosemite. It was taken at the suggestion of Albert Bierstadt, who, it is believed, will make the same scene the subject of a painting. At the suggestion of Mr. Clarence King, the artist has made several pictures of the ancient glacier channel at Lake Tenaya, and other glacier indications."

page 94. hoped first to hire Watkins: King, letter of Aug. 13, 1872, to Chief of Engineers of the U.S. Army (National Archives microfilm), mentions the previous winter's plan to employ Watkins; on April 10 of that year, in a letter to the same authority, he requested funding for employing Timothy O'Sullivan for work in the Sierra; because of the heavy snow there (and heavy photographic equipment), O'Sullivan was instead dispatched to another, more easterly part of the Fortieth Parallel Survey.

page 95. "invites comparison with Watkins": William Henry Pettee, letter to J. D. Whitney, Jan. 27, 1871, in the Pettee Papers, Huntington Library, Box 2 (10). Fascinatingly, Pettee goes on to say, "If you think it worth while I will inquire of him how much he charges for his services etc. If the funds, though, are short, it may not be feasible to make the photographic trip into the High Sierras of which I have heard you speak so often."

page 96. "At no very remote period": Bradley and Rulofson Catalog, 1873, 33.

page 97. vying to publish the results: Mozley card of corrections for page 40 reads, "Muybridge's Yosemite prospectus was issued from Nahl's studio. Both Houseworth and Bradley and Rulofson were competing to publish the photographs."

page 97. it may have been taken by Charles Leander Weed: Peter Palmquist, conversation with the author, fall 2000. Palmquist points out that the experienced Weed could have helped Muybridge deal with mammoth-plate photography, a new medium for the latter man.

page 97. The William Towne who appears in a . . . hotel register: Towne signed in with Muybridge at the Casa Nevada that day, a building no longer in existence up Little Yosemite Canyon near Nevada Falls. Information from microfilm of hotel ledger, Yosemite Research Library. Further information on Towne is in Palmquist, *Pioneer Photographers.*

page 97. "thirty-four hands all told": *Philadelphia Photographer,* Jan. 1875.

page 97. ad disparaging the photographs: Houseworth Yosemite advertisement in *Chronicle,* May 21, 1871; CPRR advertisement in *Resources of California,* June 1871.

page 97. "Messrs. Bradley and Rulofson are much obliged": Kingston Scrapbook.

page 98. "Landscapes of this size are the exception": *Philadelphia Photographer,* Feb. 1874. Dr. Vogel would become Alfred Stieglitz's teacher, and thus links the pioneer photographers with the modernists in that field.

page 98. "distinguished by superb cloud effects": *Philadelphia Photographer,* Sept. 1873.

page 98. among his initial subscribers: Also see Bradley and Rulofson Catalog, which states, on page 3, "The list of subscribers for his recent magnificent series of Yosemite Photographs includes the names of every prominent artist and nearly all the principal citizens and patrons of art in California. The amount of the subscription list, exceeding twenty thousand dollars, including one thousand dollars each from the Central and Union Pacific Railroad Companies, and five hundred dollars from the Pacific Mail Steamship Company."

page 100. In 1873 he planned to work in the mammoth-plate format: Bradley and Rulofson Catalog, page 3: "Among his projected trips this season for a series of views, 20x24 inches in size, is one along the line of the Transcontinental Railroad, and another to the Columbia River." However, with the exception of two lovely mammoth plates—a lighthouse and a ladies' college—in the Oakland Museum, no Muybridge mammoth-plate photographs are known to this author to exist outside the 1872 Yosemite work and the 1878 panorama of San Francisco.

5. LOST RIVER

page 103. "He had shaped and decorated the world": Schonchin, in Alice Marriot and Carol K. Rachlin, *American Indian Mythology* (New York: Crowell, 1968), 27. Modoc myth and details recorded in *Petroglyph Point* brochure and in Helen K. Crotty, "Petroglyph Point Revisited—A Modoc County Site," in *Messages from the Past: Studies in California Rock Art,* ed. Clement W. Meighan, Monograph XX (Los Angeles: UCLA Institute of Archaeology, 1981).

page 104. He photographed from, so far as the newspapers tell, May 2 to May 14: *Yreka Journal* of May 7 cites a May 3 report stating, "Yesterday, Gen. Jeff. C. Davis . . . and E. J.

Muybridge, photograph artist sent by Gen. Schofield to take views of the country arrived"; and on May 14 reports, "Mr. Muybridge and Mr. Ward, photographer and topographical engineer, who have been doing the Lava bed, return to-morrow."

page 104. "The wide spread and accurate knowledge": Mozley, 46.

page 104. "The extraordinary system of natural fortifications": Bradley and Rulofson Catalog, 31.

page 108. "the efforts of efficient and conscientous instructors": John Meacham, March 8, 1871, letters to the Oregon Superintendency, National Archives, Record Group 77.

page 108. "I was met by 'Capt. Jack' and 'Black Jim'": I. Applegate, letter of Nov. 30, 1871, National Archives, Record Group 77.

page 109. tied to specific places: "Indian tribes combine history and geography so that they have a 'sacred geography,' that is to say, every location within their original homeland has a multitude of stories that recount the migrations, revelations, and particular historical incidents that cumulatively produced the tribe in its current condition. . . . The most notable characteristic of the tribal traditions is the precision and specificity of the traditions when linked to the landscape, a precision lacking in most other religious traditions." Vine DeLoria Jr., *God Is Red* (New York: Grosset and Dunlap, 1973), 122.

page 111. "to sign their death warrants": Keith A. Murray, *The Modocs and Their War* (Norman: University of Oklahoma, 1959), 97.

page 112. surrounded the Stronghold with a tule-reed rope painted red: Murray, *The Modocs,* 69; Cora Du Bois, *The 1870 Ghost Dance,* Anthropological Records, vol. 3, no. 1 (Berkeley: University of California Press, 1939), 11.

page 112. Smoholla or Shouting Mountain: Vittorio Lanternari, *The Religions of the Oppressed: A Study of Modern Messianic Cults* (New York: New American Library, 1965), 127.

page 113. "the 'Supreme Ruler' was to bring the spirits": Russell Thornton, *We Shall Live Again: The 1870 and 1890 Ghost Dance Movements as Demographic Revitalization* (New York: Cambridge University Press, 1986), 3.

page 113. "and said all were to believe that the dead were coming back": DuBois, *1870 Ghost Dance Religion,* 10.

page 113. "will come back, and people will never die anymore": In Philleo Nash, "The Place of Religious Revivalism in the Formation of the Intercultural Community on Klamath Reservation," in *Social Anthropology of North American Tribes: Essays in Social Organization, Law, and Religion,* ed. Fred Eggan (Chicago: University of Chicago Press, 1937), 415.

page 113. only one more creek to cross: DuBois, *1870 Ghost Dance Religion,* 12.

page 114. spiritualist movement: On spiritualism my main source is Barbara Goldsmith's magnificent *Other Powers: The Age of Suffrage, Spiritualism, and the Scandalous Victoria Woodhull* (New York: Alfred A. Knopf, 1998), which tells of the soul-generating electrical device.

page 114. "Any sufficiently advanced technology": David A. Kaplan, *The Silicon Boys and Their Valley of Dreams* (New York: William Morrow, 1999), 40, and various other places.

page 114. evening calls from the dead: *Chronicle,* Feb. 17, 1878.

page 115. "He may be tempted to inquire": Thomson, "Taking a Photograph," in *Science for All,* ed. Robert Brown (London: Cassell, Petter, Galpin & Co., 1878), 1:258.

page 115. "In the year 1887 it occurred to me": Edison, *Century Magazine,* June 1904, and as the handwritten frontispiece in W. K. L. Dickson and Antonia Dickson's 1895 *History of the Kinetograph, Kinetoscope and Kinetophotograph* (also reproduced in Kingston Scrapbook). Note that he is probably lying about the year he became involved with cinema, since it almost certainly postdated his 1888 meeting with Muybridge.

page 116. "There are a lot of people telling this news but they aren't telling it right": DuBois, *1870 Ghost Dance Religion,* 5.

page 116. "The dead were not coming back": Ibid., 10.

page 116. "She prayed so earnestly": Bertha Berner, *Mrs. Leland Stanford: An Intimate Account* (Stanford, Calif.: Stanford University Press, 1935), 42–44.

page 117. "I give up my home on Lost River": A. B. Meacham, *Wigwam and War-Path; or, The Royal Chief in Chains* (Boston: John P. Dale, 1875), 447.

page 118. Schonchin John, "eyes burning with passion": Ibid., 491.

page 120. "All you fellows that ain't dead": Murray, *The Modocs,* 231.

page 120. "Jack's legs gave out": Ibid., 269 (and *New York Times,* June 17, 1875).

page 120. photographer Louis Heller: See Peter Palmquist, "Imagemakers of the Modoc War," in *Journal of California Anthropology,* winter 1977.

page 121. "It is doubtful": http://www.cheewa.com/modocart.htm.

page 121. "The lava beds": Bancroft, *History of Oregon II,* vol. 30 of *The Works of Hubert Howe Bancroft* (San Francisco: History Company, 1888), 636.

page 122. Jonathan Crary, *Techniques of the Observer: On Vision and Modernity in the Nineteenth Century* (Cambridge: The MIT Press, 1990), 10.

6. A DAY IN THE LIFE, TWO DEATHS, MORE PHOTOGRAPHS

page 127. "Muybridge came to my house Saturday morning": *Chronicle,* Feb. 6, 1875.

page 128. "The spies of Europe knew him": *Napa Reporter,* Nov. 28, 1874, citing the *Chicago Tribune* "of a recent date."

page 128. a gullible young heir named Arthur Neil: *Alta,* March 15 and 16, 1873; *Bulletin,* March 14 and 17, 1873; and *Chronicle,* March 16, 1873.

page 129. "Larkyns would take him by the nose and lower jaw": *Examiner,* Oct. 19, 1874.

page 129. "In the early part of 1873 he came up into the gallery": *Chronicle,* Dec. 21, 1874. The "produce dealer Mr. Selleck" may be an error of transcription; Muybridge may have been talking about his old friend the photodealer Silas Selleck—or about Joseph E. Selleck, the produce commissioner who the *Langley Directory* of San Francisco for 1874 lists as residing at 37 South Park with Charles and Edwin Selleck, apparently brothers, sons, or cousins of Silas; that year Silas Selleck is only listed at his business address, 415 Montgomery; the 1872–73 directory lists Silas and Edwin Selleck at 415 Montgomery, but Joseph at 343 Brannan, and Edwin being listed with both Silas and Joseph makes it clear they are related. The Muybridges themselves lived in South Park earlier in their married life; see note to page 131, below.

page 129. Flora Muybridge had been born Flora Downs: *Daily Evening Post,* Feb. 5, 1875, which also gives the date of their wedding.

page 130. "He permitted her to go to the theaters": William Wirt Pendegast, in *Daily Morning Call,* Feb. 7, 1875.

page 130. "We never had any trouble to speak of": *Chronicle,* Dec. 21, 1874.

page 130. "Because of the limited number of women": Starr, *Americans and the California Dream,* 360.

page 130. "You know my right in the premises as a married man": *Chronicle,* Dec. 21, 1874.

page 131. "Another lady friend": *Chronicle,* Oct. 20, 1874.

page 131. a catalog of celebrities: A copy of this is to be found at Bancroft Library. It dates from 1878, and it may be because Flora was dead that she is not mentioned by name there—though she was also anonymous in the *Philadelphia Photographer.*

page 131. Brandenburg album: The album is now in the collection of the museum at Stanford. Anita Ventura Mozley, a curator there then and one of the important scholars on Muybridge, apparently performed the initial identification of the album with Flora, and it is she who, in Mozley's *Stanford Years* catalog, noted "a steamship that had run aground in the Golden Gate," the SS *Costa Rica,* as the latest Muybridge photograph in the album. Photographs of Ralston's house may be later, taken when Florado was born, but this is uncertain. Phillip Prodger concurs that the album is Flora's.

page 133. "a tall gentleman with a high white hat": *Chronicle,* Oct. 19, 1874.

page 134. "the city's most modish meeting place": Muscatine, *Old San Francisco,* 232.

page 134. Susannah Smith Muggeridge, Muybridge's mother, died: Typescript of will in Haas papers.

page 134. "Mrs. Muybridge ordered me to bring the baby in": *Chronicle,* Feb. 6, 1874.

page 136. They left June 15: *Sacramento Daily Union,* Feb. 8, 1875; also see *Chronicle,* Dec. 21, 1874: "I had been negotiating several months with the Pacific Mail Steamship Company for a trip down the coast on one of their steamers to photograph the coast. I had my arrangements completed, and expected to go in a short time, but the agent of the company delayed from time to time, and I did not get away as I expected to. My wife had no relatives in the city, and I did not like to leave her alone with her baby while I was gone on a trip from which I should probably not return in less than five or six months. So I told her I would send her up to Oregon to her uncle, who was living in Portland, and give her money to pay her expenses there while I was away if she would go. She consented, and I gave her the money."

page 136. "Muybridge since I came here": Trial transcription of letter from Flora Muybridge to Sarah Smith, dated The Dalles, July 11, 1874, in Napa County Historical Society Archives.

page 136. "As I closed the door": *Chronicle,* Feb. 6, 1875.

page 137. "He threw himself on a lounge": *Chronicle,* Oct. 20, 1874.

page 137. "from Calistoga to the Yellow Jacket Mine": George Wolfe testimony in trial transcript from surviving courtroom documents at Napa County Historical Society.

page 138. "a view over the whole of Knight's Valley": Harry Larkyns, *Stock Reporter,* Sept. 4, 1874.

page 138. "I will only detain him a moment": *Chronicle,* Oct. 20, 1874.

page 139. "a well-known actress of the California Theater": *Chronicle,* Oct. 21, 1874.

page 139. "Muybridge is forty years old": *Chronicle,* Dec. 21, 1874.

page 141. Because Pendegast was a friend of Stanford's: In a letter of April 20, 1956, in the Robert Haas files at the Kingston-on-Thames Local History Center, Pendegast's daughter Janet Pendegast Leigh writes of how Stanford sent a special railroad car and himself rushed to be present at Pendegast's funeral, not long after the trial. The Central America album Muybridge gave Pendegast's widow with a note of his gratitude is now at the California State Library, Sacramento; a similar one given to the Stanfords is at their university.

page 141. used an insanity defense: Defense testimony in most newspaper accounts of the time; I have drawn primarily from the *Sacramento Union* and *Chronicle.*

page 141. "seemed happy, then turned suddenly": *Sacramento Union,* Feb. 5, 1875.

page 142. "The speech was one of the most eloquent": *Sunday Chronicle,* Feb. 7, 1875.

page 142. "I cannot ask you to send this man forth": *Napa Register* (weekly edition), Feb. 13, 1875. In this *Register* article, the reporter speculated that a man had to be insane to give an interview to the daily newspapers.

page 144. "The virtue of women rests not": Ibid.

page 144. "a convulsive gasp escaped": *Sunday Chronicle,* Feb. 7, 1875.

page 145. filed for divorce: Divorce reports appear in *San Francisco Call,* Jan. 10, 1875; *Chronicle,* Jan. 11, 1875, March 10, 1875, March 23, 1875, March 27, 1875, and May 1, 1875.

page 145. 600 applications for divorce: Benjamin E. Lloyd, *Lights and Shades in San Francisco* (San Francisco: A. L. Bancroft, 1876), 280.

page 145. "The doctrine": Goldsmith, *Other Powers,* 208.

page 145. "Mothers of humanity, yours is a fearful duty": Smith, *Rise of Industrial America,* 260

page 147. "While the relentless wife": *Chronicle,* March 23, 1875.

page 147. "a stroke of paralysis": *Examiner,* July 19, 1875; "a complication of spinal complaint," in *Chronicle,* July 19, 1875.

page 147. "the poor woman": *Chronicle,* July 19, 1875.

page 147. "I am sorry": Ella Clark to the librarians at the State Library, Sacramento, where the brief narrative is recorded on an index card under "Muybridge."

page 148. Muybridge moved the toddler: Letter of July 24, 1961, from the California State Library to Gordon Hendricks states that Florado was entered in the Protestant Orphan Asylum on September 16, 1876, and though some sources say Muybridge remained away until 1877, his participation in the Mechanics' Institute Fair that year and his gift of an album to Mrs. Pendegast in December of that year confirm he was back by 1876. Further information is contained in a June 23, 1961, letter from the library to Hendricks (in the Hendricks files, AAA). In Muybridge's defense it should be said that children were more readily consigned to orphanages then, that a motherless child was often considered an orphan, and that it is hard to imagine what else he could have done with the child but pay foster parents to raise it, and foster children were often little more than indentured servants then.

page 148. The Pacific Mail Steamship Company had been a powerful entity, and other background information: E. Bradford Burns, *Eadweard Muybridge in Guatemala, 1875: The Photographer as Social Recorder* (Berkeley and Los Angeles: University of California Press, 1985).

page 148. "vistas fotographicas de este Republica": in Kingston Scrapbook, 15.

page 150. He came back with nearly 200 large and 150 stereo images: These are not the usual full-plate view-camera images, but a wider format akin to the "boudoir format" in which he made one of his San Francisco panoramas in 1877, possibly with the same camera (as the 1878 panorama seems to have been made with the Yosemite mammoth-plate camera that was afterward marooned at the Palo Alto estate for more than a decade).

page 151. one to Frank Shay: Because Muybridge gave his work away strategically, it seems more likely that he gave the work to Shay after the latter became a secretary with whom he had much contact rather than while he was still a functionary in a large bureaucracy peripheral to Muybridge's work.

7. SKINNING THE CITY

page 155. Muybridge's first large panorama: The three important sources on the panoramas are Mark Klett and Eadweard Muybridge, *One City/Two Visions* (San Francisco: Bedford Arts Press, 1990), an artists' book that reproduces both Muybridge's 1878 panorama and Klett's 1990 rephotograph of it from the sixteenth floor of what is now the Mark Hopkins Hotel (and reproduces it on a scale that allows many of the details to be examined); David Harris with Eric Sandweiss, *Eadweard Muybridge and the Photographic Panorama of San Francisco, 1850–1880* (Cambridge: MIT Press, 1993); and Paul Falconer's June 1978 *CHSQ* essay on the 1877 panorama, "Muybridge's Window to the Past." Several of the ideas and some of the information in this chapter come from conversations and correspondence with Klett (including ideas about the changed seventh plate of the 1878 panorama, the decision to use vertically oriented photographs, and the relationship to the motion studies, which Harris also notes). The photohistorian Geoffrey Batchen also provided valuable information on the Sydney panorama and its makers.

page 155. "'Occident' Photographed at Full Speed": *Alta,* Aug. 3, 1877.

page 156. "The moving panorama anticipated": Stephan Oettermann, *The Panorama: History of a Mass Medium* (New York: Zone, 1997), 323.

page 157. In 1851 no fewer than five daguerreotype panoramas were made: They and subsequent panoramas are chronicled in Harris, *Eadweard Muybridge.*

page 158. a seven-stereocard panorama of San Francisco: In the Bradley and Rulofson catalogue of 1873, it precedes the photographs of the October 1868 earthquake in San Francisco as numbers 428 to 434; the earthquake images begin with the number 445.

page 159. Carleton Watkins made one of the first large panoramas: Watkins photographed from Charles Crocker's tower, which would have provided a similar 360-degree view, but stuck with the more conventional panorama format of about 180 degrees.

page 159. panorama of Sydney: "In 1876 Holtermann brought the mammoth negative to the Centennial Exhibition in Philadelphia," Beaumont Newhall, *The History of Photography* (New York: Museum of Modern Art, 1962), 80.

page 159. Watkins and Muybridge both had mammoth-plate photographs of Yosemite: See *Philadelphia Photographer,* July 1876, which also mentions "a number of 16x20 views of Yosemite Valley by Messrs. Thomas Houseworth & Co.," which may be either old Weed or Watkins photographs.

page 159. Muybridge went to Nob Hill: Between June 10 and early July of 1877 are the dates deduced by Falconer, "Muybridge's Window to the Past," *CHSQ,* June 1978. That panorama was advertised in a September 1877 broadside from Morse's Gallery at 417 Montgomery, contained in the Kingston Scrapbook, which offers it for sale mounted for ten dollars or unmounted "properly secured upon a roller" for eight. Early July is, of course, corroborated by the newspaper pieces about the panorama at that period.

page 159. he also made a seven-image panorama from the windows of the Stanfords' Nob Hill home: Harris's catalog notes that this photograph exists in multiple versions; those in the San Francisco Public Library have clouds added.

page 160. "He condenses an entire rotation of the seeing eye": Frampton, "Fragments of a Tesseract," *Circles of Perpetual Confusion,* 76.

page 161. in most versions the clock is at quarter to two: Though Falconer gives different times for the 1877 panoramas, it is he who first noted that there were two versions of the plate; my own citation of the time comes from careful examination of the four 1877 panoramas at the California Historical Society, the one in the collection of Paul Sack, and the one reproduced in Harris's book. The CHS owns three with the clock at the earlier time, and Stanford's own deluxe edition—with much better print quality and a fine binding—in which the clock is at the later time.

page 162. The Great Strike broke out spontaneously across the country: See Robert V. Bruce, *1877: Year of Violence* (Indianapolis: Bobbs-Merrill, 1959); David T. Burbank, *Reign of the Rabble: The St. Louis General Strike of 1877* (New York: Augustus M. Kelly, 1966); and the brief account in Howard Zinn, *People's History of the United States* (New York: New Press, 1997).

page 163. "corn in sacks, cotton in bales": Bruce, *1877,* 172.

page 163. "The 'communists' of 1877": Burbank, *Reign of the Rabble,* 79–80.

page 163. Red flags flew: Bruce, *1877,* 88.

page 164. supplementary troops were sent east on the Central Pacific: *Alta,* July 21 and 22, 1877.

page 166. "As among the twenty-seven thousand houses, more than four fifths were wooden": J. S. Hittell, *History of San Francisco,* 425.

page 167. "as the hired advocates of Stanford and Co. would have us believe": *Examiner,* July 24, 1877.

page 169. "The SP offered the most obvious instance": Kevin Starr, *Inventing the Dream: California Through the Progressive Era* (New York: Oxford University Press, 1985), 199.

page 170. Yung mounted an outsize coffin: Rand Richards, *Historic San Francisco* (San Francisco: Heritage House Publishers, 1991), 147–48. When Watkins made a partial panorama from Crocker's house, he left out the looming spite fence.

page 170. "I will give the Central Pacific": *Bulletin,* Nov. 5, 1877; Ira B. Cross, *A History of the Labor Movement in California* (Berkeley: University of California Press, 1935), 100.

page 171. "De Marie Antoinette au dernier Marquis de Villette": Tutorow, *Leland Stanford,* 209.

page 171. "one of the 'hardened' was abusing": Kevin MacDonnell, *Eadweard Muybridge: The Man Who Invented the Moving Picture* (Boston: Little, Brown, 1972), 149, cited as coming from the *Sacramento Union,* Feb. 5, 1875. This problematic book (which Anita Mozley excoriated for its errors in the *London Review of Books*) is copyrighted by the well-known photohistorian Bill Jay, which raises interesting questions about its authorship.

page 171. deluxe album of the Stanfords' Nob Hill home: San Francisco Public Library and Cantor Center, Stanford University, both own copies.

page 172. "created some indignation": *Bulletin,* Jan. 28, 1875.

page 172. "I shall hope to live to sit up yonder balcony": *Chronicle,* May 19, 1875; Mozley, 64.

page 173. an early 1878 fire: Haas, 87, claims, "Early in 1878, the fire at Morse's that destroyed the glass-plate negatives of Muybridge's Central American views also consumed the negatives of the two 1877 panoramas." This seems to be the source of all subsequent statements that the negatives were burned, prompting the making of a new panorama, and the only source I can find for Haas is Peterson, the Stanford Museum's not entirely reliable curator during the first decades of the twentieth century, asserting (as quoted without source in Mozley, 55) that "the original negatives [of the Central America prints] were destroyed by a fire a few weeks after these albums were made." But the one given to Mrs. Pendegast was made by 1876, judging by the dedication's date, before there were panoramas to burn, and another was given to Stanford's private secretary Frank Shay in 1879 or later—Shay testified in the 1883 *Muybridge v. Stanford* trial that they first met in 1879; either way a fire would be too soon or too late to make the 1878 panorama a replacement for a burned 1877 panorama, if the panorama and Central America images supposedly burned together. Otherwise one must believe in *two* fires. Muybridge wrote on April 14, 1879, to the Mechanics' Institute (letter now in Bancroft Library), "As I am about sending the negatives [of the Central America pictures] to Europe; and in consequence of the great expense attending their production, there being little probability of any other series ever being made, I thought it advisable to renew my offer, with the proviso that instead of $200 cash the price of the entire series—I will accept $100—and a life membership." Further, he used the same photographic key—a copy photo of the panorama with the places numbered and listed—with both panoramas. Finally, on September 5, 1893, he wrote to the executors of Stanford's estate requesting that some of his property at Palo Alto be delivered to his friend John T. Doyle, including "4 boxes of size about 30 inches long x 15 x 15 inches, containing some landscape and other negatives, stereoscopic views of California, and other effects" (letter now in Bancroft Library). If the Central America negatives weren't burned, the key wasn't burned, many negatives were still around in the 1890s, and no one has turned up a primary source for the fire, then I think there was no fire, at least not a fire burning the negatives in question. No primary source has been cited by earlier scholars, and I have not been able to find in the *Philadelphia Photographer* or the *San Francisco Chronicle* during January–June 1878 mention of a fire having to do with Muybridge or Morse's Gallery. And then there is the question of why an incomparable panorama would be made as a replacement for a good panorama; Mark Klett believes that the 1877 panorama was instead a practice run to figure out some of the technical details for the 1878 version. No negatives of Muybridge's are known to exist; what happened to the Central America negatives that he may have shipped to Europe or to the boxes he requested go to Doyle is unknown.

page 174. panoramic photographers assembled their image out of horizontal photographs: The Bernard Otto Holtermann and Charles Bayliss panorama of Sydney is a notable exception, and its scale and format are a likely influence on Muybridge's final masterpiece in the genre.

page 176. "If he had to remake a photo": Klett, correspondence with the author, 2000.

8. STOPPING TIME

page 181. "if you could limit man's wants": *Examiner,* June 22, 1893, article reprinting a long speech with Stanford's obituary.

page 181. "Few of Stanford's charges knew the meaning of fear": Tutorow, *Leland Stanford,* 165.

page 183. "very rapid work": "Before going to Central America on a professional tour, the photographer did not believe the feat possible, but some very rapid work in the southern country led him to regard it as worthy of a trial"; clipping dated Aug. 4, 1877, no recognizable publisher, Kingston Scrapbook.

page 183. "had occasion to make a series of experiments": *Bulletin,* Aug. 3, 1877.

page 183. "iron was employed in their development": *Photographic News* (London), March 17, 1882. The sentence continues, "and no additional care or particular method was had recourse to." Also see *Philadelphia Photographer,* March 1879; Muybridge wrote to the magazine, "The chemical formulae I have not yet perfected, and I consider it inadvisable to publish them at present. Whether they are equal to the various 'lightning processes,' I do not know; but that they will admit of an exposure of a two-thousandth part of a second, is proved by the fact of the trotting horse not having progressed one-quarter inch during the exposure. They will, however, be neither patented nor kept secret, when they have been improved as far as I can improve them."

page 184. "I take pleasure": Sherman Blake, San Francisco, letter of May 6, 1929, to Walter R. Miles, Stanford University Library Special Collections, from the Miles file. The location given does not match any other account; most assume that this phase took place in Palo Alto, and of course the multiple-camera photographs were taken at Palo Alto. Blake would have been younger than the age he gives, but the vividness of his account and much of the background he supplies about Morse, the handling of the horses, and the photographic techniques and tools make his account hard to dismiss. It may be that as an older man he dropped a few years from his age. He mentions the Bay District Track again in a letter of May 31, 1929, from the same file and mentions a single thread used to trip the shutter, making it clear that he is talking about the single-camera work of 1877. Tutorow notes on page 161 of *Leland Stanford* that "Stanford's interest in racing led him at this time to buy some stock in the Bay District Track just north of the Golden Gate Park." And Haas—page 109—notes that by 1878, Stanford had moved his horses to Palo Alto. An interim between leaving the Sacramento house and developing the Palo Alto property in which Stanford made use of the Bay District Track, particularly given his part ownership, makes considerable sense. Haas, page 93, mentions that Occident raced on the Bay District Track in 1874. Muybridge's own article of Feb. 6, 1881, in the *Examiner* mentions Sacramento as the site of the July 1877 work and Palo Alto as the site of subsequent work, but does not mention the Bay District Track.

page 185. "This picture has been retouched": *Alta,* Aug. 3, 1877.

page 185. a photograph of a painting of the photograph: Mozley, 62–63.

page 186. Stanford directed . . . Montague: *Edward J. Muybridge v. Leland Stanford,* Suffolk Superior Court, Massachusetts, surviving papers—mostly statements for the defense—in the Huntington Papers.

page 186. "I discussed this business with him": Testimony of John D. Isaacs, July 18, 1883, Huntington Papers.

page 187. "to reap the full benefit of the time ball": *Scientific American,* Nov. 30, 1878.

page 187. According to Muybridge scholar Phillip Prodger: In conversation with the author, June 2001.

page 187. when Stanford hammered the last electrically wired spike: *California Spirit of the Times,* June 22, 1878.

page 187. Stanford's costs: A Huntington Papers estimate brings the total by 1884 to $52,817.76, including $21,463.44 for the book and an estimated $14,000 for "1st exh." Muybridge was given $2,000 at the end of his work there, more a gift than anything resembling wages.

page 187. "see how we were getting along": Knowles testimony, July 24, 1883, Huntington Papers.

page 188. "not under direct control": Muybridge, *Notices of the Proceedings at the Meetings of the Members of the Royal Institution of Great Britain, with Abstracts of the Discourses Delivered at the Evening Meetings,* vol. X, 1882–1884. Also published in the *Journal of the Franklin Institute,* April 1883, 264. Both provide the text of Muybridge's March 13, 1882, talk before the Prince of Wales. The clock was reproduced in *La Nature* as a "horloge pneumatique" and may have been a device for setting off several cameras simultaneously. *La Nature,* Jan. 4, 1879, in Kingston Scrapbook. In a letter to Eakins of May 7, 1879, Muybridge wrote, "I commenced these experiments last year with a clockwork arrangement but relinquished it for the automatic in consequence of the extreme difficulty in getting the clock to run with a speed exactly coinciding with the speed of the horse. I have the clock and will use it for birds; possibly for dogs, but for animals under control the automatic arrangements are unquestionably the best."

page 189. he took out patents: U.S. patent 212,864 (March 4, 1879), for "a novel arrangement for exposing the sensitive plates of photographic cameras, for the purpose of taking instantaneous impressions of objects in motion" (British patent 2,746, July 9, 1878); U.S. patent 212,865 (March 4, 1879), for "a double-acting slide, with the means for operating the same, and to a novel background, which is graduated or marked so as to gauge the position of the horse and the posture of his limbs"; U.S. patent 251,127, assigned to the Scoville Manufacturing Company, of Dec. 20, 1881, for "a picture-feeding device for magic lanterns to change from one picture to the other thus effected instantaneously, and without leaving the light from the lantern upon the screen without a picture, so as to dazzle the eyes"; U.S. patent 279,878 (June 19, 1883), for "effectually photographing changing or moving bodies in their different phases or positions."

page 189. "We began our experiments the next May": Muybridge, letter published in *La Nature,* Feb. 1879.

page 190. copy thousands of documents for the city of San Jose: *San Jose Mercury News,* Nov. 9, 1877.

page 190. "He was living at the Palo Alto Ranch": Shay Testimony, July 23, 1883, Huntington Papers.

page 191. "like that made by the wings of a woodcock": *California Spirit of the Times,* June 22, 1878.

page 191. "There is a feeling of awe in the mind of the beholder": Ibid.

page 192. San Francisco's *Illustrated Wasp* and Britain's *Punch* published parodies: Both are in Muybridge's Kingston Scrapbook.

page 192. "illustrating the geology of the Sierras": *Sacramento Bee,* Sept. 18, 1878. These were undoubtedly some of his 1872 Yosemite pictures.

page 193. Rulofson wrote in to . . . denounce the motion studies as "bosh": A few months later Rulofson fell to his death in what is sometimes suspected to have been a suicide. He had gone upstairs to inspect a new story being added to his gallery. A false step on an unfinished wall sent him plummeting to Montgomery Street below, and a friend of Horace Greeley's who happened to be present found in his coat a miniature that he recognized as that of the linguistic prodigy and murderer Edward Ruloff, who had been executed in New York for his crimes. See Robert Bartlett Haas, "William Herman Rulofson: Pioneer Daguerreotypist and Photographic Educator," *CHSQ,* Dec. 1955.

page 193. Martha Sandweiss pointed out: In the opening passages of "Undecisive Images: The Narrative Tradition in Western Photography," *Photography in Nineteenth-Century America* (Fort Worth: Amon Carter Museum, 1991), 100.

page 194. "All experience, in matters of philosophical discovery": Poe, "The Daguerreo-type," 1840, reprinted in Jane M. Rabb, *Literature and Photography: Interactions, 1840–1990* (Albuquerque: University of New Mexico, 1995), 5.

page 195. Thomas Jefferson's great land survey of 1785: See J. B. Jackson, "Jefferson, Thoreau and After," in *Landscapes: Selected Writings of J. B. Jackson,* ed. Ervin H. Zube (Amherst: University of Massachusetts Press, 1970).

page 195. Charles Willson Peale painted himself in 1822: The picture is reproduced in and discussed at length in the opening passages of Alan Trachtenberg's *Reading American Photographs: Images as History, Matthew Brady to Walker Evans* (New York: Hill and Wang, 1989). It's worth noting that Muybridge is the source of what may be the most significant grids in twentieth-century art, those of the minimalist artist Sol LeWitt, whose sequential work draws directly from Muybridge. (See notes for chap. 10.)

page 196. "It is the artist who tells the truth": Marc Gotlieb, *The Plight of Emulation: Ernest Meissonier and French Salon Painting* (Princeton, N.J.: Princeton University Press, 1996), 181.

page 197. The painting was later criticized: Mozley, 103.

page 197. "All these years my eyes had deceived me" and following, Gotlieb, *Plight of Emulation,* 178–80.

page 197. "His commitment to the veracity of his representations": Ibid., 182–83.

page 198. "They first started in by taking pictures of horses": Nicholas T. Smith, treasurer of the Southern Pacific Railroad, trial testimony, Huntington Papers.

page 198. "desire to extend the investigation": Handwritten draft letter of Muybridge's to Stanford, May 2, 1892, Bancroft Library; also reproduced in Mozley, 127–29.

page 198. apparently prompted by a studio visit: *Examiner,* Feb. 6, 1881.

page 199. "In order to display as completely": *Chronicle* article, reprinted in Oct. 1878 *Philadelphia Photographer,* also in Kingston Scrapbook.

page 200. That fall of 1879 Maybridge also debuted his zoopraxiscope: See Haas, 117–20.

page 201. "The illusion . . . was easily explained": Laurent Mannoni, *The Great Art of Light and Shadow: Archaeology of the Cinema,* trans. Richard Crangle (Exeter: University of Exeter Press, 2000), 216, 222.

page 202. "in quick succession": Mozley, 71; Kingston Scrapbook, 30.

page 203. "What attracted the most attention": *San Francisco Call,* May 5, 1880. The San Francisco Art Institute, heir to the SFAA, likes to call this the first public film screening, though of course much had to be done before the actual medium of film would arrive.

page 203. He ordered a horse's skeleton: It was photographs of this skeleton that are known to have been used directly in the zoopraxiscope rather than being "translated" into drawings for projection.

page 203. "He lied to me, and I think he behaved very shabbily": Stillman testimony, 1883, Huntington Papers.

page 203. Despite his reservations, Muybridge wrote an introduction: This was published in the *Examiner,* Feb. 6, 1881, and is one of the most useful accounts of the Palo Alto experiments.

page 203. Muybridge didn't think the book "would be successful": Shay testimony, 1883, Huntington Papers.

page 204. "expected to be like the moon to the sun": Stillman testimony, 1883, Huntington Papers.

page 205. In 1881 he created several handmade albums: Because these were copyrighted they are often referred to as books, though they were not printed and published as books generally are. About fifteen copies are known, and as with the Central America albums, different versions exist.

page 204. Stanford sold to him for the sum of one dollar: Legal deed in Muybridge file, Bancroft Library, dated July 7, 1881.

page 204. "a number of Dallmeyer lenses": *Philadelphia Photographer,* July 1881, 259.

9. THE ARTIST IN MOTION AND AT REST

page 209. two hundred of "the most eminent": *American Register,* Paris, Dec. 3, 1881, in Kingston Scrapbook.

page 210. adapted an existing "photographic gun": see Marta Braun, *Picturing Motion: The Work of Etienne-Jules Marey, 1830–1904* (Chicago: University of Chicago Press, 1992), 55.

page 211. Braun points out that cinematic information was irrelevant: Ibid., 151.

page 212. "personality, intelligence, even the very desires of the workers": Ibid., 241.

page 212. "As we regulate the use of machines": Anson Rabinbach, *The Human Motor: Energy, Fatigue, and the Origins of Modernity* (Berkeley and Los Angeles: University of California Press, 1992), 116.

page 212. "I saw them off on the cars": Letter of Nov. 28, 1881, Huntington Papers.

page 213. "he had come to the knowledge of a new process of instantaneous photography": Stillman testimony, Huntington Papers.

page 213. "Mr. Meissonier exhibits the greatest interest in the work": Letter of Dec. 23, 1881, Huntington Papers.

page 214. "I anticipate no difficulty": Stillman's recollection, Huntington Papers.

page 214. "I should like to see your boxing pictures": *Photographic News,* March 17, 1882.

page 214. "and throughout his lecture": Ibid.

page 214. "After Mr. Muybridge had shown his audience": Ibid.

page 215. "I received a note requesting my presence": Handwritten draft letter to Stanford, May 2, 1892, Bancroft Library; also reproduced in Mozley, 127–29.

page 216. "Muybridge has commenced a suit by attachment": Huntington Papers. Muybridge also filed suit against the publishers and also lost that suit.

page 218. "Godfather of Movies" and "Grand Dad of Movies": *New York Evening World,* June 8, 1923; *Brooklyn Standard,* June 8, 1923. The *Brooklyn Standard,* clearly drawing from an interview, declares he "designed the counterpart of what today is the moving picture camera," a feat not even Muybridge accomplished.

page 220. Blanche Epler, aged twenty: According to notebooks in Muybridge's handwriting, Eastman House Library, Rochester, New York.

page 221. "a rather remarkable man": Letter to Walter Miles, May 10, 1928, Miles file, Stanford University Library Special Collections.

page 222. Beard believed that "modern civilization": In *American Nervousness,* excerpted in *Popular Culture and Industrialism, 1865–1890,* ed. Henry Nash Smith (Garden City, N.Y.: Anchor Books, 1967), 58.

page 222. "The perfection of clocks": Ibid., 61.

page 222. "embraced a large number of actions": Typed transcript titled "Quadrupedal, Leap. Kick. Fight. Proportion," unpublished lecture, Photographic History Collection, National Museum of American History, Smithsonian Institution (no date, but likely after 1886), 8.

page 222. Photohistorian Jayne Morgan argues: "Eadweard Muybridge and W. S. Playfair: An Aesthetics of Neurasthenia," *History of Photography,* autumn 1999.

page 223. "Muybridge was not using his camera as an analytical tool,": Braun, *Picturing Motion,* 249. Braun may overstate the errors and the attempt to deceive in Muybridge's work. She writes, "Muybridge's claim to science, a claim that has never been challenged, rests on the viewer's unquestioning acceptance of the structure of the sequence. As such it is suspect" (252). In fact, Muybridge's claim to science lies in his capture of hitherto invisible motions, of sequences of motion, and of their reanimation by means of the zoopraxiscope, and Braun only calls into question the second of these achievements. In some cases the sequences do indeed seem to have been renumbered to suggest a continuity that had been ruptured, in others—such as #43—the numbering clearly indicates the omissions. But her analysis is in other respects original and important.

page 223. "Muybridge's concern, then, is with narration": Ibid., 249.

page 226. "tesseract of water": Frampton, "Eadweard Muybridge: Fragments of a Tesseract," in *Circles of Confusion* pointed out the relationship between the waterfalls and the motion-studies water.

page 228. "sporting world": Letter to the *Orange Journal,* in Charles Musser, *Origins of the Cinema,* vol. 1 of *History of the American Cinema* (Berkeley and Los Angeles: University of California Press, 1994), 53.

page 228. "Mr. Edison said that Prof. Muybridge": Ibid., 62, quoting *New York World,* June 3, 1888. Thomas Anschutz is sometimes also cited as an influence on the Edison workshop, but since Anschutz was himself only improving upon the motion studies and zoopraxiscope, the source is still ultimately Muybridge.

page 229. "that grand opera can be given at the Metropolitan Opera House": This quote appears several places, including Kingston Scrapbook; see notes to chap. 5.

page 229. "He permitted her to go to the theaters": See notes to chap. 6.

page 230. "mounted on boards and set up in the library": Gordon Hendricks, *Origins of the American Film* (New York: Arno Press, 1972), 27.

page 230. "more than 300 participants": Mannoni, *Great Art of Light and Shadow,* 391.

page 231. "The importance of this development": Eric Rhode, *A History of the Cinema from Its Origins to 1970* (New York: Hill and Wang, 1976), 18–19.

page 232. "a panorama of the Bernese Alps": Rossiter Johnson, ed., *A History of the World's Columbian Exposition Held in Chicago in 1893* (New York: D. Appleton, 1989), 3:434.

page 233. "the celebrated Neapolitan painter Count Antonio Coppola": Julie K. Brown, *Contesting Images: Photography and the World's Columbian Exposition* (Tucson: University of Arizona Press, 1994), 104.

page 233. "asked in 1893 for the first time": *The Education of Henry Adams* (New York: Modern Library, 1931), 342.

page 233. "bring together evidences of the amazing material productiveness": Alan Trachtenberg, *The Incorporation of America: Culture and Society in the Gilded Age* (New York: Hill and Wang, 1982), 216.

page 234. "Sitting Bull's original cabin": Johnson, *History of the World's Columbian Exposition,* 444.

page 235. "You have a great deal to live for": Tutorow, *Leland Stanford,* 222.

page 236. "millinery": Roxanne Nylan, former Stanford archivist, in conversation with the author.

page 236. "It will be our aim": *Examiner,* June 21, 1893.

page 237. "An aristocracy of brains": Starr, *Americans and the California Dream,* 321.

page 237. "Nowhere are the conditions of life happier and better": *Examiner,* June 21, 1893.

page 237. "Life in California is a little fresher": Starr, *Americans and the California Dream,* 313.

page 238. "Edward Muggeridge has come to Kingston": Rachel Rickard, "née Smith," to Elizabeth Selfe, Nov. 6, 1894, hand-copied for Robert Haas by Norma Selfe, Haas Papers.

page 238. "as young as he did twenty years ago": *Photographic Times,* June 1897, quoted in Hendricks, 223.

page 238. "much pleased to donate a copy": Letter to "the Librarian, State University, Berkeley" of June 20, 1903, Gordon Hendricks files.

page 238. His effects were valued: Hendricks, 226.

10. FROM THE CENTER OF THE WORLD TO THE FINAL FRONTIER

page 241. artists have: Lucy Lippard writes of sequential and serial 1960s art in "The Dematerialization of Art," in her book *Changing* (New York: E. P. Dutton, 1971): "Motion is the
source of pattern-making, and it might seem that film rather than painting or sculpture
would be the visual art most suited to the portrayal of motion and time. But paintings like
those of Larry Poons and sculpture such as Sol LeWitt's offer successful means of present-
ing time-motion without anything actually moving (as, in another way, do Oldenburg's
soft sculptures). They are like time exposures in photography, revealing time-space patterns that are invisible to someone seeing them in sequence alone . . . (one of LeWitt's influences, and also one of Duchamp's, was Muybridge)" (256–57). And in *Sol LeWitt: A
Retrospective* (New Haven: Yale University Press, 2000), Anne Rorimor writes, "In the following year [1964], with the realization of *Muybridge 1,* LeWitt furthered his investigation of pictorial planarity and spatial reality with relation to duration. Familiarity with the
studies of . . . Muybridge . . . aided him in a concerted search for ways to counteract the
static nature of singular objects" (61).

page 246. "Hollywood is afflicted with total amnesia": Quoted in Jerome Charyn, *Movieland:
Hollywood and the Great American Dream Culture* (New York: Putnam, 1989), 94.

page 246. "gone from picturesque dilapidation": Mike Davis, *Ecology of Fear: Los Angeles
and the Imagination of Disaster* (New York: Metropolitan Books, 1998), 395.

page 251. "Imagine an underground chamber like a cave": Plato, *The Republic,* trans.
Desmond Lee (New York: Penguin, 1974), 317.

page 255. "The revolution will end": David Denby, "The Speed of Light: The High-Stakes
Race to Build the Next Internet," *New Yorker,* Nov. 27, 2000, 133.

ACKNOWLEDGMENTS

This project was pure pleasure from beginning to end, not only for the resonance of its stories, but for the excitement of the chase and the generosity of the many who helped. For comments on the manuscript and consultations on the history of photography, I want to thank the photographer Mark Klett, who through his own work has become one of the most thoughtful and informed historians of western photography in Muybridge's time, and the photography historians Geoffrey Batchen and Peter Palmquist, who did much to steer me straight through the complicated terrain of nineteenth-century photography. For advice, information, and suggestions at various stages in the process, thanks are also due to Byron Wolfe, John Rohrbach, Phillip Prodger, John Martini, Art Shimamura, Frish Brandt, Jeffrey Fraenkel, Chip Lord, Lisbeth Haas, Roxanne Nilane, Charl Lucassen, Catherine Harris, Ellen Manchester, Julian Borrill, Malcolm Margolin, Susan Schwartzenberg, Lucy Lippard, and David Dodge.

This book was researched in many libraries and archives, and the time spent there and help offered deepened my longtime gratitude and enthusiasm for those institutions and the people who work in them. Bancroft Library was extraordinarily welcoming and encouraging, particularly David Kessler, Baiba Strads, Jack Von Au, and James Eason there. I also want to thank the libraries of the University of California at Berkeley; Stanford Library and Archives and archivist Maggie Kimball there; the Cantor Art Center at Stanford and Dolores Kincaid; the California Historical Society library and archive; the Fine Arts Library of the University of New Mexico; George Eastman House International Museum of Film and Photography in Rochester and librarian Becky Simmons there; the San Francisco Public Library; Yosemite Research Library and historian Jim Snyder, curator Barbara Beroza, and anthropologist Craig Bates there; California State Library,

Sacramento; Kingston-upon-Thames Local History Room; the Archives of American Art; the National Museum of American History and curator Michelle Delaney there; the Huntington Library in San Marino and curator Jenny Watts there; and the Napa County Historical Society.

Finally, before I thought a publisher would provide significant support for this book I applied for a Guggenheim grant; receiving it was an honor and an added impetus to do the work as best I could every step of the way.

PHOTOGRAPH CREDITS

ALL PHOTOGRAPHS IN THIS BOOK ARE BY EADWEARD MUYBRIDGE UNLESS OTHERWISE INDICATED IN THE CAPTIONS.

Images on pages 182, 188, and 206–207: copyright Addison Gallery of American Art, Phillips Academy, Andover, Massachusetts. All rights reserved.

Frontispiece portrait of Muybridge and images on pages 12, 20, 25, 31, 48, 49, 52, 55, 59, 63, 68, 75, 85, 87, 90, 95, 99, 101, 105, 106–107, 119, 143, 153, 157–161, and 239: courtesy of University Archives, Bancroft Library, University of California, Berkeley.

Images on pages 150 and 151: courtesy of the California History Room, California State Library, Sacramento, California.

Frames of Muybridge running on pages 3–23: courtesy of the Huntington Library, San Marino, California.

Images on pages 1 and 192: courtesy of the Library of Congress.

Images on pages 168 and 169: courtesy of the San Francisco History Center, San Francisco Public Library.

Images on pages 125, 132, 135, 140, and 217: Iris & B. Gerald Cantor Center for Visual Arts at Stanford University, Stanford Family Collections.

Images on pages 79, 177, and 199: courtesy of the Department of Special Collections, Stanford University Libraries.

Images on pages 224 and 225: from the collections of the University of Pennsylvania Archives.

Images on pages 16 and 227: collection of the author.

INTERNET SOURCES FOR MORE PHOTOGRAPHS:

The great abundance and variety of Muybridge's work can only be hinted at in this book, but there are two particularly rich sources for viewing it online. Bancroft Library at the University of California, Berkeley, has put virtually its whole Muybridge collection online, including its nearly complete collection of the Yosemite mammoth plates and the huge array of stereos from the Lone Mountain Albums. It can be viewed at:

http://www.oac.cdlib.org/dynaweb/ead/calher/

The independent scholar Charl Lucassen in the Netherlands has an excellent Web site on many aspects of the motion-studies images, processes, and devices, along with animations of some of the motion studies. It can be viewed at:

http://web.inter.nl.net/users/anima/chronoph/index.htm

INDEX